Traditional
JIGS & FIXTURES
for HANDTOOLS

A Manual of Devices for Woodworking

also by
Graham Blackburn

FICTION

For Love or Money?
The Castilian Suite
The Stanford Solution
Tango Slim

NON-FICTION

Illustrated Housebuilding
*The Illustrated Encyclopedia of
Woodworking Handtools, Instruments, & Devices*
Illustrated Basic Carpentry
The Postage Stamp Gazetteer
Illustrated Furniture Making
Illustrated Interior Carpentry
*The Illustrated Encyclopedia of Ships, Boats,
Vessels, & other Water-borne Craft*
The Illustrated Dictionary of Nautical Terms
The Parts of a House
An Illustrated Calendar of Home Repair
Quick & Easy Home Repair
Floors, Walls, & Ceilings
Creative Ideas for Household Storage
Year-round House Care
Furniture by Design
Traditional Woodworking Handtools
Traditional Woodworking Techniques
Furniture Design & Construction

Andante: a memoir

*for all
those woodworkers
who would rather work by hand
than by machine*

*Joiner using a Diagonal Bit Holder
(from A. J. Wilkinson & Co.'s 19th cent. catalogue)*

Traditional Jigs & Fixtures *for* Handtools

A Manual of Devices for Woodworking

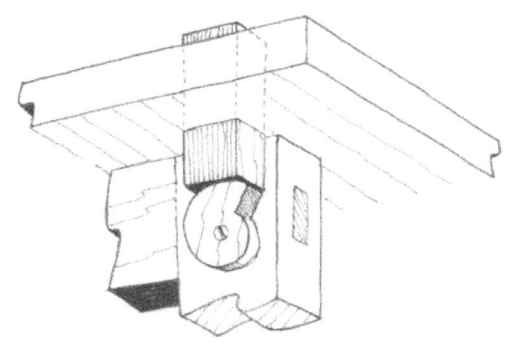

written & illustrated
by
GRAHAM BLACKBURN

Copyright © 2014, 2021 by G. J. Blackburn

All rights reserved.
No part of this book may be reproduced in any form or
by any means without the written permission of the publisher.

Published by
CEDAR LANE PRESS
PO BOX 5424
LANCASTER, PA 17606-5424
WWW.CEDARLANEPRESS.COM

Library of Congress Card Number: 2021930291
International Standard Book Number: 978-1-950934-69-0

Designed by Graham Blackburn
Set in 11 point Caslon

First Edition
0 9 8 7 6 5 4 3 2 1

Printed in the United States of America

ACKNOWLEDGEMENTS

It would be impossible to list all those anonymous woodworkers
who over the ages have contributed to this particular store of knowledge,
but I would like to thank in particular Reginald Smith, my school shop teacher,
George Harris, the cabinetmaker to whom I was unoffcially apprenticed
during my college years, and several colleagues I have had the privilege
of working with in America, namely: Paul Potash, Paul Schürch, and
David Marks, whose contributions have been especially helpful.

CONTENTS

	PREFACE	xiv
	INTRODUCTION	xvi
1.	HOLDING	1

      I. Workbench Aids: Bench Stops: *Round Bench Stop, Square Bench Stop, Capped & Pinned Bench Stop, Cam-Fixed Bench Stop, Screw-Fixed Bench Stop, Manufactured Metal Bench Stop, V-Block (V-Board, Bench Clamp, Top Clamp), Bench Dogs, Bench Hook (Side Hook, Side Rest);* **Holdfasts:** *Basic Holdfast, Screw Holdfast, Bridge Clamp*
      II. Vise Fixtures: Deadmen: *Fixed Deadman, Free-Standing Deadman, Sliding Deadman, End Bracket;* **Auxiliary Vise Jaws:** *Replacement Jaw Facings, Finishing Jaws, Vertically Tapered Jaws, Matching Taper Jaw;* **Cradle Jaws:** *Vertical Cradle Jaws, Horizontal Cradle Jaws, Tall Jaws, Box Jaws*
      III. Additional Holding Fixtures: *Right-Angled Bracket, Floor Clamp, Handscrew Jaw Extender*

2.	**MEASURING & MARKING**	21

      Straightedge, Pinch Rods, Diagonal Strips, Winding Sticks, Flexible Straightedge, Asymmetrical Straightedge, Brick Batten Stop, Story Stick, Mullet, Patterns & Templates, Beam Compass; **Usermade Gauges:** *Pencil Gauge, Bossed Curve-Gauge, Panel Gauge, Dowelled Curve-Gauge, Parallel Marking Gauge;* **Preset Gauges:** *Notched Preset Gauges, Rabbeted Preset Gauge, Bored Trysquare, Drawer-Pull Guide, Drawer-Pull Centering Positioner, Cabinet Door-Handle Guide, Shelf-Support Layout Guide, Grasshopper Gauge (Handrail Gauge), Cylinder Gauging Cradle, Corner Scribe, Sliding Bevel Spacer;* **Dovetail Guides:** *Dovetail Marking Guide, Side Dovetail Guide*

3. SAWING — 41

Saw Bench, Saw Horse, Ripping Horse, Sawbuck (Saw-Goat);
Bench Aids: *Pivoting Saw-Stop, Kerfed Bench-Hook, Fretsawing Bracket, Fretsawing Block;* **Sawing Guides:** *Depth Stop, Dowel Length-Stop, Shoulder Guide, Angle Guide;* **Mitering Aids:** *Miter Block (Mitre Block), Miter Box (Mitre Box), Mitered-Dovetail Block, Miter-Sawing Saddle*

4. PLANING — 53

Face-Planing Stop; **Edge-Planing Fixtures:** *Roman Pegs, Strip Clamp, Edge-Planing Clamp, Planing Board, Cammed Planing Board, Sticking Board, Dowel Box (Rounding Cradle), Planing Cradle;* **Shooting Boards (Chute Boards):** *Basic Shooting Board, Wedged Shooting Board, Compound Angle Shooting Board, Miter Shooting Board, Donkey's Ear Shooting Board, Shooting Block;* **Fixtures for Accuracy:** *Rabbeting Guide, Fielding Guides, Mitered-Dovetail Guide, Depth & Width Stops, Square-Edge Guide, Planing Push Guide*

5. JOINERY — 67

Simple Scratch Stock, Rounded-Edge Scratch Stock; **Dowelling:** *Dowel Groover, Dowel Marker;* **Miters & Dovetails:** *Mitered Moulding Guide (Miter Template), Dovetail Paring Guide, Mitered-Dovetail Paring Block;* **Mortising:** *Mortising Block, Mortising Handscrew, Turning Box (Moulding Box, Fluting Box), Hand-Router Shoe, Angled Circle-Cutting Guide*

6. BORING — 77

Splintering Guard; **Straight Boring Guides:** *Trysquare Guide, Framing Square Guide, Vertical Boring Guide, Thin-Stock Boring Guide, Block Boring Guide;* **Angled & Spaced Guides:** *Angle Boring Guide, Spaced-Hole Boring Guide, Evenly-Spaced Hole Guide, Corner Boring Guide;* **Depth Stops:** *Tape Depth Guide, Block Depth Guide (Block Stop), Adjustable Depth Stop*

7. **ASSEMBLY & FINISHING** 85
   I. Assembly: Dent Protection: *Hammer Shield, Pliers Shield, Fulcrum Raiser, Striking Block;* **Clamping:** *Floor Frame-Container, Frame Clamp, Door Rocker;* **Gluing Aids:** *Edge Clamp, Peg Form, Wall Form, Solid Bending Form;* **Gluing & Adhesive Tape:** *Glue-Block Protector, Squeeze-Out Protector, Glue-Surface Protector, Tape Repair*
   II. Finishing: Sanding: *Sandpaper Divider;* **Sandpaper Holders:** *Sanding Plane, Curved Sanding Planes, Sanding Rubbers, Sanding Shooting Board, Lipping Sander, Straddle Sander;* **Finish Protection:** *Finishing Support Board, Finish Protectors*

APPENDICES:

1. SHARPENING 99
2. SELECT BIBLIOGRAPHY 107
3. FIGURES 111
4. INDEX 115

ILLUSTRATIONS

A list of all illustrations, both in the main text as well as in the Sharpening Appendix.

CHAPTER 1
- FIG. 1 BENCH STOPS
- FIG. 2 VARIOUS BENCH STOP DIMENSIONS
- FIG. 3 CAM-FIXED BENCH STOP
- FIG. 4 CAM-FIXED STOP DETAILS
- FIG. 5 SCREW-FIXED BENCH STOP
- FIG. 6 METAL BENCH STOP
- FIG. 7 V-BLOCK BENCH STOP
- FIG. 8 BENCH DOGS
- FIG. 9 WOODEN & METAL BENCH DOGS
- FIG. 10 BENCH HOOKS
- FIG. 11 BASIC HOLDFAST
- FIG. 12 TOP VIEW OF CABINETMAKER'S BENCH
- FIG. 13 SCREW HOLDFAST
- FIG. 14 BRIDGE CLAMP
- FIG. 15 FIXED DEADMAN
- FIG. 16 FREE-STANDING DEADMAN
- FIG. 17 SLIDING DEADMAN
- FIG. 18 END BRACKET
- FIG. 19 REPLACEMENT VISE FACINGS
- FIG. 20 FINISHING JAWS
- FIG. 21 VERTICALLY TAPERED JAWS
- FIG. 22 MATCHING TAPER JAWS
- FIG. 23 VERTICAL CRADLE JAWS
- FIG. 24 HORIZONTAL CRADLE JAWS
- FIG. 25 TALL JAWS
- FIG. 26 CLAMPING WITH TALL JAWS
- FIG. 27 BOX JAWS
- FIG. 28 RIGHT-ANGLE BRACKET
- FIG. 29 FLOOR CLAMP
- FIG. 30 HANDSCREW JAW EXTENDER

CHAPTER 2
- FIG. 31 STRAIGHTEDGE
- FIG. 32 PINCH RODS
- FIG. 33 DIAGONAL STRIPS
- FIG. 34 WINDING STICKS
- FIG. 35 FLEXIBLE STRAIGHTEDGE
- FIG. 36 ASYMMETRICAL STRAIGHTEDGE
- FIG. 37 BRICK BATTEN STOP
- FIG. 38 STORY STICK
- FIG. 39 MULLET
- FIG. 40 PATTERNS & TEMPLATES
- FIG. 41 BEAM COMPASS
- FIG. 42 BEAM COMPASS WITH TRAMMEL POINTS
- FIG. 43 PENCIL GAUGE
- FIG. 44 BOSSED CURVE-GAUGE
- FIG. 45 PANEL & DOWELLED CURVE-GAUGE
- FIG. 46 PARALLEL MARKING GAUGE
- FIG. 47 NOTCHED PRESET GAUGES
- FIG. 48 NOTCHED PRESET GAUGE
- FIG. 49 BORED TRYSQUARE
- FIG. 50 DRAWER-PULL GUIDE
- FIG. 51 DRAWER-PULL CENTERING POSITIONER
- FIG. 52 CABINET DOOR-HANDLE GUIDE
- FIG. 53 SHELF-SUPPORT GUIDE
- FIG. 54 GRASSHOPPER GAUGE
- FIG. 55 CYLINDER GAUGING CRADLE
- FIG. 56 CORNER SCRIBE
- FIG. 57 SLIDING BEVEL SPACER
- FIG. 58 DOVETAIL MARKING GUIDE
- FIG. 59 SIDE DOVETAIL GUIDE

CHAPTER 3
- FIG. 60 SAW BENCH
- FIG. 61 SAW BENCH DIMENSIONS
- FIG. 62 SAW HORSE
- FIG. 63 SAW HORSE DIMENSIONS
- FIG. 64 RIPPING HORSE
- FIG. 65 SAWBUCK
- FIG. 66 DUTCH ZAAG-BOC
- FIG. 67 BENCH STOP DAMAGE

TRADITIONAL JIGS & FIXTURES

FIG. 68 PIVOTING SAW STOP
FIG. 69 KERFED BENCH HOOK
FIG. 70 FRETSAWING BRACKET
FIG. 71 FRETSAWING BLOCK
FIG. 72 DEPTH STOP
FIG. 73 DOWEL LENGTH STOP
FIG. 74 SHOULDER GUIDE
FIG. 75 ANGLE GUIDE
FIG. 76 MITER BLOCK
FIG. 77 MITER BOX
FIG. 78 COMPOUND MITER BOX
FIG. 79 MITERED-DOVETAIL BLOCK
FIG. 80 MITER-SAWING SADDLE

CHAPTER 4
FIG. 81 FACE-PLANING STOP
FIG. 82 ROMAN PEGS
FIG. 83 STRIP CLAMP
FIG. 84 EDGE-PLANING CLAMP
FIG. 85 PLANING BOARD
FIG. 86 CAMMED PLANING BOARD
FIG. 87 STICKING BOARD
FIG. 88 PLANING CRADLE
FIG. 89 CRADLE INTERNAL ANGLES
FIG. 90 BASIC SHOOTING BOARD
FIG. 91 SHOOTING END GRAIN
FIG. 92 WEDGED SHOOTING BOARD
FIG. 93 COMPOUD ANGLE SHOOTING BOARD
FIG. 94 MITER SHOOTING BOARD
FIG. 95 DONKEY'S EAR SHOOTING BOARD
FIG. 96 SHOOTING BLOCK
FIG. 97 USERMADE SHOOTING BLOCK
FIG. 98 RABBETING GUIDE
FIG. 99 FIELDING GUIDES
FIG. 100 MITERED-DOVETAIL GUIDE
FIG. 101 DEPTH & WIDTH STOPS
FIG. 102 BEVELED WIDTH STOP
FIG. 103 SQUARE-EDGE GUIDE
FIG. 104 PLANING PUSH BLOCK

CHAPTER 5
FIG. 105 FACE-PLANING SCRATCH STOCK
FIG. 106 SCRATCH STOCK BLADE
FIG. 107 ROUNDED-EDGE SCRATCH STOCK
FIG. 108 DOWEL GROOVER

FIG. 109 SAW HORSE DOWEL GROOVER
FIG. 110 DOWEL MARKER
FIG. 111 MITERED STUCK MOULDING
FIG. 112 MITERED MOULDING GUIDE
FIG. 113 DOVETAIL PARING GUIDE
FIG. 114 MITERED DOVETAIL PARING BLOCK
FIG. 115 MORTISING BLOCK
FIG. 116 MORTISING HANDSCREW
FIG. 117 TURNING BOX
FIG. 118 TURNING BOX DIMENSIONS
FIG. 119 HAND-ROUTER SHOE
FIG. 120 ANGLED CIRCLE-CUTTING GUIDE

CHAPTER 6
FIG. 121 AVOIDING SPLIT-OUT
FIG. 122 SPLINTERING GUARD
FIG. 123 TRYSQUARE GUIDE
FIG. 124 FRAMING SQUARE GUIDE
FIG. 125 VERTICAL BORING GUIDE
FIG. 126 THIN STOCK BORING GUIDE
FIG. 127 BLOCK BORING GUIDE
FIG. 128 ANGLE BORING GUIDE
FIG. 129 SPACED HOLE GUIDE
FIG. 130 EVENLY-SPACED HOLE GUIDE
FIG. 131 CORNER BORING GUIDE
FIG. 132 TAPE DEPTH GUIDE
FIG. 133 BLOCK DEPTH GUIDE
FIG. 134 ADJUSTABLE DEPTH STOP

CHAPTER 7
FIG. 135 HAMMER SHIELD
FIG. 136 PLIERS SHIELD
FIG. 137 FULCRUM RAISER
FIG. 138 STRIKING BLOCK
FIG. 139 FLOOR FRAME-CONTAINER
FIG. 140 FRAME CLAMP
FIG. 141 DOOR ROCKER
FIG. 142 EDGE CLAMP
FIG. 143 PEG FORM
FIG. 144 WALL FORM
FIG. 145 SOLID BENDING FORM
FIG. 146 GLUE BLOCK PROTECTOR
FIG. 147 SQUEEZE-OUT PROTECTOR
FIG. 148 GLUE-SURFACE PROTECTOR
FIG. 149 TAPE REPAIR

ILLUSTRATIONS

FIG. 150 SANDPAPER DIVIDER
FIG. 151 SANDING PLANE
FIG. 152 CURVED SANDING PLANES
FIG. 153 SANDING RUBBERS
FIG. 154 SANDING SHOOTING BOARD
FIG. 155 LIPPING SANDER
FIG. 156 STRADDLE SANDER
FIG. 157 FINISHING SUPPORT BOARD
FIG. 158 FINISH PROTECTORS

SHARPENING APPENDIX
FIG. A1 HAND-GRINDER BLADE SUPPORT
FIG. A2 SHARPENING STONE FLATTENER
FIG. A3 WEDGED STONE-HOLDER
FIG. A4 BEVEL SUPPORT
FIG. A5 SCRAPER-PLANE BLADE SUPPORT
FIG. A6 SPOKESHAVE SHARPENING HOLDER
FIG. A7 DRAWKNIFE REST

PREFACE

One of the chief attractions of woodworking as a trade or a hobby has always been the satisfaction of producing something ourselves by hand. We are, after all, by definition tool-using creatures. Today's world, however, is become so complicated that there are ever fewer opportunities for indulging this urge. Few people can build their own computer, make a cell phone, or even fix their cars anymore. Woodworking is one of the rare opportunities that remain to us for creative self-expression. But even woodworking, by taking advantage of modern technology, has frequently become far removed from what it once was. For many people woodworking now means acquiring expensive powertools and machines such as tablesaws, shapers, jointers, planers, routers, and a host of other items. The expense and increasing technical complications, not to mention the potential dangers of equipping a shop this way, have turned woodworking, especially as a hobby, into something very far removed from the more hands-on approach of using hammer and saw.

As a result there is, fortunately, a renewed interest in more traditional methods. Many woodworkers are once again discovering the pleasure and advantages of using handtools. These provide not only less expensive, safer, and greener methods of doing things, but also ways of working with wood that at the same time are often quicker, better, and offer more choices than does a reliance on machinery. There is even an increasing supply of quality handtools alongside a mountain of secondhand tools. To pick up a plane and immediately produce a shaving is a different and more personal experience than donning earplugs and safety glasses, turning on dust extractors, clearing the area of onlookers, and starting an expensive stationary machine.

Unfortunately traditional woodworking is not quite as simple as merely picking up a handplane. The plane needs to be understood, and you must learn how to tune and sharpen it. While this may not be particularly difficult, especially since there are now many good books on the subject and an increasing number of opportunities to attend schools and workshops, what is often ignored are the jigs and fixtures that traditional woodworkers employed with handtools such as planes and saws to guarantee speed, accuracy, and efficiency. A few of these things survive, and may even have been incorporated into the tool itself — in the form of fences and depth stops, for example. But the vast majority of these aids were usermade as the occasion demanded, and so do not appear in today's standard tool catalogs. The result is often unnecessary frustration with traditional handtool woodworking, and a temptation to return to powertools. Of course, practice and experience will improve your technique no matter how you work, with or without extra jigs and fixtures, but there is little point in attempting to do something unaided when a simple device will go a long way to guaranteeing the desired perfection.

There is undoubtedly no end to the number of jigs and fixtures that have been or may be invented to facilitate traditional woodworking. Furthermore, experience with just a few of them will invariably suggest many others; and modifications are virtually limitless.

Traditional Jigs & Fixtures is an attempt to re-introduce many of these items. The selection contained here primarily includes the traditional usermade ones, together with those I personally grew up with, plus a few more recent adaptations and even some newer manufactured items. The usermade jigs are mostly very simple to construct and use, but the incorporation into your shop of any of these items will make all the difference between frustration and success.

Publisher's Note:
This edition of 'Traditional Jigs & Fixtures' is a much revised and corrected edition of the work originally entitled 'Jigs & Fixtures for the Hand Tool Woodworker' published by Popular Woodworking Books, Cincinnati, Ohio.

INTRODUCTION

THE LINE BETWEEN A JIG OR FIXTURE AND AN ACTUAL TOOL IS OFTEN BLURRED. A TOOL MAY BE THOUGHT OF AS SOMETHING THAT WORKS UPON AND ALTERS THE WORKPIECE DIRECTLY, LIKE A SAW, A PLANE, OR A DRILL WHILE A JIG OR A fixture is something that helps and improves that tool's use. Indeed, what contemporary woodworkers often take for granted as manufactured 'tools' often started out as usermade jigs and accessories. Items such as squares, bevels, and gauges were once all typically made by the craftsman rather than being bought in a tool shop or from an online catalog. Indeed, few self-respecting craftsmen would waste money buying such items, for it used to be considered self-evident that a craftsman who could not make a simple trysquare would stand little chance of being able to construct a more complicated piece of furniture. Nowadays, however, not only is a trysquare thought of as a tool but it is also generally bought rather than made. Even simpler items, such as dovetail marking guides, are sometimes sold as 'tools', and in expensive velvet-lined boxes to boot!

Now of course you should by all means feel free to indulge the desire to treat yourself to a gorgeous item for your chosen hobby, but surely the pleasure and rewards of traditional woodworking derive from doing it yourself rather than relying exclusively on store-bought or pre-manufactured items. Otherwise we might just as well sit back and let a pre- programmed computer numerical control (CNC) machine produce the ideas that pop into our head. If the end product is the sole goal this is fine, but if it is the process that provides the pleasure and satisfaction of being a 'tool-using animal' then the hands-on approach is better. It is to this end this book will be more than useful, both as a means to producing better work as well as to making the process more rewarding.

METHODS AND MATERIALS

HOW VARIOUS JIGS AND FIXTURES ARE MADE is usually self-evident. Since in most cases it is the underlying principle that is important, feel free to improvise, alter, and adjust to suit your own particular needs and situation. The materials you use may be varied: hardwood, carefully assembled and polished for posterity, or something far simpler picked up from the scrap heap. Even materials perhaps esthetically at odds with tradition, such as plastic, plywood, or particleboard may be equally effective if carefully made. More important from a practical point of view is accuracy or adjustability, but always remember that handtool use does not usually imply freehand use.

Most items are illustrated both realistically and in use. The measurements that are given in the working drawings need not be adhered to slavishly or thought of as absolute; their purpose is merely to make clear the basic structure of the realistic drawings and what will work as a starting point. Many of the jigs and fixtures illustrated here may be equally efficient if made considerably larger — or even smaller. It will depend largely on the scale of your particular project.

ORGANIZATION

TO MAKE THEIR DISCOVERY EASIER THE JIGS and fixtures included in this book have been grouped under various chapter headings that follow the standard workflow that governs most projects: from holding, through measuring and marking, sawing, planing, cutting, and boring, to assembly and finishing. Such groupings are not necessarily definitive, however, since a particular jig might be equally useful under another heading. For this reason a complete alphabetical index of all jigs and fixtures is also included, together with cross-references to their appearances in different chapters.

Also included with these appendices is a short section on various jigs and fixtures useful in the sharpening process. Although this book as mentioned in the preface is concerned primarily with discovering how you may use handtools more effectively, rather than learning what they are and how to tune and fettle them as well as what they are intended to do, I have nonetheless thought it helpful to include a few items that may make the sharpening process in particular easier.

For more information on the tools themselves, reference to several of my earlier books — such as *Traditional Woodworking Handtools*, and *Traditional Woodworking Techniques* — will be more appropriate.

One last note on terminology: since there is very little consistency in the English naming of woodworking items and terms — preferences changing from one side of the Atlantic to the other, as well as from one generation to the next — I have listed the items included in this book using the most common contemporary American usage, with alternative names from other eras and places included in parentheses.

TRADITIONAL JIGS & FIXTURES

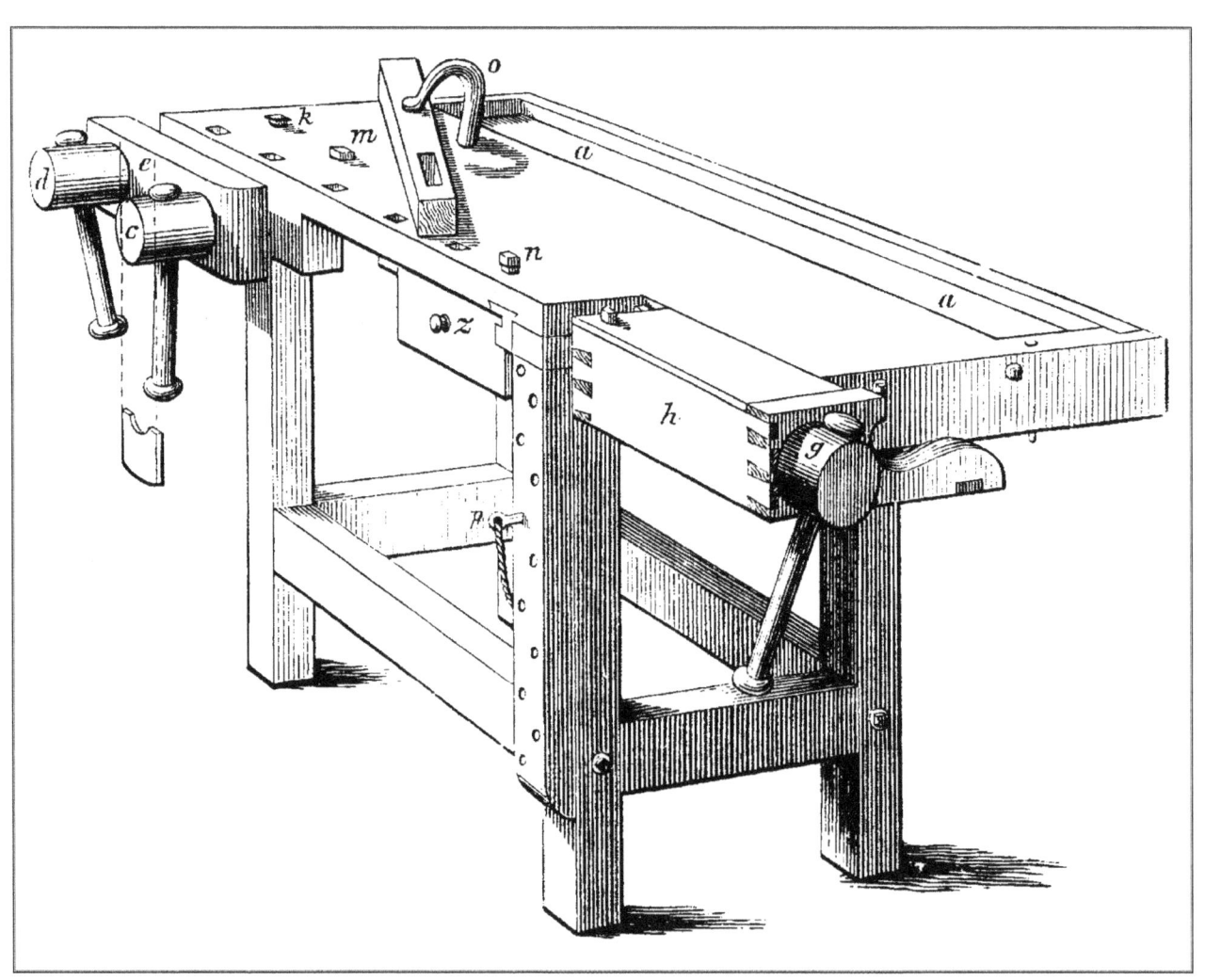

THE SUTCLIFFE BENCH
a. tool tray; c. face-vise handle; d. face-vise handle; e. face-vise jaw; g. tail-vise handle; h. tail-vise jaw; k. bench stop; m. bench stop; n. bench dog; o. holdfast; p. deadman pin; z. tool drawer

I

JIGS & FIXTURES FOR HOLDING

VERY LITTLE HAND WOODWORKING APART FROM WHITTLING IS DONE LITERALLY BY HAND ALONE. YOU MIGHT BE ABLE TO HOLD A PIECE OF WOOD IN ONE HAND AND CARVE IT WITH A KNIFE HELD IN THE OTHER HAND, BUT BEYOND THIS SOMETHING ELSE IS REQUIRED. This first chapter is therefore all about fixtures designed for securing the workpiece. It is divided into three main sections: workbench aids; vise fixtures; and additional holding fixtures.

1. WORKBENCH AIDS

THE WORKBENCH IS FOR THE TRADITIONAL woodworker the most important item in the workshop. Even in a shop that depends solely on powertools and machines some kind of worksurface is needed if only for assembly. But the moment handtools are involved, a bench becomes essential. I consider my cabinetmaker's workbench my single most important tool, but in fact it is probably truer to call it my most important jig or fixture.

Its history may be traced back to low Roman benches which were used primarily for supporting wood when being sawed. Today's benches are used for much more.

There is also a wide variety of styles available, including the so-called German, British, Scandinavian, and other European benches, as well as benches designed for specific kinds of woodworking, such as cabinetmaking, joinery, or carving.

It is an unfortunate fact that although making one's own bench can be a fine place to start when setting up a shop, you might not actually know what works best for you until after you have made — or bought — your first bench. Nevertheless, whatever kind of bench you end up with there are a number of items that will improve its efficiency. These are chiefly items you can make and install to improve the holding ability of this most fundamental piece of equipment.

To start with, a bench needs to be a firm and secure workplace. It should be heavy and stout enough to support the work and not budge, rock, or wobble when items are being planed or sawed on it. Although most manufactured benches are provided with some form of vise it can have many other features. Of these, certainly the simplest fixture on any bench is a bench stop, of which there are a number of varieties listed below.

BENCH STOPS:

A BENCH STOP MAY BE NOTHING MORE THAN A dowel let into the surface of the bench at the far left-hand end of the bench — assuming you are right-handed and generally work from right to left — secured at whatever height is convenient by a friction fit alone. If available, hardwood such as oak is preferable to a piece of softwood for reasons of strength. The size need not be much more than 1in. or 1-1/2in. square, by a length sufficient to penetrate the thickness of the bench top and protrude perhaps a maximum of 2in.

ROUND BENCH STOP

THE EASIEST WAY TO CREATE A ROUND BENCH stop — ideal for a bench without bench dogs *(see page 6)*, or indeed for any other work surface such as the top of a sawhorse or a temporary outfeed table — is to use a length of dowel. Commercially available dowel rods are rarely perfectly round; therefore boring a hole in the surface to receive the dowel the same nominal diameter as the dowel will usually guarantee a sufficiently tight friction fit as the slightly out-of-round dowel is forced into the perfectly round hole. For most purposes a 1/2in. diameter rod will be sufficient.

SQUARE BENCH STOP

A SQUARE BENCH STOP IS A LITTLE MORE difficult to make since its hole must be mortised fairly accurately to match. It may, of course, not be exactly square; the important thing is that it presents a flat surface to the workpiece, which is often a little more secure than a round surface. Use hardwood such as oak rather than softwood such as pine. If the stop and its hole are slightly rectangular rather than perfectly square, orient the side that faces the

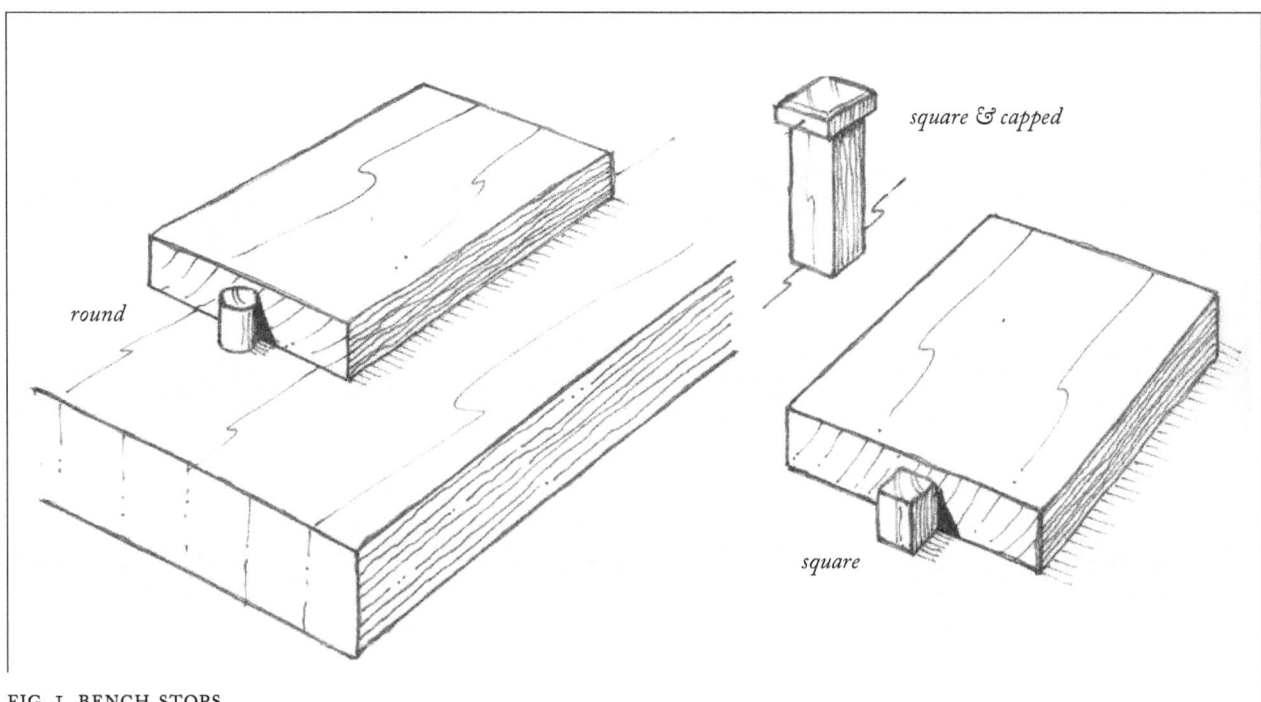

FIG. 1 BENCH STOPS

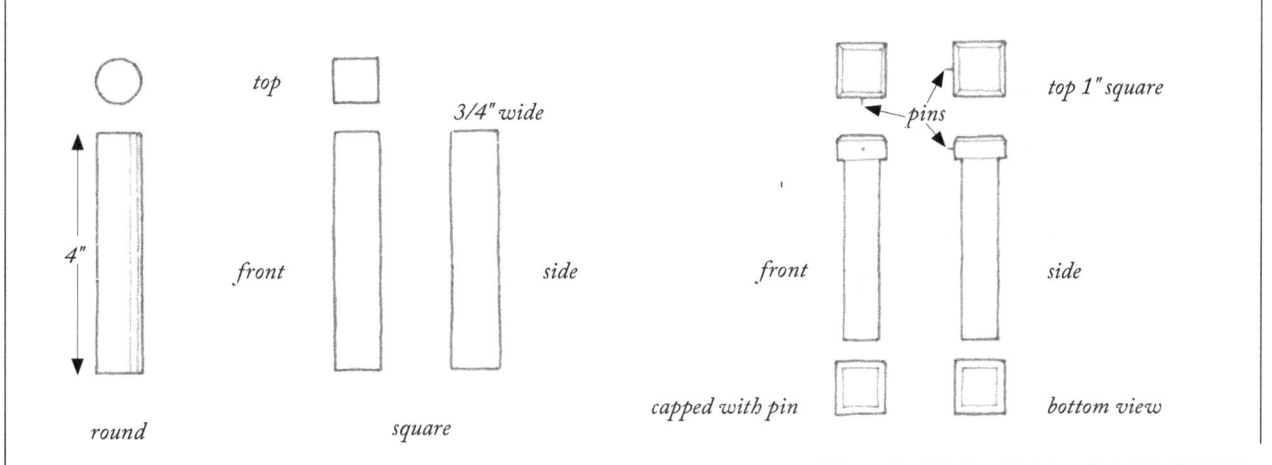

FIG. 2 VARIOUS BENCH STOP DIMENSIONS

workpiece so that it is side grain rather than face grain against which the workpiece bears, since this is stronger.

CAPPED & PINNED BENCH STOP

THE THREE ADVANTAGES OF THIS KIND OF stop — a flat face against which the work may bear, an added pin to prevent the work from sliding off, and a cap to prevent the stop from disappearing below the surface of the bench — all entail a little more work.

The remarks concerning size, length, and grain direction mentioned above apply here equally. The cap represents the most important consideration: whether you decide to make it integral by reducing the shaft of the stop where it is inserted through the worksurface or whether the cap is a separate added piece. The former method is stronger, the second method perhaps quicker, provided the cap is substantial enough and pre-bored to accept a screw that fixes it to the shaft. Only the smallest pin is necessary, but to avoid the possibility of the pin damaging any finished surface of the workpiece make the stop perfectly square so that it may be rotated when needed.

CAM-FIXED BENCH STOP

SLIGHTLY MORE CONVENIENT IS AN ADJUSTABLE bench stop, especially if secured at the desired height by means of a cam or a screw tightened against it below the surface of the bench.

FIG. 3 shows the cam variety with the cam rotated to support the stop. When the cam is rotated clockwise the stop sinks down flush with the surface of the bench. It is prevented from falling out completely by the flat step cut in the cam.

Note that the cam is a section of a spiral — not of a circle *(see* FIG. 4, *next page)*. The more exaggerated the spiral the greater the protrusion of the stop that rests on it will be as the cam is rotated. An easy way to lay out the cam is to describe two concentric circles, the larger one with a diameter 1in. greater than that of the smaller one, and simply within the space of one revolution freehand a connecting line. At the point where this line connects to the outer diameter cut a perpendicular step back to the inner circle. Having made sure that the hole for the screw that attaches the cam to the bench is exactly

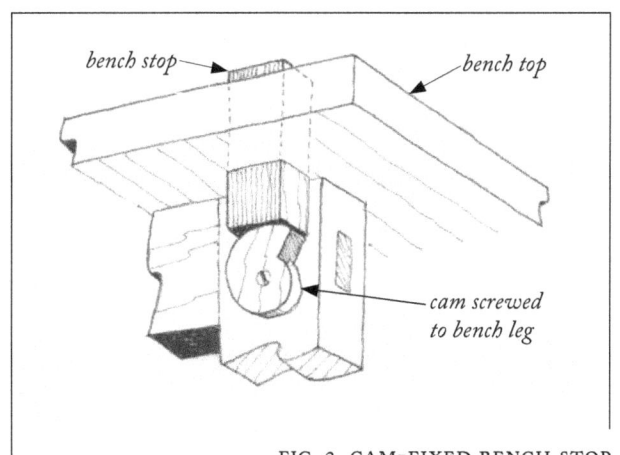

FIG. 3 CAM-FIXED BENCH STOP

TRADITIONAL JIGS & FIXTURES

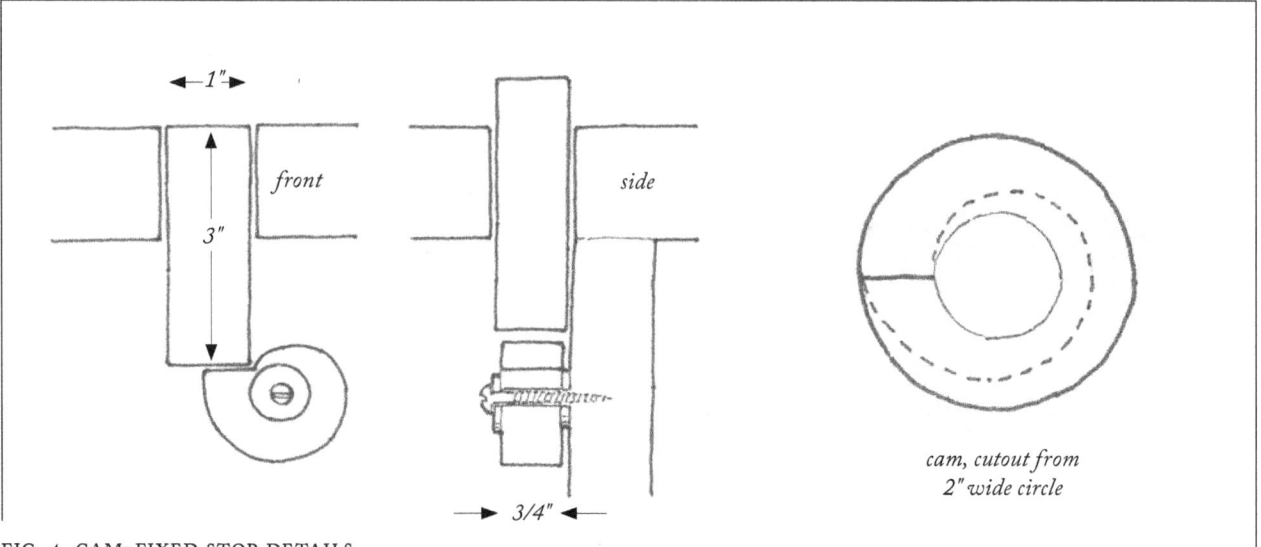

FIG. 4 CAM-FIXED STOP DETAILS

in the center of both circles, attach the cam to the bench with the top resting on the step at the point where this allows the top of the stop to be flush with the top of the bench. Although a countersunk woodscrew may be used to attach the cam, a slightly better method is to use a roundhead screw and two washers: one behind the head of the screw and the other between the cam and the bench. This will prevent the screw from becoming either too loose or too tight as the cam is repeatedly used. The screw should, of course, be inserted tightly enough so that the cam remains at whatever height it is raised or lowered to.

SCREW-FIXED BENCH STOP

A SIMPLER ARRANGEMENT IS THE SCREW variety where a screw is used to tighten against the stop either through an adjacent part of the bench's substructure — such as a leg or a section of skirting, or through a separate piece attached to the underside of the top.

The screw is actually a wingnut-bolt that works within a tapped hole. The size known as 1/4 by 20 is most useful. The 1/4 refers the largest diameter of the bolt; the 20 refers to the pitch of the thread, or how many threads per inch. Buy a bolt that is somewhat longer than the thickness of the wood through which it is to be inserted, and bore a hole for it a little smaller than 1/4in. The first time you insert the bolt into this hole the threads will cut their way into the wood and remain threaded, keeping the bolt secure.

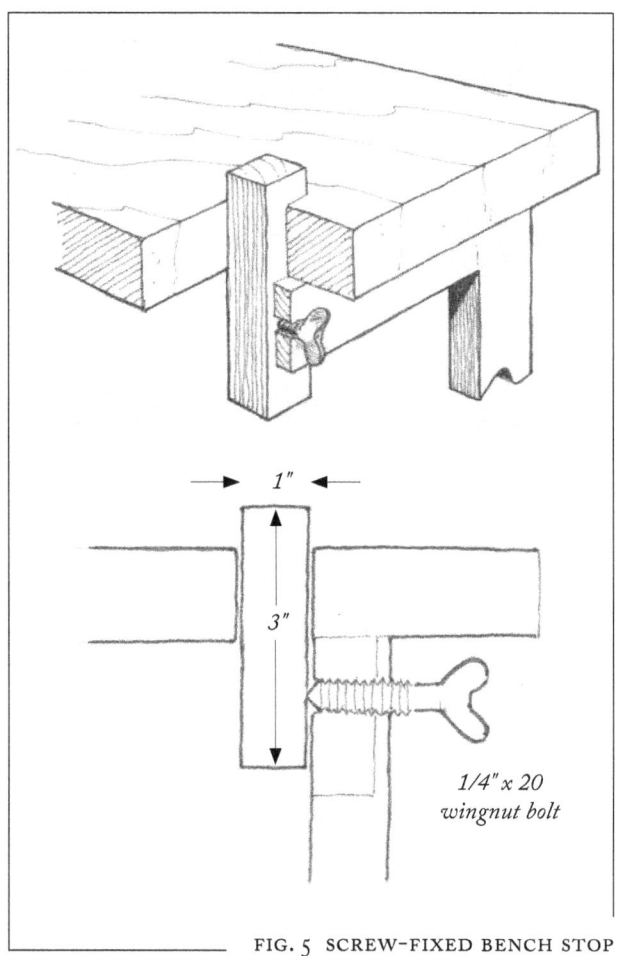

FIG. 5 SCREW-FIXED BENCH STOP

MANUFACTURED METAL BENCH STOP

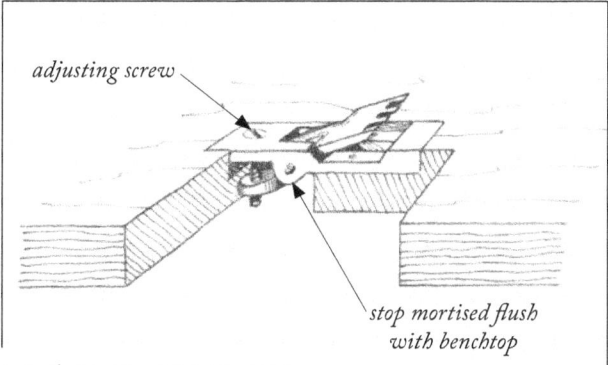

FIG. 6 METAL BENCH STOP

MANUFACTURED METAL BENCH STOPS THAT are controlled either by a spring or a height-adjusting screw have also been available for a long time. These are usually designed to be mortised flush into the bench top wherever convenient. The better ones are made of soft metal designed to minimize damage to any cutting edges that may come in contact with them. It is, however, sometimes advisable to insert a spacing block between the workpiece and any kind of stop to protect a finished edge.

The only detail to be aware of with this item is its placement. It is usually well to imitate the placement of such items as are sometimes included with store-bought benches, namely close to the front edge of the bench at the left-hand end — assuming you are right-handed; left-handers who work in the opposite direction will want to mortise this item into the right-hand end.

V-BLOCK
(V-BOARD, BENCH CLAMP, TOP CLAMP)

THE ADVANTAGE OF A BENCH STOP IS THAT IT CAN be pushed down level with the top of the bench when not needed, thereby leaving a continuously flat worksurface with no obstruction. On the other hand, it is not always as secure a means of stopping or holding the workpiece as a V-block. V-blocks, of whatever size, and however positioned — longitudinally or laterally — are more permanent, usually being nailed or screwed to the surface of the bench, but are inevitably in the way. If you find nailing or screwing something to the worksurface to be objectionable, they may instead be designed so that they can be clamped to the end of the bench top or, if large enough, be fitted with dowels that fit into dog holes or other purpose-bored holes in the bench's surface.
(See also Chapter 4: Wedged V-block.)

Cut a V-block from the end of a length of 3/4in.-thick one-by-twelve. For most work this need only be about 12in. long. But for securing especially heavy pieces making it from 5/4in.-thick stock will be much better.

The angle of the V should be no more than 30°; a greater angle will have less holding power and a smaller angle may be liable to split. Plywood has the advantage of being less liable to split no matter how much pressure is brought to bear on it, but other sheet goods such as medium density fiberboard (MDF) have less strength.

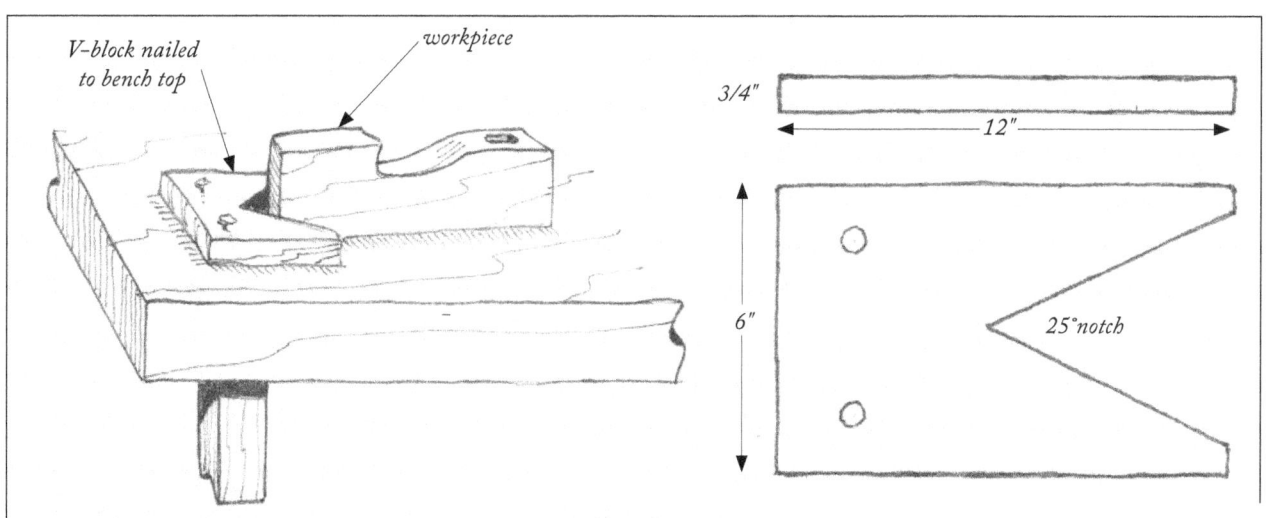

FIG. 7 V-BLOCK BENCH STOP

TRADITIONAL JIGS & FIXTURES

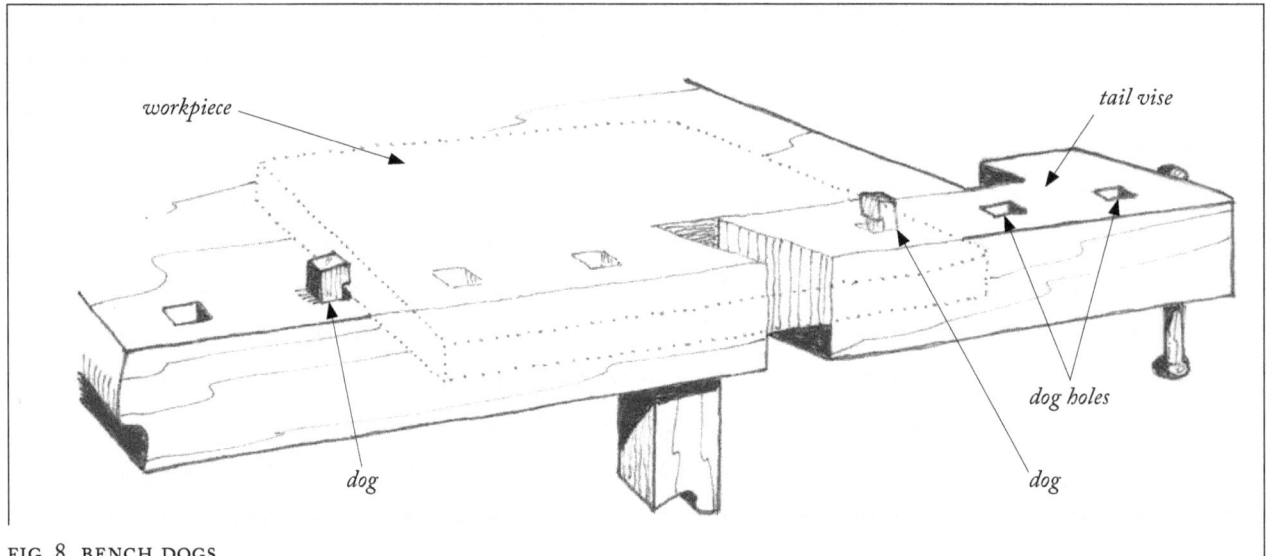

FIG. 8 BENCH DOGS

BENCH DOGS

THE TERM 'BENCH DOG' COMMONLY REFERS TO a particular kind of bench stop that is located in a series of so-called 'dog holes' mortised at regular intervals along the front edge of a bench.

Like bench stops, bench dogs may be made of wood or metal. They may be round or square, and they may be usermade or manufactured. Large cabinetmaker's benches fitted with tail vises are usually provided with dog holes in the tail vise itself, as well as along the front edge of the bench, so that a workpiece may be held securely between a dog positioned in one of the front edge mortises and a dog in the tail vise that can be tightened against it. (A tail vise is a vise fixed to the end of a bench in addition to the one — known as a face vise — fitted at the front).

Store-bought manufactured dogs are commonly made from metal, as are dogs provided with new benches, but wooden, usermade dogs are far safer, especially when used to hold workpieces that are being planed, for should the plane run into the dog a wooden one will not damage the plane iron, whereas a metal dog, even if made of a softer metal than cast iron, might inflict serious damage and necessitate a lengthy resharpening. Furthermore, be aware that not all metal dogs are made the same size. They must be large enough to fit in the dog hole with a slight amount of friction (some have springs for this purpose) so that they will stay at whatever height is needed, but not so large that adjusting them up or down requires the use of a mallet or a hammer.

Make your own wooden dog from a piece of hardwood that has been cut so that its top inch or so fits nicely into any pre-existing dog hole and when pushed down flush with the bench's surface rests on the step that reduces the dog hole's width. Cut the lower end of the shank that fits into this reduced width at a slight angle of 10° or so. Glue a thin (1/8in.–1/4in.) hardwood strip to this angled section, making it long enough to extend just below the head of the dog, and the dog will be easily held at any required height.

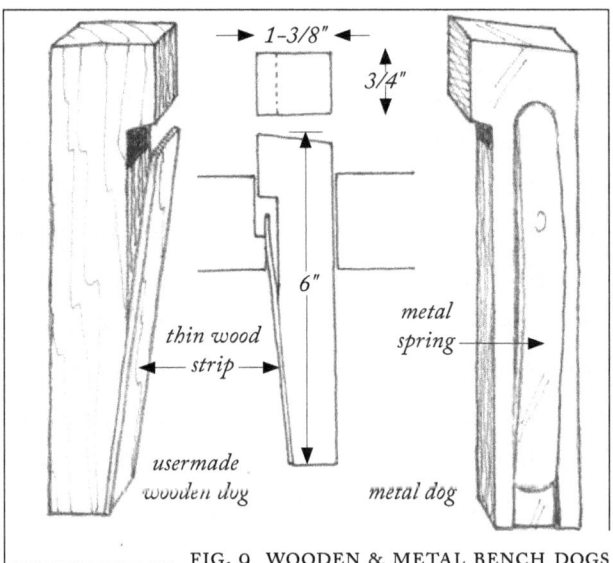

FIG. 9 WOODEN & METAL BENCH DOGS

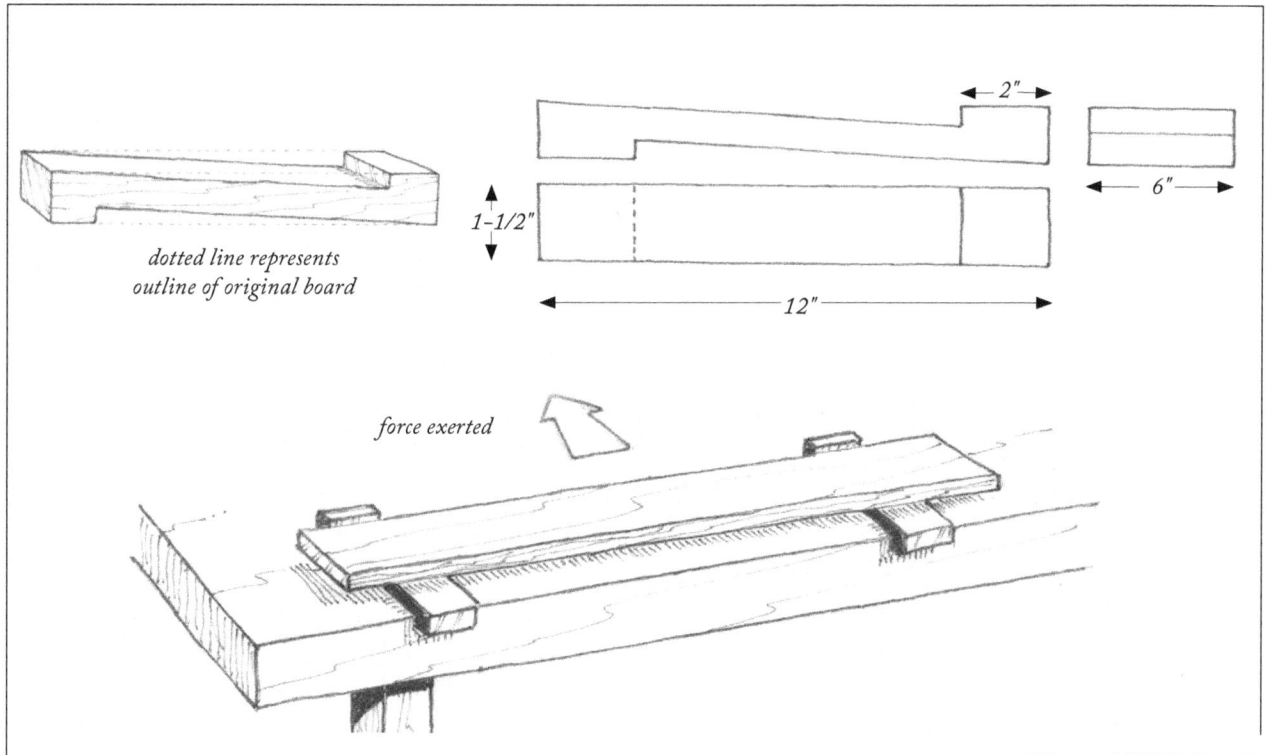

FIG. 10 BENCH HOOKS

BENCH HOOK
(SIDE HOOK, SIDE REST)

NOT EVERYTHING MAY BE CONVENIENTLY HELD at the edge of the bench. Bench hooks offer a little more choice, especially where operations such as sawing and chiseling need to be performed across the workpiece rather than along it such as planing.

The simplest form of bench hook is a narrow piece of wood cut in its thickness so that the bottom hooks against the edge of the workbench and the top provides a stop against which the workpiece may be pushed and thereby securely held while being worked on.

Cut a hook or step into a piece of 6in. or wider piece of scrap, such as a 1 ft.-long length of two-by-six, on both ends but on opposite sides. The hook parts need only be half the thickness of the two-by-six with the flat remaining parts of the two-by-six roughly chiseled or hatcheted from the uncut ends in a gentle slope down to the bottom of the sawcut at the hooked ends. Make the vertical cut that defines the hook no less than 2 in. in from the end, or it will risk being knocked off should the supported workpiece be attacked too vigorously, such as when mortising with a mallet.

For sawing or boring — operations usually undertaken transversely rather than longitudinally as is typically the situation when planing — and where a large or long workpiece needs support or simply to be held off the surface of the bench, a pair of bench hooks of roughly equal size can be used to keep the workpiece at an equal height.

More common, and often more useful than one or two narrow bench hooks made from two-by-fours, is a much wider bench hook capable of supporting a workpiece on its own bed. Even so it is often necessary to use a second bench hook or a piece of scrap of similar thickness to keep the end of a very long workpiece from sagging. It is best to make the hooked sections of a wide bench hook from separate pieces nailed, screwed or glued to the base. Exercise care in using metal fasteners when doing this since they can interfere with sawcuts that might be made in the hooked sections should the bench hook be used not merely for holding but also as a sawing guide as described later.
(For detailed construction suggestions see Chapter 3: Bench Hook.)

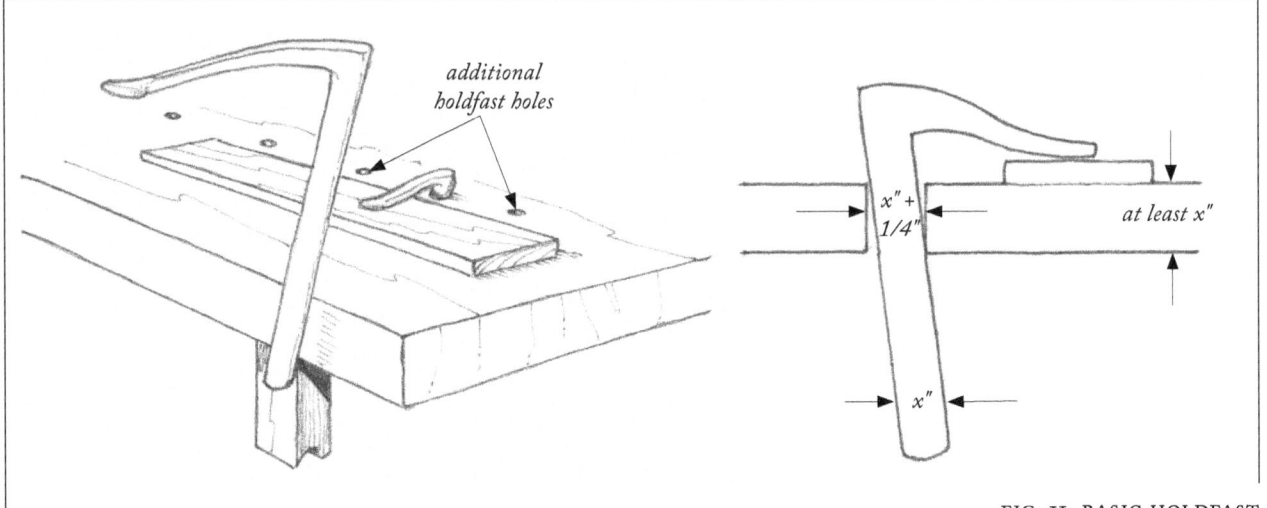

FIG. 11 BASIC HOLDFAST

HOLDFASTS:

WHILE VISES, ALONE, AND SOMETIMES IN conjunction with bench dogs as explained above — are good for securing relatively narrow workpieces such as boards to be planed, bored, or sawed, irregularly shaped pieces may be better held by a holdfast. The holdfast, being invariably made out of metal, is now usually a bought item since few woodworkers, even the most traditionally inclined, own or have access to a small forge.

The exact location of holdfast holes is usually accomplished by trial and error, but if centered in the front-to-back width of the worksurface and spaced regularly apart at 12 in. intervals this will often be found to be most useful.

BASIC HOLDFAST

THE SIMPLEST DESIGN IS NO MORE THAN AN upside-down, L-shaped piece of metal that is dropped into a hole slightly larger than the diameter of its shank so that the short perpendicular arm bears on the workpiece. Provided the bench top is sufficiently thick, tapping the shaft into the hole with the short end of the holdfast resting on a workpiece at least 1/2 in. thick will cause the long arm of the holdfast to become wedged into its hole very securely. A simple tap behind the arm releases the holdfast.

The diameter of the hole into which the holdfast is inserted is critical. If it is too wide or too narrow it will in both cases be difficult to get the shank

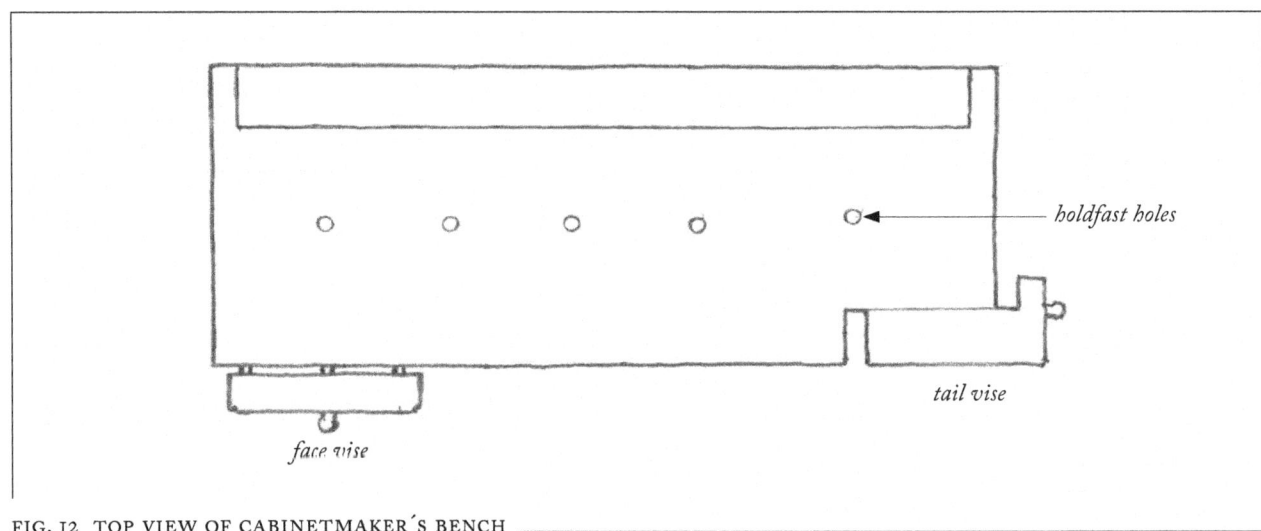

FIG. 12 TOP VIEW OF CABINETMAKER'S BENCH

securely wedged. A good rule of thumb is to bore a hole wider than the diameter of the shaft by a little less than a quarter of the shaft's diameter; for example, a 3/4in.-diameter shaft will wedge securely in a 7/8in.-diameter hole. Equally important is the depth of the hole, for if the wood in which the hole is bored is too thin (unlikely in the case of most benches, but possible if you attempt to use a holdfast in a saw horse) the wedging will be insecure. The solution is simply to increase the thickness by gluing or screwing another piece of wood to the underside of the worksurface at the spot where the hole is to be bored.

SCREW HOLDFAST

A MUCH MORE SOPHISTICATED VERSION HAS A tommy-barred screw which forces the short arm against the workpiece providing even more security. This screw also eliminates the need to hit the back of the holdfast to release it. Such holdfasts may additionally be sold with one or two metal collars of exactly the right size. These collars are intended to be mortised into the bench, thus preventing a raw hole enlarging with use.

The most vexing aspect of this device is always where to bore the hole in the bench top; it being almost inevitable that wherever this is done will sooner or later be found to be in the wrong place! One of the more useful locations is in the center of the bench's width close to the tail vise if one is present, or opposite the face vise should this be the only vise, since vise and holdfast can often be used in conjunction to great effect. Ultimately, however, you may find that several positions are needed, as shown opposite in FIG. 12, and as was indeed common in eighteenth-century French workbenches, which relied almost exclusively on stops and holdfasts rather than on vises.

BRIDGE CLAMP

AN IRREGULAR WORKPIECE IS SOMETIMES BETTER secured by means of a bridge clamp — a separate piece of wood that bears upon both the workpiece and a spacer block of the same overall thickness or height as the workpiece, and which is itself clamped, often by a holdfast or even another clamp that engages it and the bench.

If the irregular workpiece that needs to be secured has been so formed by having been bandsawed, the offcut often provides the ideal matching surface to engage the workpiece securely, and may be used on its own if long enough or fixed to the underneath of a separate board.

Both clamp and spacer block can be conveniently made from any sufficiently large piece of scrap, a softwood bridgepiece such as pine being less likely to damage the workpiece than a hardwood bridge. Owing to the irregularity of such a jig it is seldom useful to keep it after use, a new one being made when next the need arises.

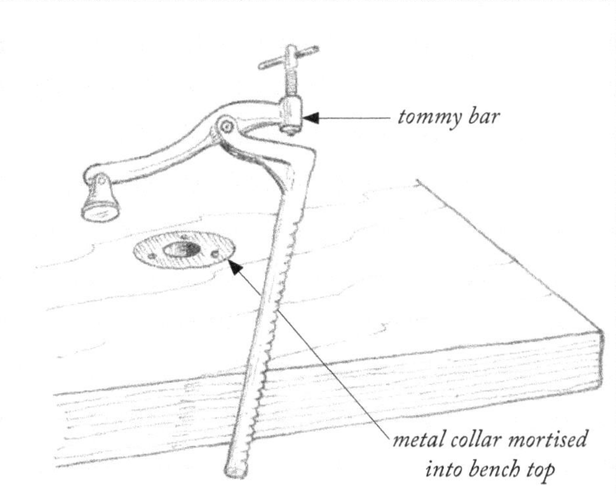

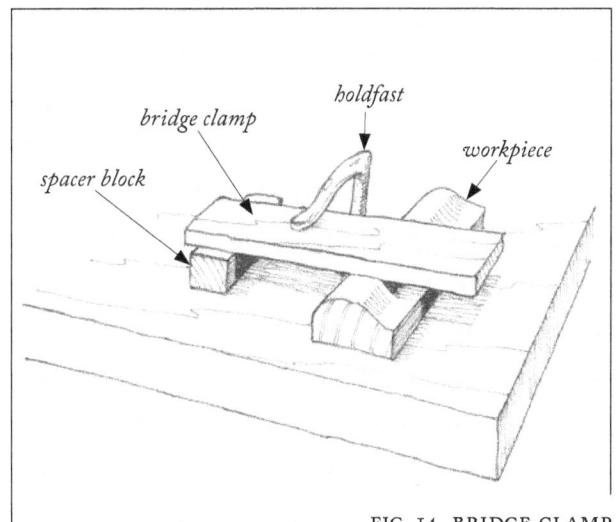

FIG. 13 SCREW HOLDFAST

FIG. 14 BRIDGE CLAMP

II: VISE FIXTURES

SINCE MOST WORKBENCHES ARE PROVIDED WITH vises, which like benches themselves come in a wide variety, their description, like that of benches is not strictly within the purview of this book. But whatever kind of vise your bench may be fitted with there are a number of items that can be made to increase their utility. The first group of these will enable really long workpieces — that might otherwise prove difficult to be held in the average vise — to be held more securely than by clamps or holdfasts.

DEADMEN:

A DEADMAN IS THE SOMEWHAT MACABRE NAME given to a vertical board or post bored with a number of holes at different heights, into one of which a peg or dowel may be placed on which the end of a long workpiece held in the face vise is supported. Several varieties are possible as described below.

FIXED DEADMAN

SIMPLE HOME-MADE BENCHES MAY HAVE THE right-hand leg bored, or if this is not feasible may have a separately-made deadman simply clamped to a convenient part of the bench's substructure, such as a leg.

FREE-STANDING DEADMAN

THE SIMPLEST KIND OF FREE-STANDING deadman may be nothing more than a length of two-by-four long enough to be stood on the floor and held in the jaws of a tail vise (if one is present) as shown opposite in FIG. 16.

A two-by-four, or something of similar size and length, bored on its wide face rather than on its narrow side, is usually the most convenient way to provide a deadman. The advantage of boring the wide face is that a second column of staggered holes may be bored to allow a greater choice of height positions for the workpiece. Boring the holes at a very slight angle up from perfectly horizontal decreases the likelihood that the workpiece will slip off the inserted pegs.

Regular 1/2 in.-diameter hardwood dowels which, when inserted into a two-by-four deadman, protrude 2 in. or so are usually sufficient, but the owner of a particularly finely made workbench might make a planed, chamfered, and polished deadman as a matching accessory to be proud of.

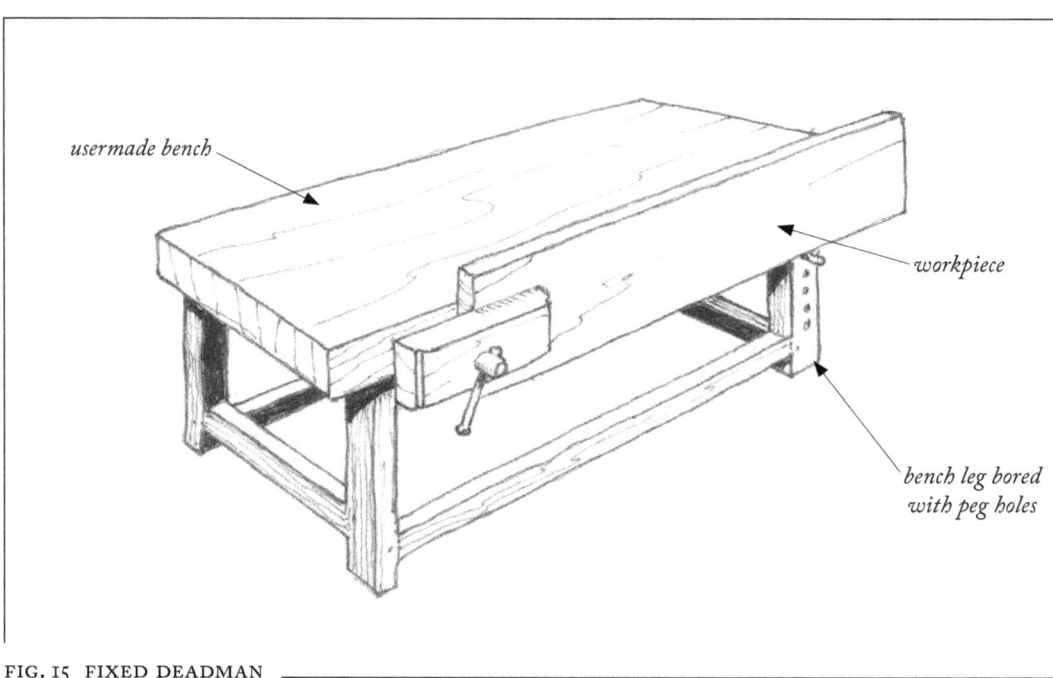

FIG. 15 FIXED DEADMAN

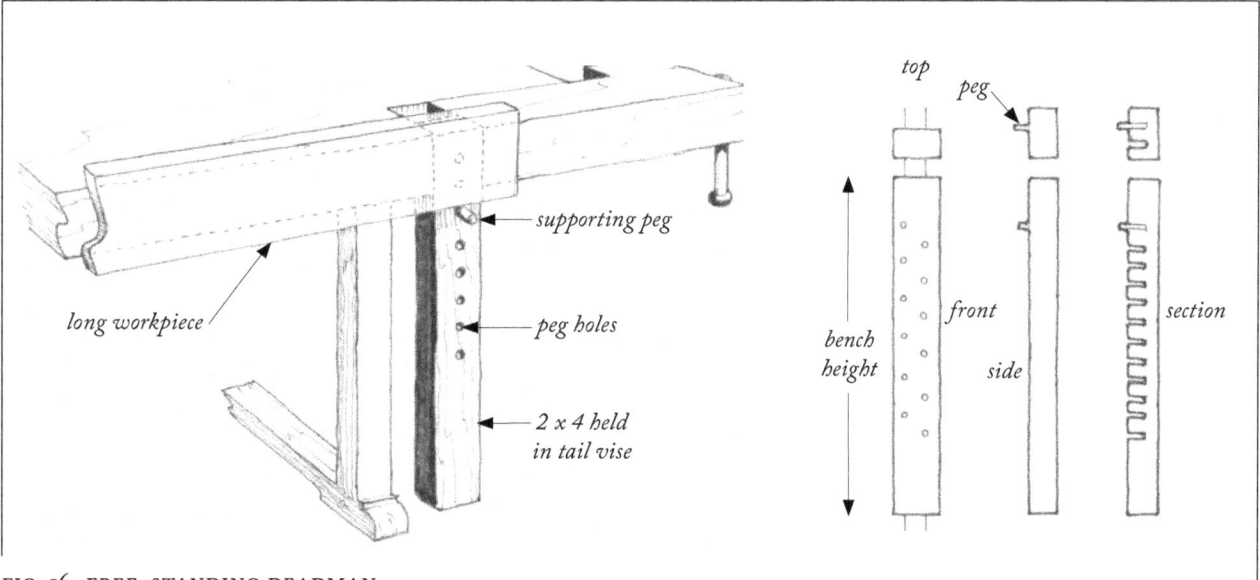

FIG. 16 FREE-STANDING DEADMAN

SLIDING DEADMAN

MANY SOPHISTICATED NINETEENTH-CENTURY cabinetmaker's benches were often fitted with sliding deadmen. These are vertical, bored members both ends of which are V-notched to run on rails similarly shaped to receive them (as shown below in FIG. 17) at the front of the bench.

It is sometimes possible to retrofit a bench with a sliding deadman, especially if the underneath of the bench is free of drawers, cupboards, and shelving. All that is required are two rails between which the deadman may be slid from side to side as needed to accomodate different lengths of any given workpiece. One method is to cut a tongue at each end of the deadman and fit these tongues into grooves cut in the rails. Better (because the groove in the lower rail can become clogged with shavings) is to V-notch the ends of the deadman to slide over a reverse V-shaped profile formed on the inner edges of the rails. Making the ends of the deadman wider than its center, and keeping the rails waxed, makes this fixture much easier to use than a straight deadman.

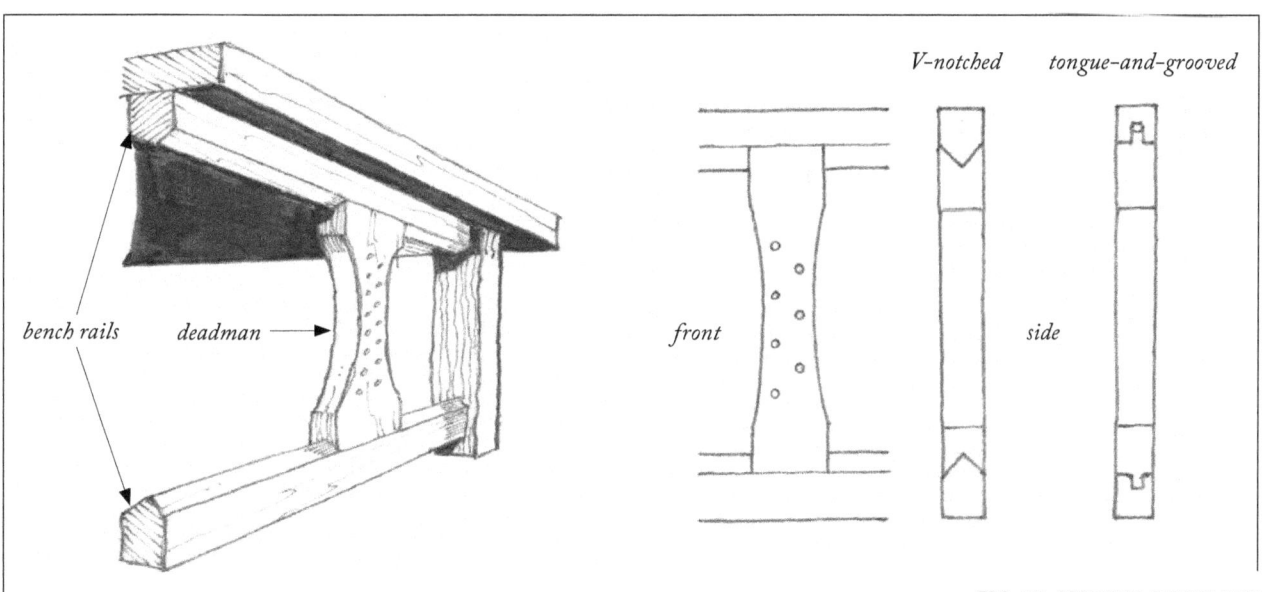

FIG. 17 SLIDING DEADMAN

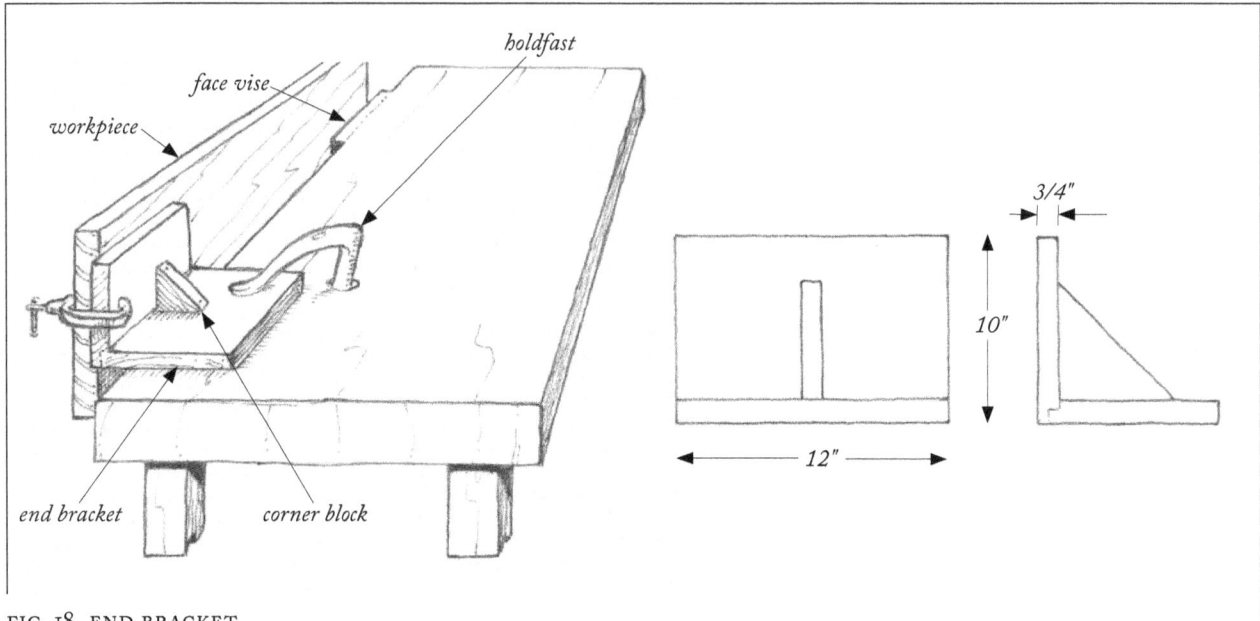

FIG. 18 END BRACKET

END BRACKET

A SIMPLE RIGHT-ANGLED BRACKET CLAMPED TO the top of the bench by a holdfast and to which in turn is clamped the workpiece, cannot only take the place of a deadman for supporting the end of a long workpiece, but may also be more convenient than trying to hold an especially long vertical workpiece in a vise.

The essence of this jig lies in the accurate verticality of the upright piece to which the workpiece is attached. If the two pieces are simply rabbetd together the temptation is to orient the grain horizontally in relation to the bench top as shown in FIG. 18 — which leaves the upright piece more vulnerable to being broken off than if they had been joined with corner dovetails, for in the latter case the grain of the vertical piece would be rising from the bench rather than parallel to it. The use of plywood, of course, eliminates this concern. In any event it is wise to guarantee both the strength and the squareness of the jig by including a carefully cut corner block.

AUXILIARY VISE JAWS:

THE SECOND GROUP OF FIXTURES THAT CAN increase the utility of vises consists of a selection of modifications to the vise jaws. Although many eighteenth-century British benches had vises whose jaws could be closed parallel or not parallel depending on the shape of the workpiece being held, and although some modern (and relatively expensive) so-called universal vises also have jaws that may be similarly adjusted in or out of parallel, most contemporary vises, because of the way the guide arms and screws are made, operate on the principle that when properly installed and adjusted the jaws are will remain perfectly parallel. This is fine only if trying to hold workpieces that also have parallel faces. For everything else, including very thin items and irregular or round workpieces, something else is needed.

REPLACEMENT JAW FACINGS

DEPENDING ON THE KIND OF VISE ALREADY present on your bench, many of the following auxiliary jaws can be made to simply sit in the vise resting on the guide arms or adjusting screw. If, however, because of the placement of these parts this is not practical it is often possible to replace the existing wood facings of many metal jaws with slightly larger pieces whose sides are rabbeted, over which auxiliary jaws can be slipped and held. The tongues formed by these rabbets, and which slide

TRADITIONAL JIGS & FIXTURES

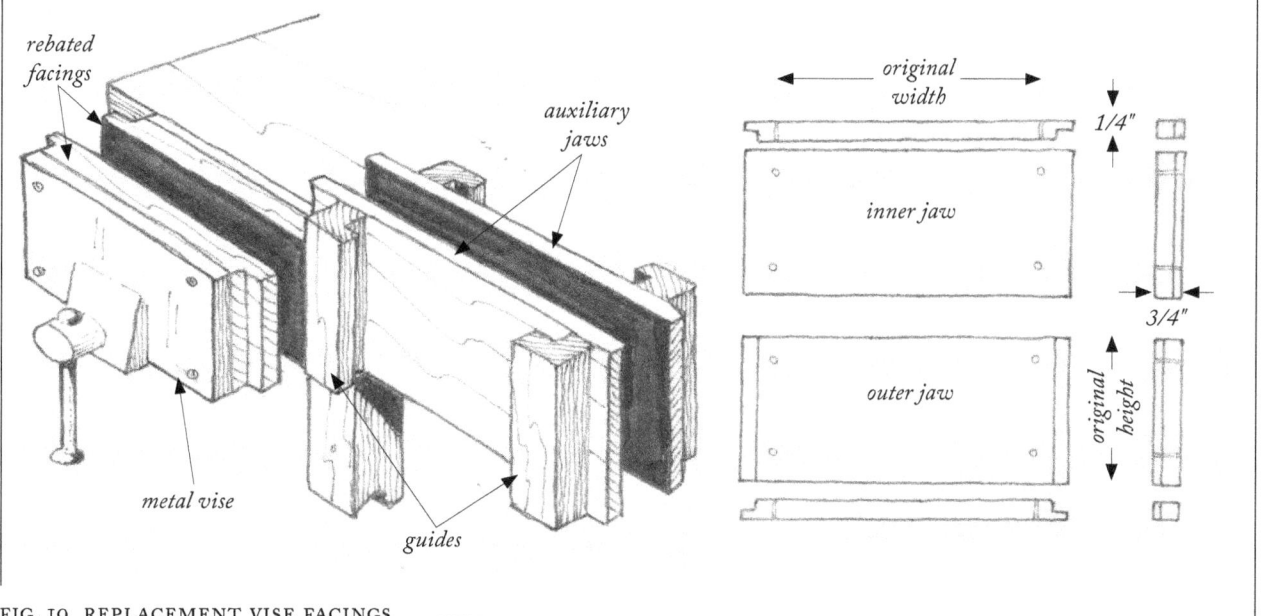

FIG. 19 REPLACEMENT VISE FACINGS

into the slots attached to the auxiliary jaws, should be thick enough merely to fit comfortably into the slots, since no pressure is ever exerted on them, everything being held within the vise.

Detach — usually by unscrewing — the existing facings, and use these pieces as templates from which to cut new, 4in.-wider facings.

Cut 1in. rabbets in the ends of these new facings and attach them to the vise, making sure that the rabbeted ends are clear of the metal jaws so that any auxiliary jaws fitted with guides as shown can be easily but securely slipped over them. The vise can now be used as before but with the added ability of being able to accept any of the auxiliary jaws described below.

FINISHING JAWS

A PAIR OF BOARDS SOMEWHAT LARGER THAN THE jaws of your vise, if covered with soft material such as felt, old but clean toweling, or even carpet, is useful when securing finished workpieces should you be concerned about damaging the surfaces of the workpiece. It is best to attach the protective material to one side only of the jaws. If carpeting,

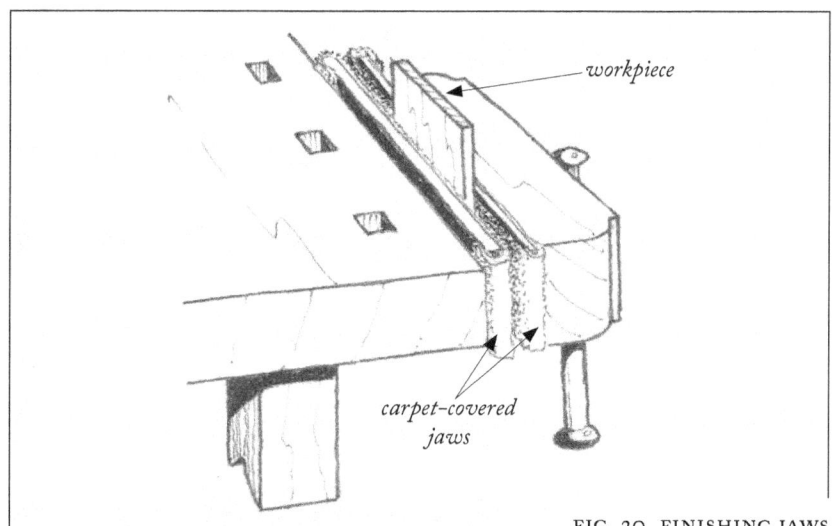

FIG. 20 FINISHING JAWS

HOLDING

TRADITIONAL JIGS & FIXTURES

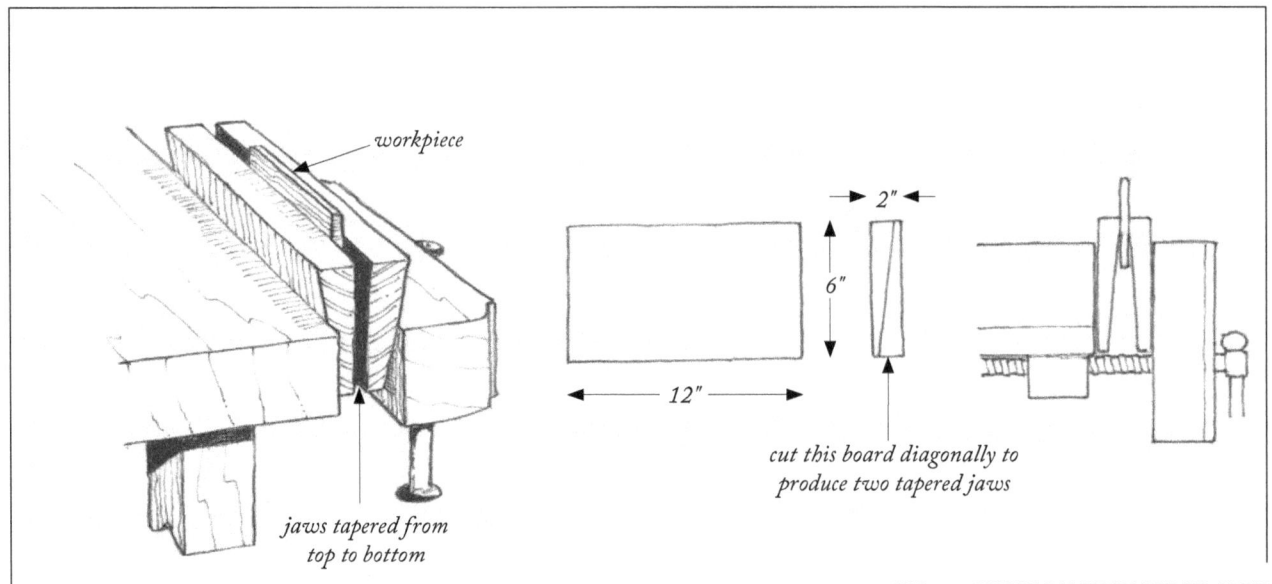

FIG. 21 VERTICALLY TAPERED JAWS

for example, is wrapped around the ends, take care to ensure that the center of the finishing jaws are not able to deflect, for otherwise the workpiece may not be held securely.

Protective material like carpet may be quickly attached with small tacks or staples to the backs of the jaws, or even with an adhesive suitable for gluing fabric to wood.

VERTICALLY TAPERED JAWS

FOR VERY THIN WORKPIECES, OR WHEN CLAMPING something between vise jaws that no longer close with a perfect exactness, a pair of slightly tapered jaws, thinner at the bottom than at the top, will guarantee a secure grip since the difficulty usually lies in the ability of the vise jaws to close tightly level with the bench's working surface. *(See also Chapter 3: Saw Vise, and Chapter 5: Scraper Vise.)* In the long run it is best to restore the vise jaws so that they close properly, but this is not always possible.

Tapered jaws can be made by resawing a thicker board roughly the same width and height as the vise's jaws. If the board is about 2in. thick it should be possible to make the resaw cut at an angle, producing two identically tapered jaws. Alternatively a single board can be planed to be thinner along one long side than on the other side. The angle of resawing or the amount of planed taper will depend on the degree to which the vise jaws no longer touch at the top when closed.

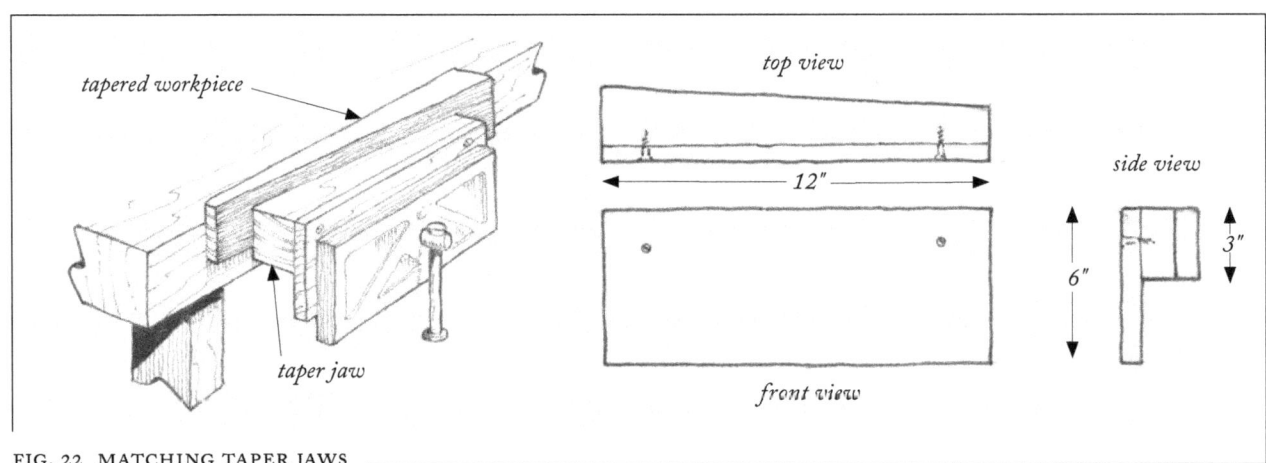

FIG. 22 MATCHING TAPER JAWS

MATCHING TAPER JAW

THE OPPOSITE PROBLEM TO SECURING STRAIGHT stock in vise jaws that do not close properly occurs when trying to secure a longitudinally tapered workpiece in a vise whose jaws do in fact close perfectly parallel. The solution is to provide an additional jaw facing to which is attached a matching taper. Very often the offcut from the tapered workpiece itself can be used — attached to an extra inner or outer jaw, or even to the workpiece itself, with double-sided tape — to make such a jaw.

The simplest form of taper jaw consists of a board a little larger than an auxiliary vise jaw to which is attached, either permanently in the case of repetitive tapers or temporarily (with double-sided adhesive tape) for different tapers. Note that when placing the workpiece in the vise for operations such as planing where grain direction is important, the taper jaw may be placed either against the outer vise jaw or the inner vise jaw — thus reversing the grain of the workpiece.

CRADLE JAWS:

ROUND STOCK PRESENTS A DIFFERENT PROBLEM from the previous examples, but a very general solution that will be found to hold a wide variety of shapes is to make a pair of auxiliary jaws faced with wide V-blocks. The V-blocks may be fixed horizontally or vertically as the occasion demands.

VERTICAL CRADLE JAWS

THERE IS LITTLE PROBLEM IN MAKING A PAIR OF vertical cradle jaws other than ensuring that the V-blocks that are attached to the auxiliary jaw facings are not notched too deeply or with too tight a 'V'. Such V-blocks are both a good general solution for holding shaped or irregular stock, but for a guaranteed fit when holding perfectly round stock bore a hole in a solid block to the same diameter as the workpiece and then saw the bored block in half. The resulting kerf will have removed enough wood so that the two halves, when attached

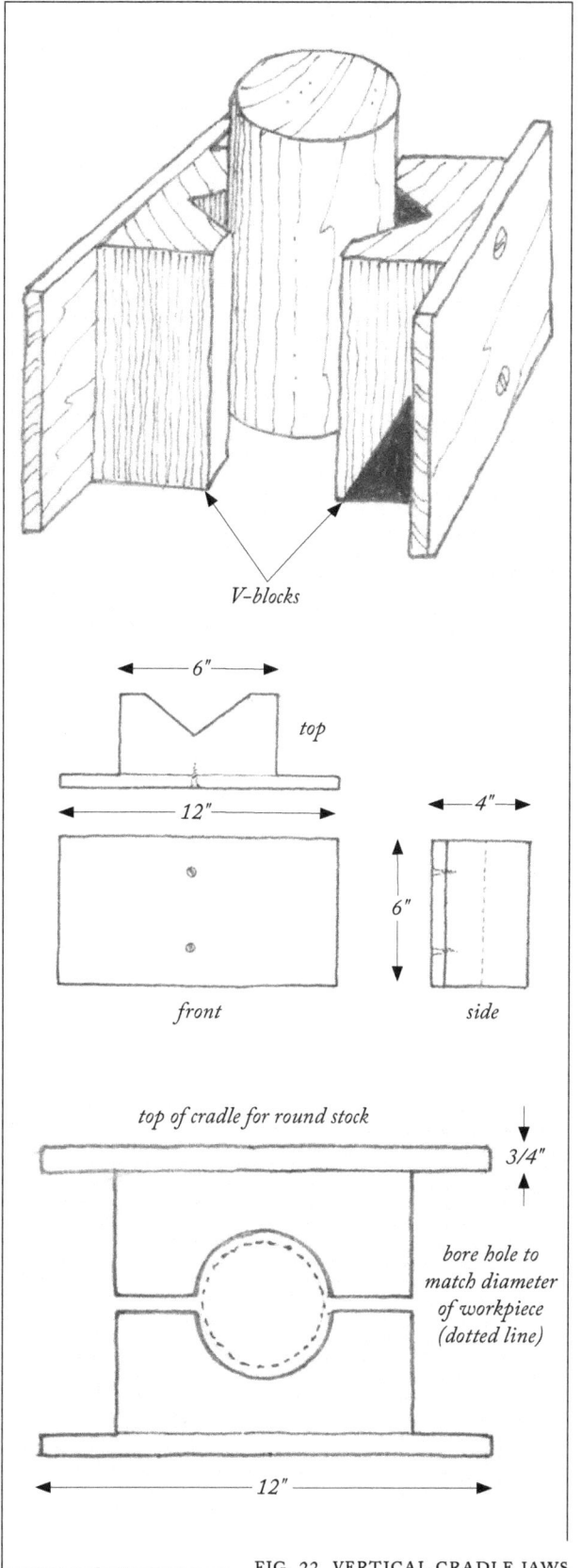

FIG. 23 VERTICAL CRADLE JAWS

TRADITIONAL JIGS & FIXTURES

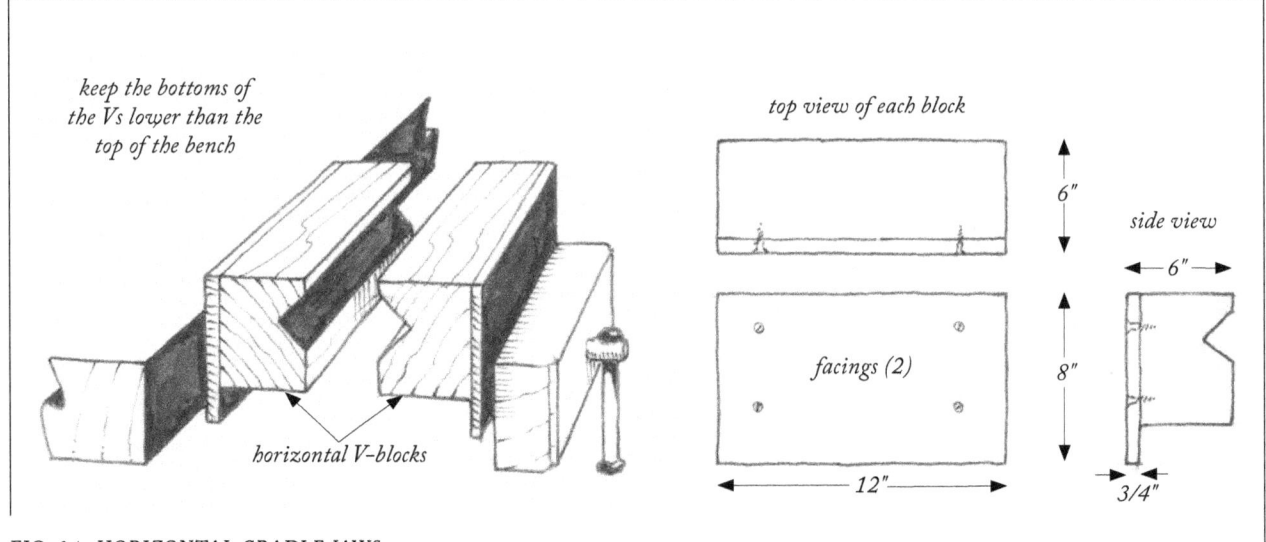

FIG. 24 HORIZONTAL CRADLE JAWS

to the auxiliary jaw facings, clamp the workpiece with the greatest security.

HORIZONTAL CRADLE JAWS

IN ORDER THAT ANY WORKPIECE HELD horizontally in horizontal cradle jaws is usefully accessible for planing, sawing, or chiseling operations, it is normally necessary that the upper surface of the workpiece be higher than the top of the bench. Provision must therefore be made to ensure that when the vise is closed the auxiliary jaws remain vertically parallel. This can be best achieved either by making sure that the bottom of the V-grooved part extends below the level of the top of the jaws or by providing them with rabbeted guides as described above so that the lower part is not squeezed and consequently causes the upper part to open and lose its grip on the workpiece.

TALL JAWS

SOME MANUFACTURED METAL VISES ARE FITTED with an adjustable depth stop in the outer jaw, but a cabinetmaker's bench used for fine furnituremaking is usually provided with vises whose wooden jaws are perfectly flush with the bench top. It is good practice, in fact, when periodically dressing the

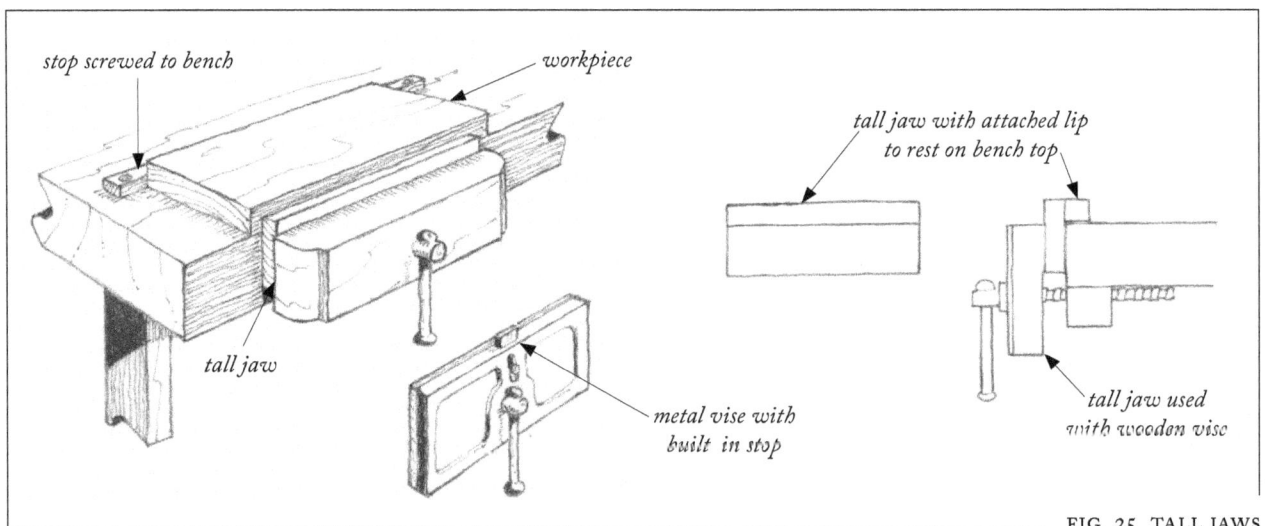

FIG. 25 TALL JAWS

TRADITIONAL JIGS & FIXTURES

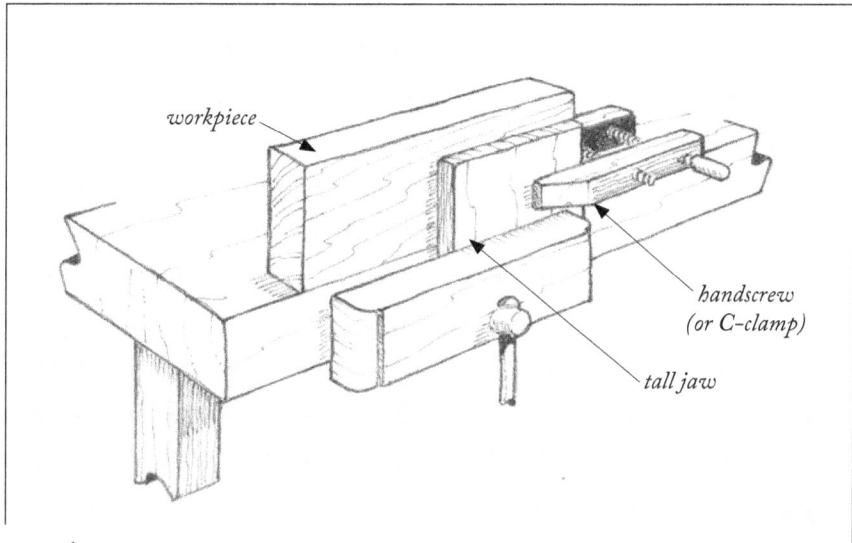

FIG. 26 CLAMPING WITH TALL JAWS

top of such benches in order to maintain perfect flatness, to plane the tops of the (closed) vise jaws together with the bench itself. For such flush-top vises an auxiliary jaw as wide as the vise itself, but taller by 1in. or so when resting on the vise's screws and guide bars, can be used similarly to the stop provided in metal-faced jaws to secure a bench-top workpiece against a facing stop strip screwed or clamped to the bench.

Almost any board that is tall enough to rest on the vise's guide bars and be higher than the top of the worksurface will suffice. Another option which can sometimes be more effective depending on the particular form of the workpiece is to use a narrower board, especially if this narrower board is provided with an attached lip so designed as to rest on the very top of the outer jaw or on the top of the bench.

An alternative method of using a tall jaw is to clamp the workpiece directly to it. This is sometimes more convenient than trying to hold the workpiece either in the vise or directly to the bench top.

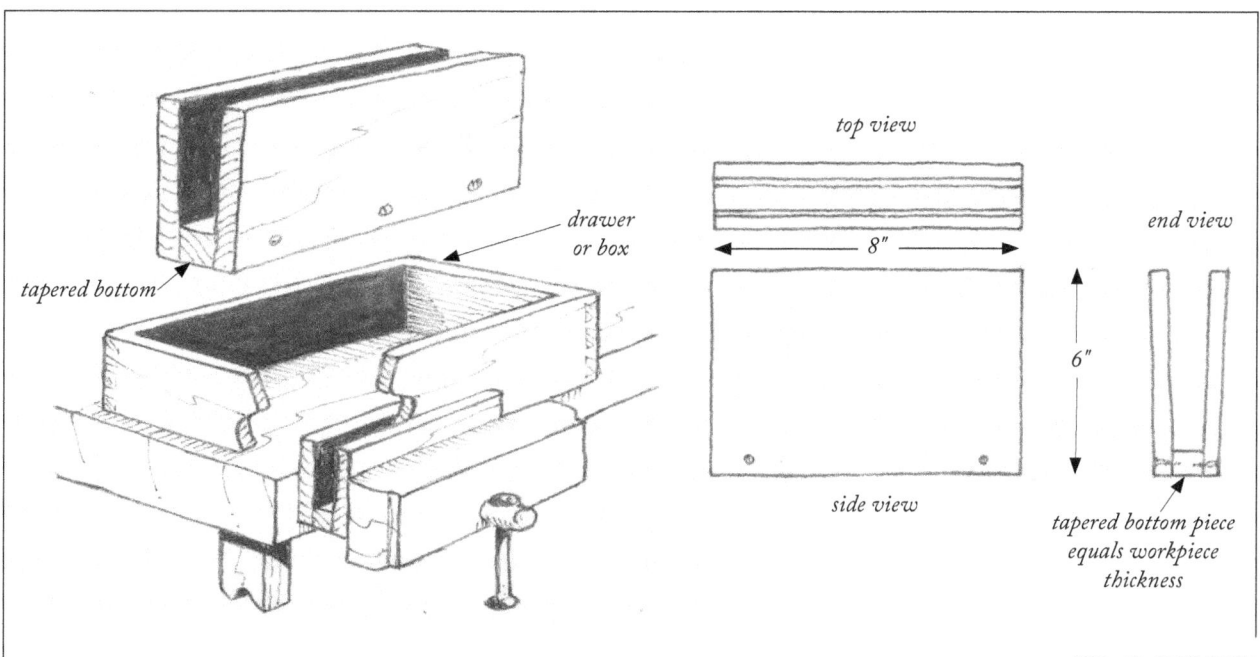

FIG. 27 BOX JAWS

HOLDING

BOX JAWS

WHEN IT IS NECESSARY TO HOLD A PARTIALLY assembled box or drawers for bottom or top edge-planing it is not always possible to secure such workpieces between bench dogs. A better method is to clamp one of the sides between box jaws as shown in FIG.27 on the previous page, which, being slightly tapered and standing proud of the bench top, secure the whole assembly without risk of deformation.

Start by preparing a length of stock approximately the same width as the thickness of the box or drawer sides to be held in the jaws. Plane a very slight angle on both sides of this piece so that when the jaws are attached to it they are further apart at the top than at the bottom. This will ensure that when the vise is closed the workpiece will be gripped tightly. It is important for this device to work that whatever is used to make the jaws is stiff enough not to deflect under pressure. Use either wood with the grain running vertically, or perhaps more reliably in this instance make the jaws from 3/4in.-thick plywood.

III. ADDITIONAL HOLDING FIXTURES

RIGHT-ANGLED BRACKET

SIMILAR TO THE COPING OR FRETSAW BRACKET shown later *(see Chapter 3)* which item can, indeed, often double for the following purpose) is an exactly-made right-angled bracket held in the vise at the required height, and to which two pieces that need to be positioned precisely for marking can in turn be clamped. If made large enough, such brackets greatly improve the ability to lay out dovetails, since by clamping the workpieces to the bracket so that their conjoined sides are flush with one side of the bracket both pieces are more accurately and securely positioned than by simply attempting to balance the two parts on each other.

For most purposes two boards about 8in. wide joined together at an exact right angle, the vertical board being twice as long as the horizontal board, will be found to be sufficient. To guarantee and maintain the perfect right angle include an exactly cut right-angled support block in the center of the boards' width.

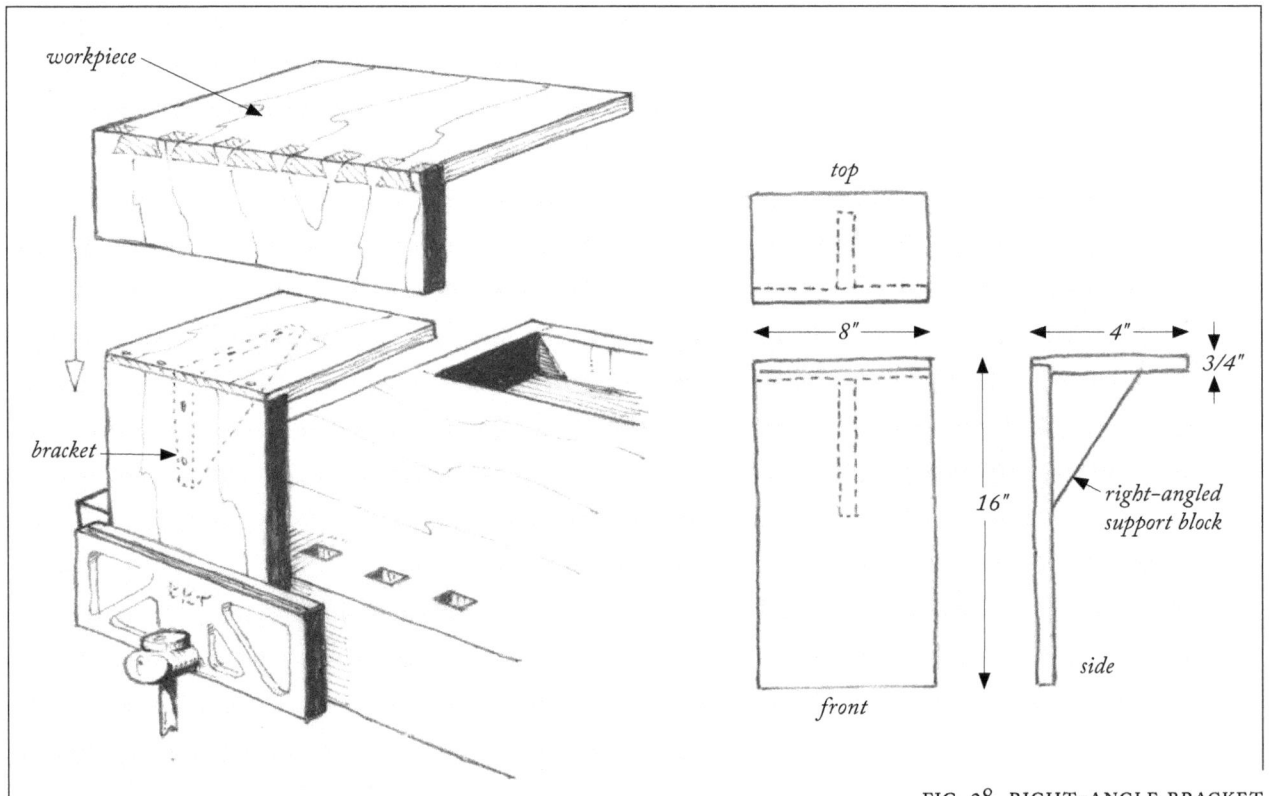

FIG. 28 RIGHT-ANGLE BRACKET

TRADITIONAL JIGS & FIXTURES

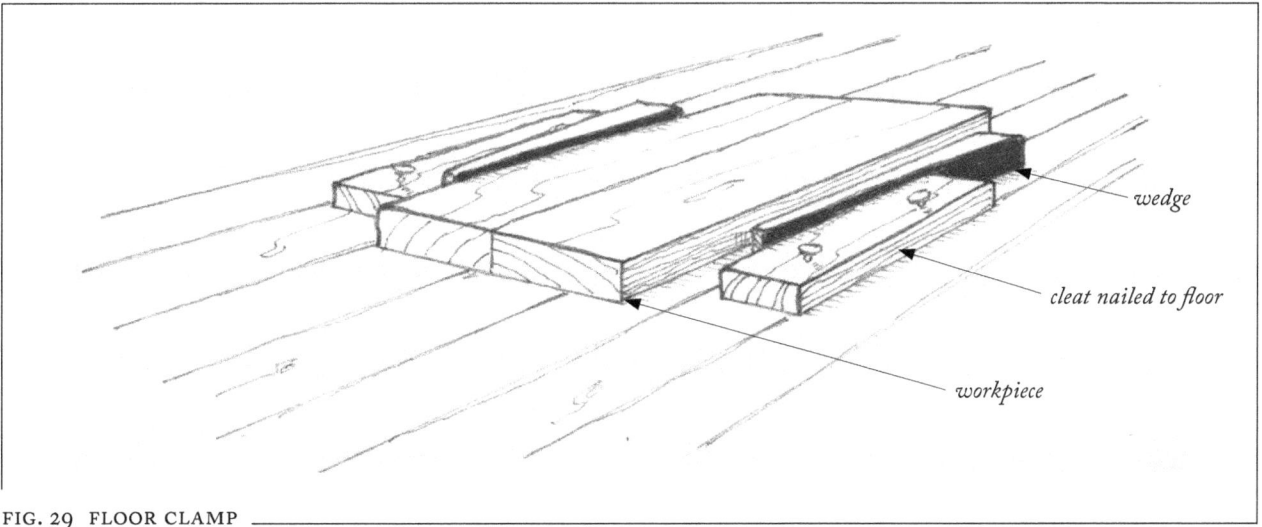

FIG. 29 FLOOR CLAMP

FLOOR CLAMP

A HOLDING METHOD PERHAPS MORE USEFUL for old shops in rough sheds or barns than in a modern building with a finished floor that you may be loathe to mar is something once commonly used by woodworkers such as bodgers and chairmakers working on seats that needed to be worked with a long-handled adze.

Known as a floor clamp, this fixture consisted of two stout cleats, securely nailed to the wooden floor, between which the workpiece — such as a seat blank or other large piece might be placed and then wedged into position.

HANDSCREW JAW EXTENDER

WOODEN HANDSCREWS ARE AVAILABLE IN VARIOUS sizes, but unless you are lucky enough to locate an antique tool or are prepared to make your own you will be limited to the modern Jorgensen™ variety with metal screws. Although these have the great advantage of strength, plus the ability to be used with their jaws positioned other than parallel to each other, and furthermore rarely sustain damage to the screws themselves, they can seldom be found with jaws larger than 10 in.

For those occasions where a deeper reach is needed, and when something needs to be

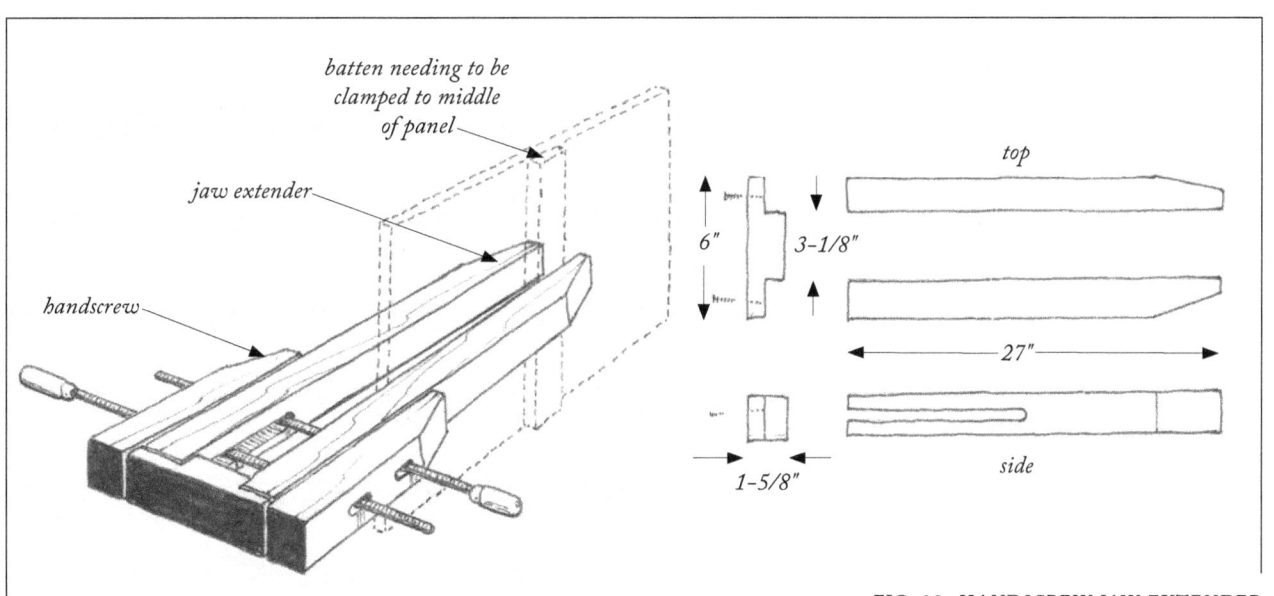

FIG. 30 HANDSCREW JAW EXTENDER

HOLDING

clamped at a distance greater than 10in. from its edge, a jaw extender is necessary.

Two pieces, made to exactly the same width as the jaws they are to extend (in order to prevent any uneven obstruction), and made approximately 2 ft. in length, and finished tapered at their end like the original jaws, are attached by loose screws to a rabbeted center piece about 6in. wide.

The screws that attach the extenders to the center piece are inserted so as to allow a small amount of sideways movement in order to accommodate the changing angle at the tip of the jaws when in use.

These pieces are then fitted over the back end of the handscrew by having the ends of the extra jaws slotted so that they may pass over the metal screws holding the jaws together. Their ends are then attached to the rabbeted ends of the center piece. Just as for the original handscrew, the material used for the jaw extenders should be straight-grained hardwood, such as maple, for optimum strength.

2

JIGS & FIXTURES FOR MEASURING & MARKING

THE FIRST OPERATION IN MOST PROJECTS GENERALLY INVOLVES GETTING OUT THE STOCK. THIS TYPICALLY INVOLVES MEASURING AND MARKING PIECES FOR BEING SAWED OR CUT OUT INTO THEIR VARIOUS CONSTITUENT PARTS, AND THEN TESTED FOR SHAPE AND SIZE. THINGS SUCH as flatness, straightness, and adjacent surface relationships all need to be checked. For many contemporary woodworkers the chief aid in all this is the tape measure. And, indeed, for a lot of woodworking this is a useful tool, but for really fine woodworking, such as furnituremaking, the traditional wooden folding-rule is far superior. The reasons why are many, and range from greater accuracy to additional uses not possible with a modern metal tape measure.

For a start, using a sharp marking knife or scratch awl to make a precise mark on the workpiece by taking advantage of the incised graduations on a wooden rule guarantees far greater accuracy than trying to take a mark from a tape measure, whose graduations may themselves may have a thickness of up to a sixteenth of an inch, not to mention the risk that the hook at the end of the tape (designed to slide sideways to permit inside and outside measurements) is frequently worn and thus no longer accurate. Then the fact that the rule is easier to hold diagonally across a workpiece, can be used as a depth gauge, or be used as a bevel to mark angles (some folding rules even have the knuckle joint graduated in degrees for this purpose), and even be used as a level when equipped with a built-in bubble, further illustrates the fact that many traditional handtools are themselves also 'jigs and fixtures' designed to facilitate better-quality woodworking.

Despite the demonstrable superiority of the wooden rule, however, marks and measurements derived from the clumsy system of inches and feet (and even the superior metric system), although often indispensable for gross overall measurements are not as convenient as many of the traditional jigs and fixtures that may be used to ensure accuracy. Measuring or marking one piece from another is invariably less prone to error than trying to calculate for example a third of 1ft. 2-3/16ins! Whether you use the width of the actual tenon to mark directly the width of its future mortise, regardless of its actual measurement in inches or fractions of an inch, or some other item such as winding sticks or pinch rods, you will be practicing a form of traditional woodworking easier and more accurate than one reliant on tape measures or calculators.

STRAIGHTEDGE

ONE OF THE SIMPLEST ITEMS YOU CAN MAKE is a straightedge longer than the typical wooden or metal rule. It is not necessary to graduate it nor indeed make it to any particular length. Anything from three to five feet will be found to be of great use in laying out straight lines for sawing to or planing. Straight-grained quarter-sawn hardwood planed or machined accurately on one side will last longest but should still be checked frequently for accuracy. To check the truth of the straightedge simply draw a line against the straight side then flip the straightedge over and draw another line. If the straightedge is in truth the lines will coincide. Varnishing or painting and hanging rather than leaning up against a wall when not in use will keep it true longer, and shaping the back side will make clear which is the straight side.

PINCH RODS

DESPITE THE AFOREMENTIONED HOOK DESIGNED to slide in and out on a metal tape measure, taking an inside measurement is a tricky operation since there is often a certain amount of inaccuracy when taking into account the thickness of the case which must be added to the last visible marking on the tape. 'Pinching' two overlapping lengths of wood together and extending them to fit in the inside space needing to be measured will give you an absolute length that can then be measured without any guesswork.

Two straightedges (or any two other pieces of convenient lengths of wood) held together may be used as pinch rods to take an internal measurement as shown. Most shops sooner or later accumulate

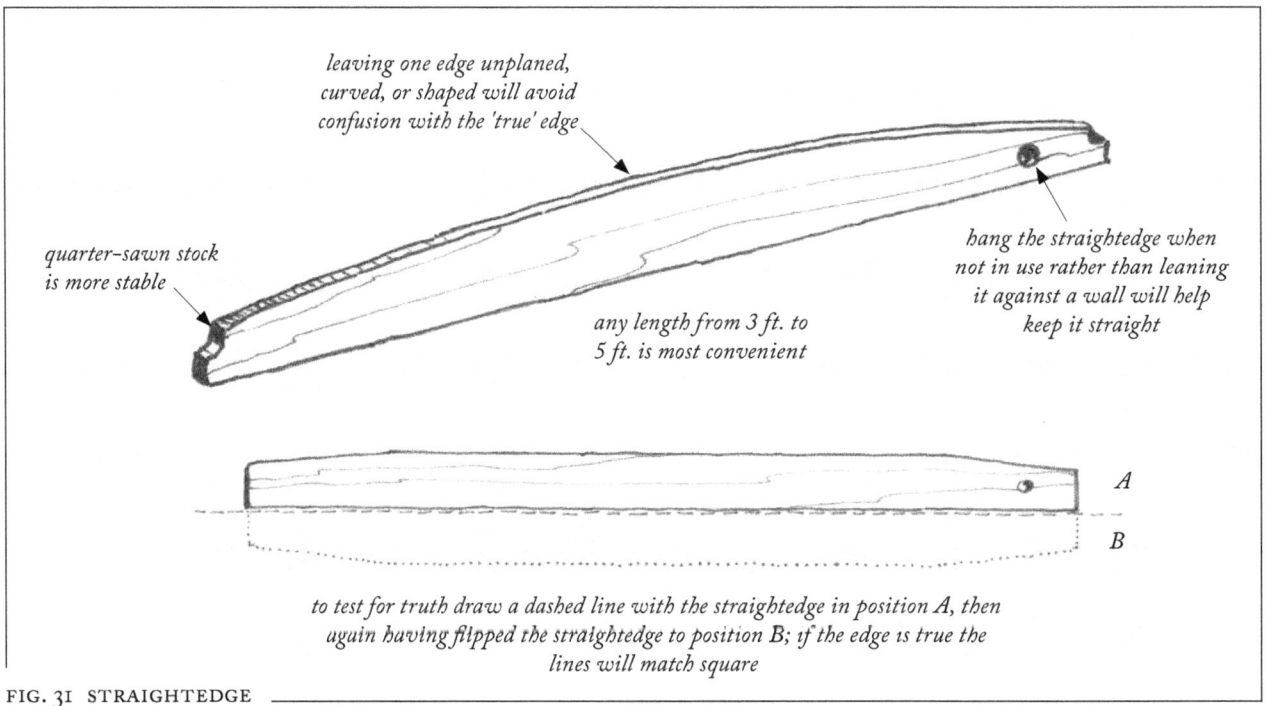

leaving one edge unplaned, curved, or shaped will avoid confusion with the 'true' edge

quarter-sawn stock is more stable

hang the straightedge when not in use rather than leaning it against a wall will help keep it straight

any length from 3 ft. to 5 ft. is most convenient

A
B

to test for truth draw a dashed line with the straightedge in position A, then again having flipped the straightedge to position B; if the edge is true the lines will match square

FIG. 31 STRAIGHTEDGE

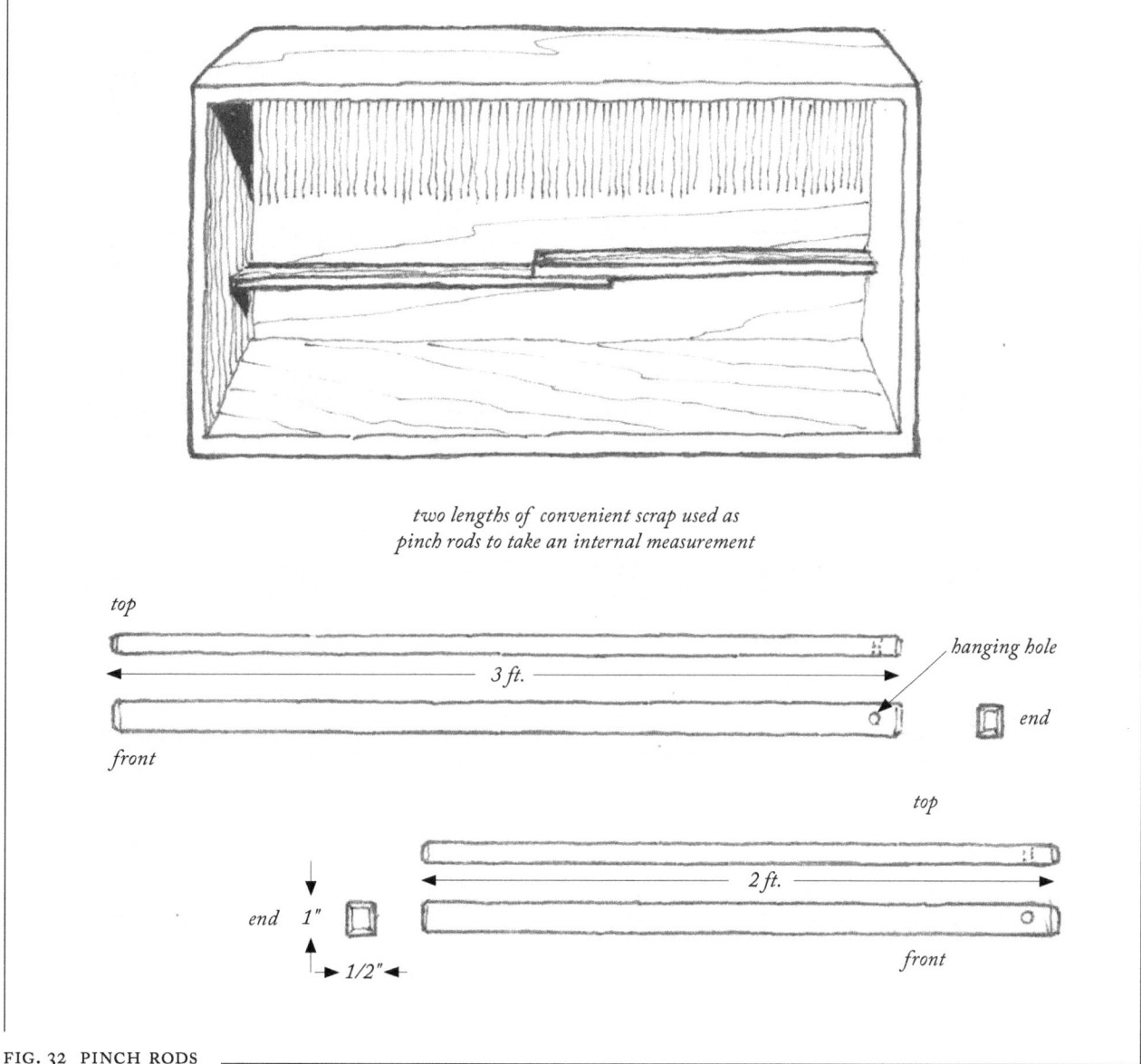

FIG. 32 PINCH RODS

enough scrap from which pinch rods may be made. Bore a hanging hole in the end of each piece and keep them handy.

DIAGONAL STRIPS

A SLIGHT MODIFICATION CAN TURN PINCH RODS into a jig for checking the rectilinearity of carcases, chests or boxes. The difference between something with square corners and something that is rhomboidal is that the diagonals of the former will be equal. By making the ends of the pinch rods pointed so that they fit into a corner, checking the length of the diagonals is made easier than trying to measure them with a tape or rule. Note also that for exact measurements the rods should be held one on top of the other and not side by side. When they are fully extended into opposite diagonal corners draw a line across both sticks. When placed into the two opposite corners this line should still be continuous if the object being tested is indeed perfectly rectilinear.

Note that if the ends are pointed at 45° they will only fit into the corners of a square; for other rectangles the ends need to be pointed more

TRADITIONAL JIGS & FIXTURES

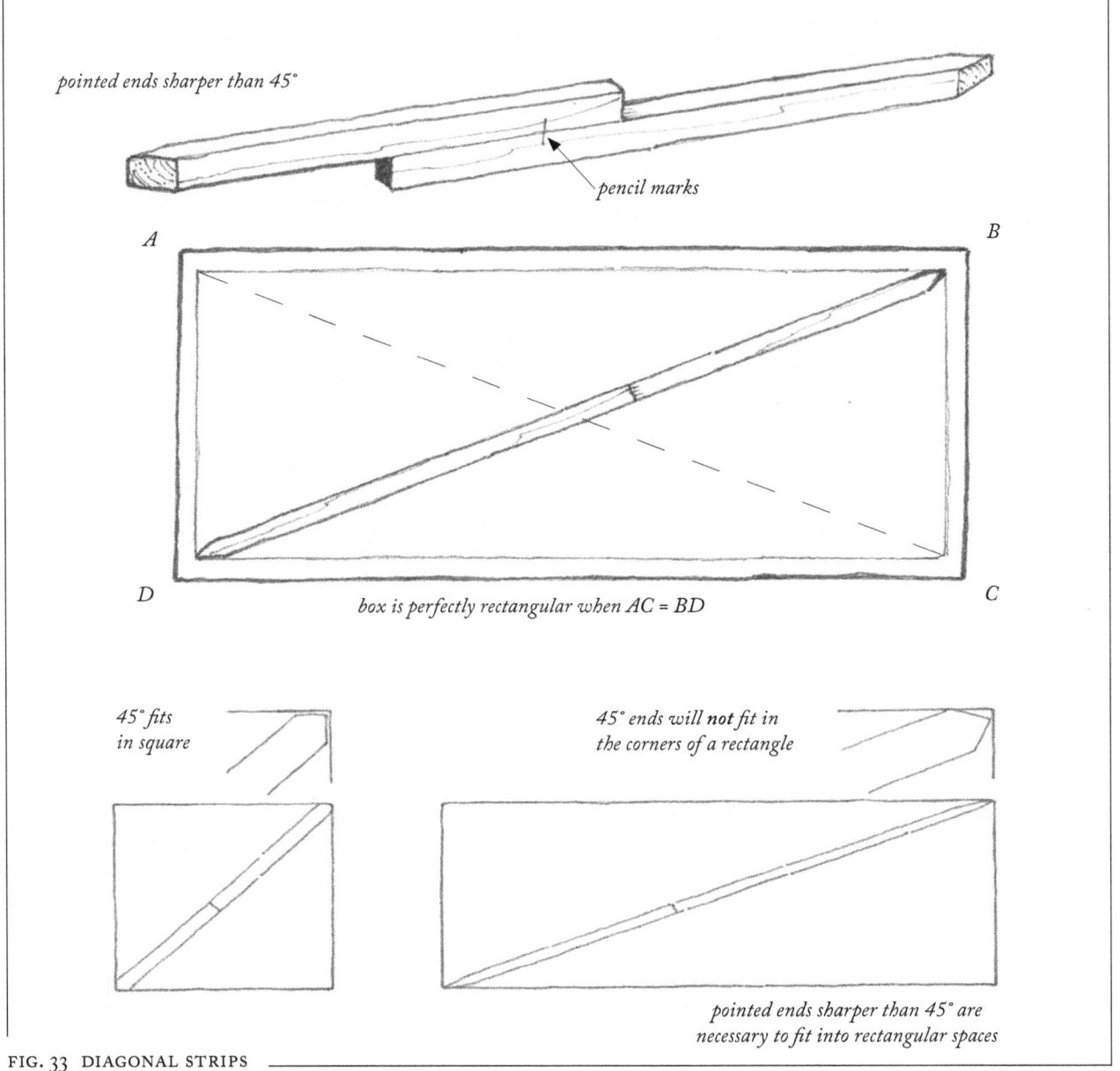

FIG. 33 DIAGONAL STRIPS

sharply. A small piece of masking tape applied over both strips provides a better (and easily replaceable) surface for marking rather than making lines directly on the wood.

WINDING STICKS

IF YOU HAVE A COMPLETELY FLAT WORKSURFACE, such as an accurately dressed bench top, it is easy to check whether a board is completely flat simply by placing it on this surface and seeing if it touches at all points or if it rocks. But it is not so easy to mark the exact spots where it is perhaps a little high or a little low, or to gauge which is the twisted end. What is needed is a pair of winding sticks, so-called because they can be used to check not only whether a board is perfectly flat but also if it is twisted or 'in winding'.

The first stick, known as the gaffer, is placed at one end of the board, and the other — known as the jack — is placed at the far end. If, when sighting across the top of the gaffer the top of

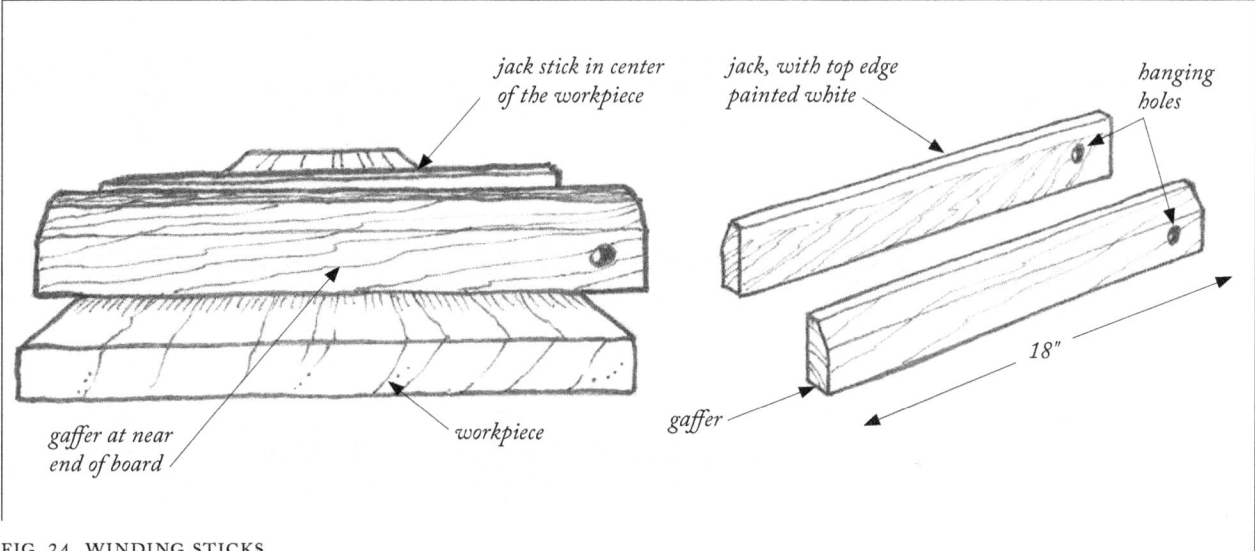

FIG. 34 WINDING STICKS

the jack appears perfectly parallel to it, the board is straight.

Similarly, by placing them parallel to each other some distance apart at different spots on the surface of any workpiece, and then sighting across the top of one to the other you will be able to discover whether or not the surface of your workpiece is truly flat.

Two similarly-sized short straightedges, perhaps no longer than 18 in. can be used as winding sticks. Make them thick enough to be stood on edge, and to make sighting easier it is a good plan to paint the top of the jack white, the better to observe how nearly the gaffer coincides with it.

FLEXIBLE STRAIGHTEDGE

AS PROFESSIONAL DESIGNERS KNOW WELL, FOR an ideally harmonious design all the parts and proportions of any given piece should relate in some way to one another. This includes regular curves, which can be designed exactly only if the major and minor axes of the ovals of which they are a section are known. The axes can be calculated and derived geometrically, but if all that is required is simply a smooth curve, regardless of any possible integral relationship with other dimensions that might describe the overall piece, then all that is necessary is a thin lathe that can be used to form a fair shape by being bent to the estimated steepness and held in place either by a string connecting the ends or by nails or blocks placed on the workpiece. To ensure a regularly fair curve, use a lathe or strip of wood of even thickness and with as even grain as possible.

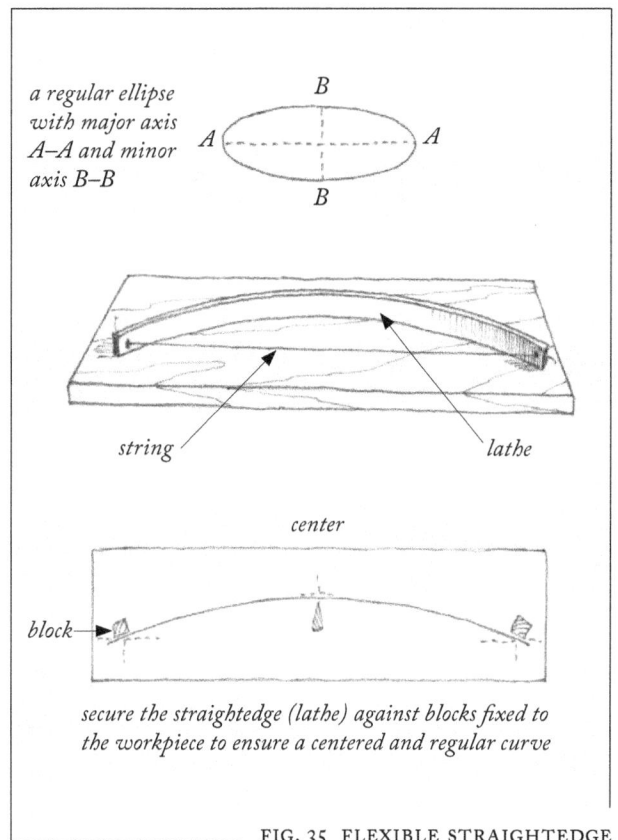

FIG. 35 FLEXIBLE STRAIGHTEDGE

MEASURING & MARKING

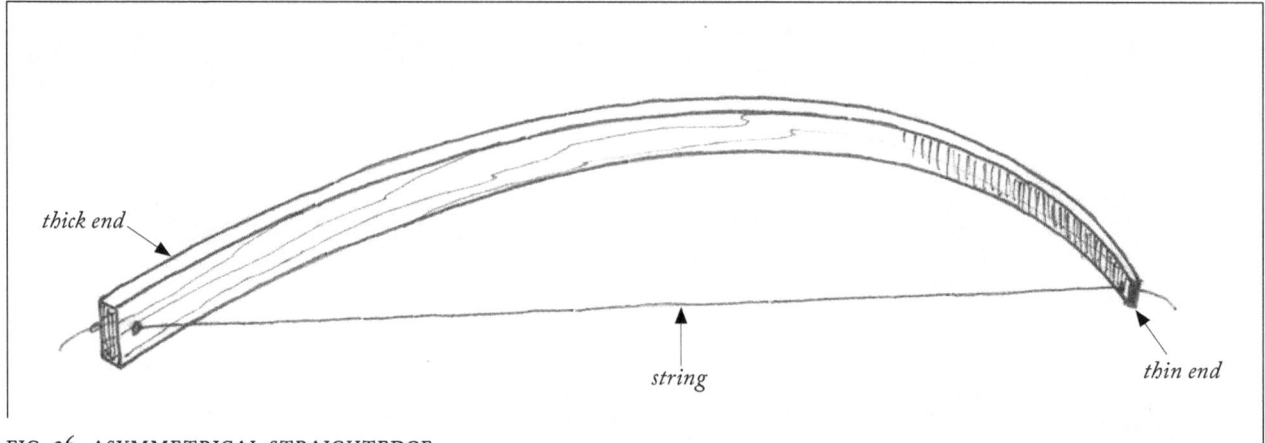

FIG. 36 ASYMMETRICAL STRAIGHTEDGE

ASYMMETRICAL STRAIGHTEDGE

IF WHAT IS REQUIRED IS AN ASYMMETRICAL curve and you want to control the exact shape (geometrically obtainable by laying out a tilted ellipse whose axes are not at right angles) then a lathe prepared so that one end is thinner than the other can, by trial and error, duplicate such a shape; the amount of thinning determining the steepness of the asymmetry.

BRICK BATTEN STOP

SELF-SUPPORTING PIVOT POINTS CAN BE A more convenient way to bend thin strips, such as battens, into required curves, than is clamping or nailing such points to the workbench. A short board provided with a pivot point at one end and two stops designed to hold a regular brick will suffice.

They are usually used in threes — one at each end of the workpiece and one at the high point of the required curve (which point may be in the middle of the batten's length if a symmetrical curve is desired, or somewhere off-center if an asymmetrical curve is desired). The stops can be positioned to produce any degree of steepness up to the point where they begin to move the bricks — such movement, should it occur, then being a useful indication that the desired curve is too steep for the flexibilty of the given workpiece.

It is best to use three identical bricks in order to ensure equal resistance against the workpiece. Wrapping the bricks in some sturdy paper helps keep things clean, but may increase the likelihood of the bricks slipping. A length of 3/4in. dowel fixed in the end of the stop forms the pivot point. If the workpiece being bent should be higher than the height of the brick, then it should be mounted so as to lie proud of the end of the stop.

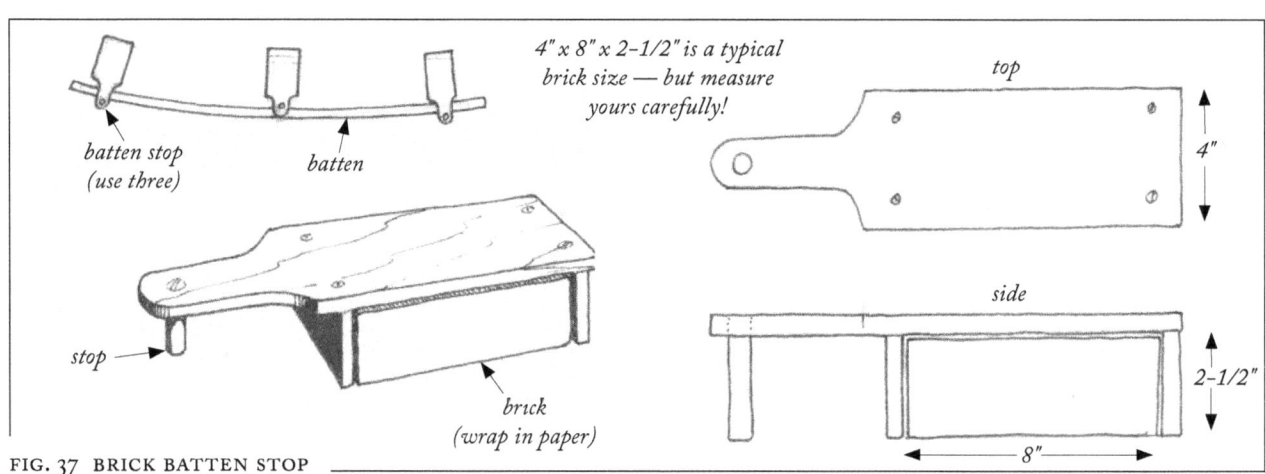

FIG. 37 BRICK BATTEN STOP

STORY STICK

MORE FAMILIAR TO CARPENTERS WHO SOMETIMES use tall story sticks to check the relative positions of window and door openings and different siding elements in house construction, a story stick can also be extremely useful to a woodworker laying out shelves, drawers, and mouldings, especially where these things are repeated. It is essentially a custom-graduated rule indicating the relative position of such elements and associated joints. Its advantage is that exact dimensions need only be measured and marked on the stick once, and then may be repeated on the workpiece with the assurance that errors will not occur.

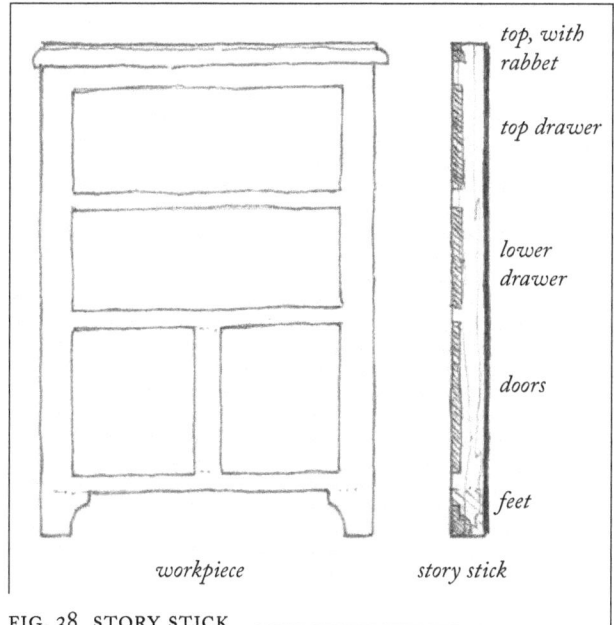

FIG. 38 STORY STICK

MULLET

A MULLET IS USUALLY OBTAINED FROM THE cut-off end of a grooved framing member, such as a rail or stile, where the groove runs out the end. Since paneling is intended to fit in the grooves of the frame, running this mullet around the edges of the panel before assembly is a quick way to ensure that the panel edges have been properly thicknessed and will, in fact, fit comfortably into the framing before proceeding.

If you make a mullet from something other than a piece of the actual grooved framing note the exact shape of the tongue formed on the panelling that is intended to fit in it. Unless it has a parallel edge make sure that the mullet's groove is wide enough to accommodate the widest section of the bevel that may enter when the panel is at its widest stage of expansion and contraction.

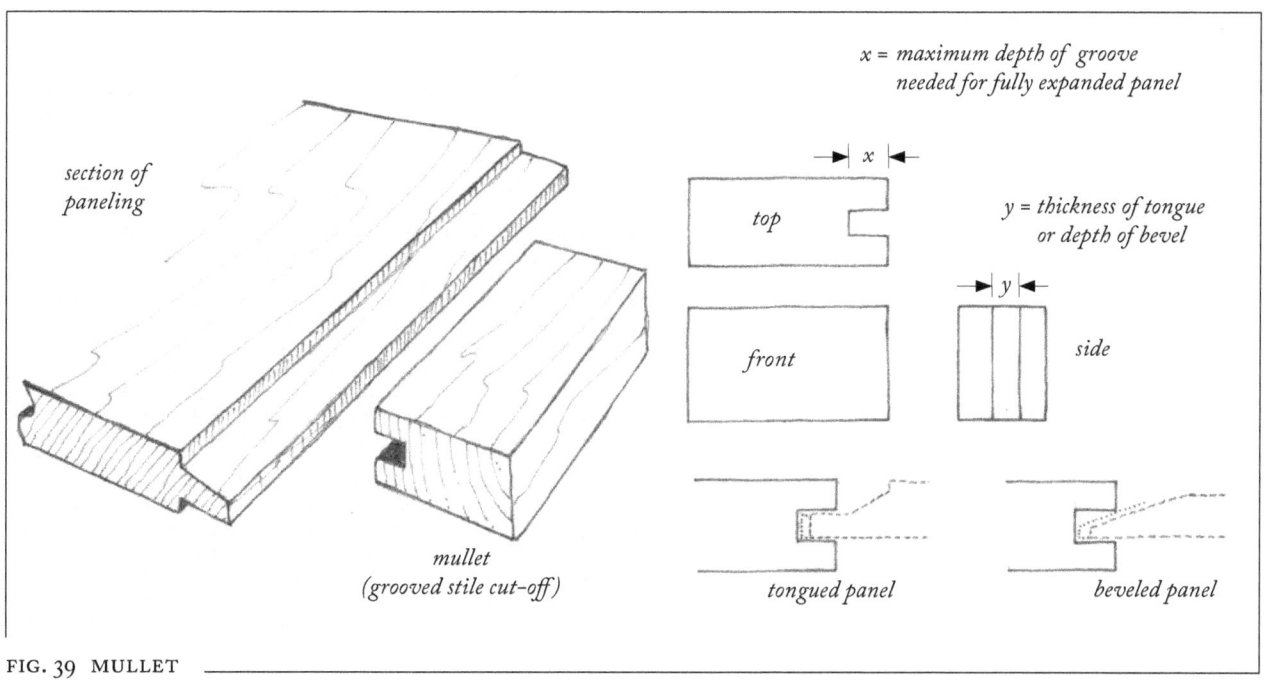

FIG. 39 MULLET

MEASURING & MARKING

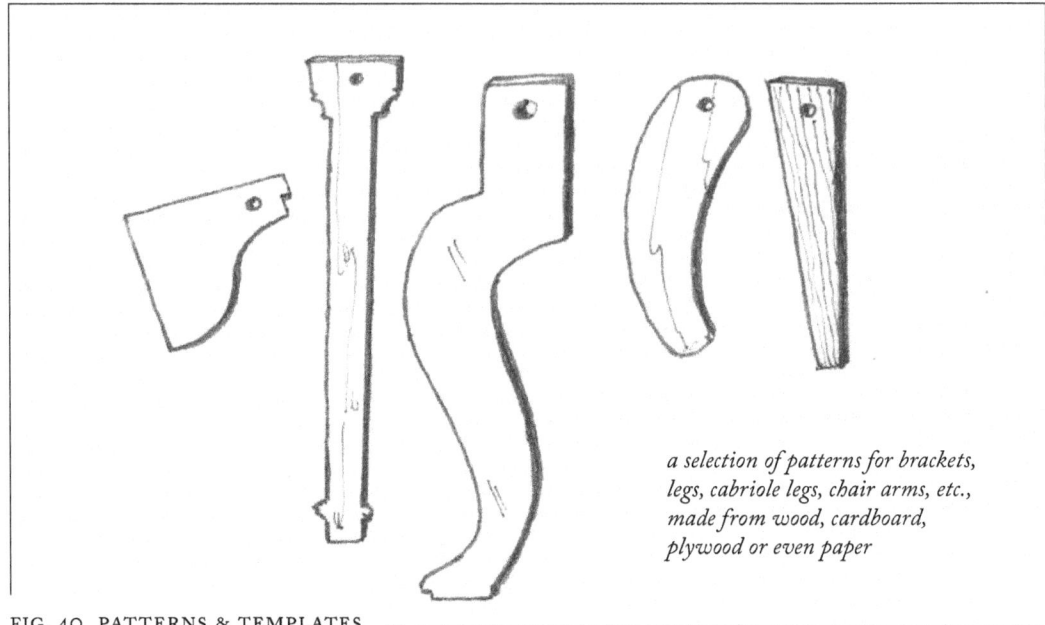

a selection of patterns for brackets, legs, cabriole legs, chair arms, etc., made from wood, cardboard, plywood or even paper

FIG. 40 PATTERNS & TEMPLATES

PATTERNS & TEMPLATES

THE BEST EXAMPLE OF USING A JIG INSTEAD of repeatedly measuring something is, of course, the use of patterns and templates. These may range from full-size cut-outs of chair backs and cabriole legs to something as small as a paper cut-out of a single dovetail joint. Even if your woodworking primarily involves making one-of-a-kind pieces, keeping any patterns or templates that you may make for unique pieces can often prove very useful when developing new but similar projects. To this end it is a good idea always to label any such pattern or template with relevant details about when and where it was used.

BEAM COMPASS

IN ORDER TO DESCRIBE AND LAY OUT LARGE circles or segments of circles recourse may be had to the beam compass. The actual beam may be nothing more than a length of wood sufficient to match the required radius of the circle to be described. A nail at one end and a pencil inserted through a hole at

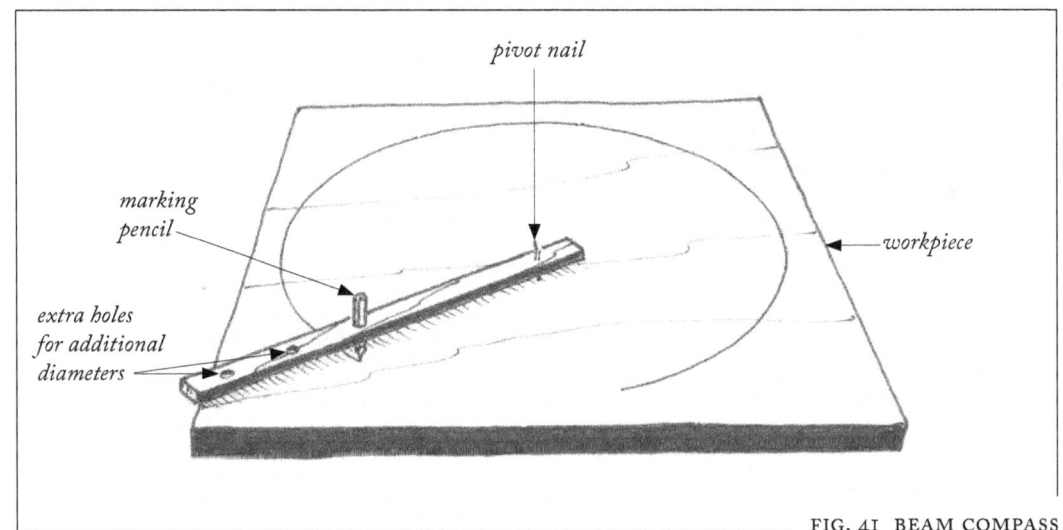

FIG. 41 BEAM COMPASS

TRADITIONAL JIGS & FIXTURES

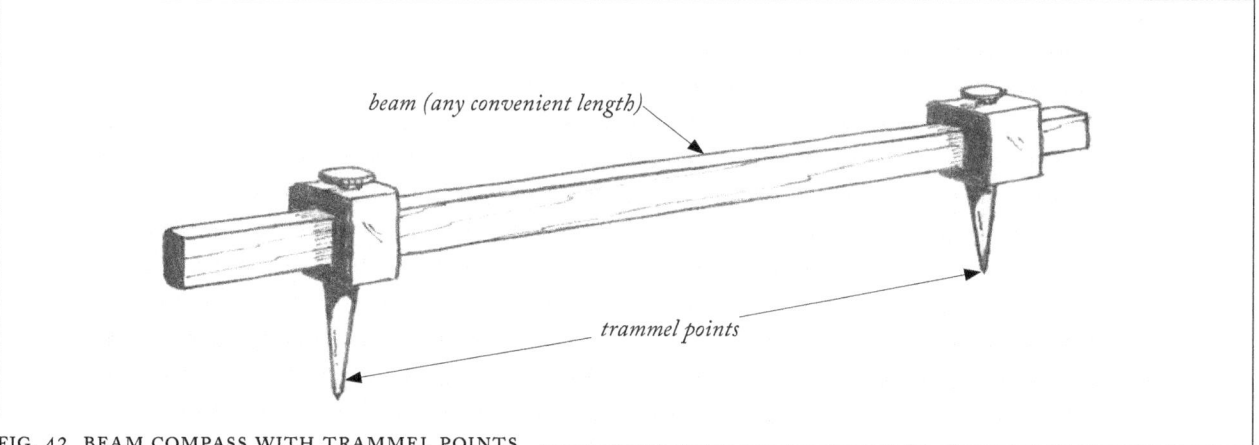

FIG. 42 BEAM COMPASS WITH TRAMMEL POINTS

the other end will serve to allow the given shape to be marked.

The actual beam may be provided by almost any length of wood, provided it is relatively straight and rigid. It is probably easiest to use something rectangular in cross-section in order that a nail forming the pivot point may be inserted at one end, and a hole (plus holes for different radii) bored for a pencil at the other end. A store-bought alternative to the slightly more traditional beam compass entails the purchase of a pair of trammel points. Trammels are sharp metal points attached to a body designed to slide over and be fixed at the required point on the beam — which of course must be of a dimension to accept the trammels.

USERMADE GAUGES:

ALTHOUGH TOOLMAKERS ARE FOREVER ENLARGING their catalogs with new and improved additions there remains a number of items which while they might be thought of as tools must still be usermade, and which therefore qualify as jigs or fixtures. One such group of items belongs under the heading of gauges — items that may be used to measure and mark workpieces for further processing.

PENCIL GAUGE

SOMETIMES A LITTLE MORE CONVENIENT THAN A regular marking gauge with a pin that leaves a scratched line on the workpiece is a pencil gauge.

While it is not too difficult to make a dedicated pencil gauge along the lines of a standard marking gauge a quicker solution is simply to bore a pencil-sized hole in the other end of the beam from the pin, saw a slot from the end of the beam into the hole, and after inserting a pencil into the hole, secure it with a screw from the side.

BOSSED CURVE-GAUGE

THE STANDARD MARKING GAUGE IS USED BY holding the flat stock or head against the edge of the workpiece. This works fine so long as the surface of the workpiece is also flat, but should a marked line be needed at a consistent distance

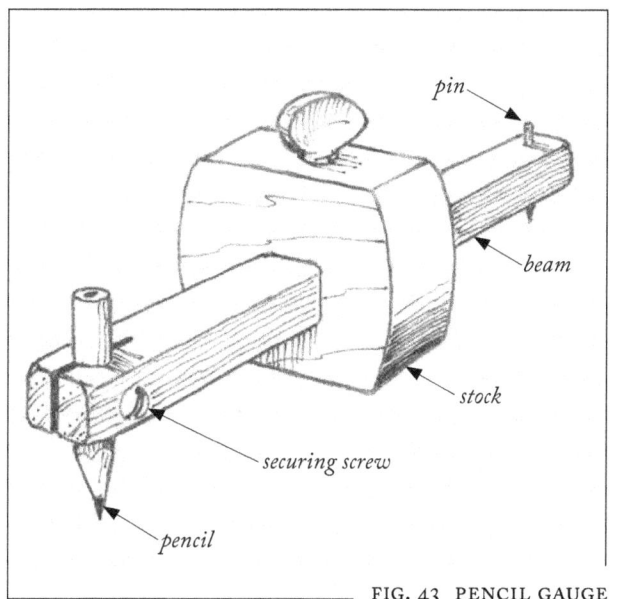

FIG. 43 PENCIL GAUGE

MEASURING & MARKING

TRADITIONAL JIGS & FIXTURES

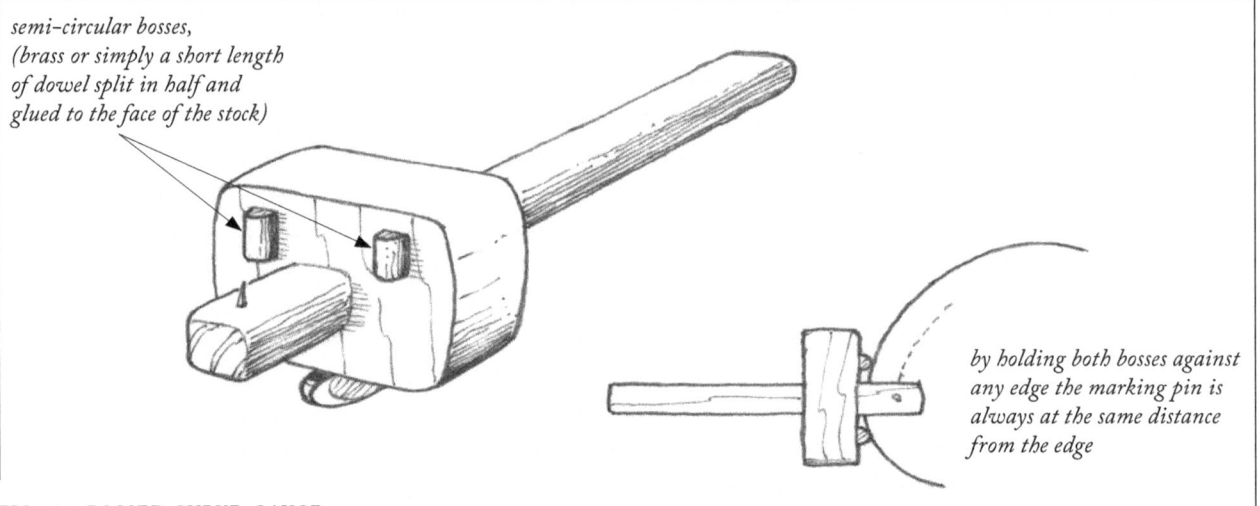

FIG. 44 BOSSED CURVE-GAUGE

from a curved surface it can be difficult to keep the pin (or pencil) perfectly tangent to the edge. The solution is to add two bosses or protrusions to the head, spaced equally from the centerline.

PANEL GAUGE

A LESS COMMON GAUGE THAN THE REGULAR marking gauge is the much larger panel gauge. With a beam measuring from 18 in. to 2 ft. its head is usually rabbeted along its lower edge, the better to ride along the edge of the workpiece being marked. As with smaller workpieces this is fine so long as the workpiece is straight, but for any kind of curved edge, either convex or concave, something else is required.

DOWELLED CURVE-GAUGE

FOR GAUGING ON A LARGE SCALE BUT WHEN working with curved workpieces the solution is an alternate head for the panel gauge with no rabbet, but provided instead with two dowels inserted in the bottom edge, both dowels being located the same distance from the center. This is also a solution that may be adopted for smaller gauges should you not want to add the bosses illustrated in FIG. 44 above.

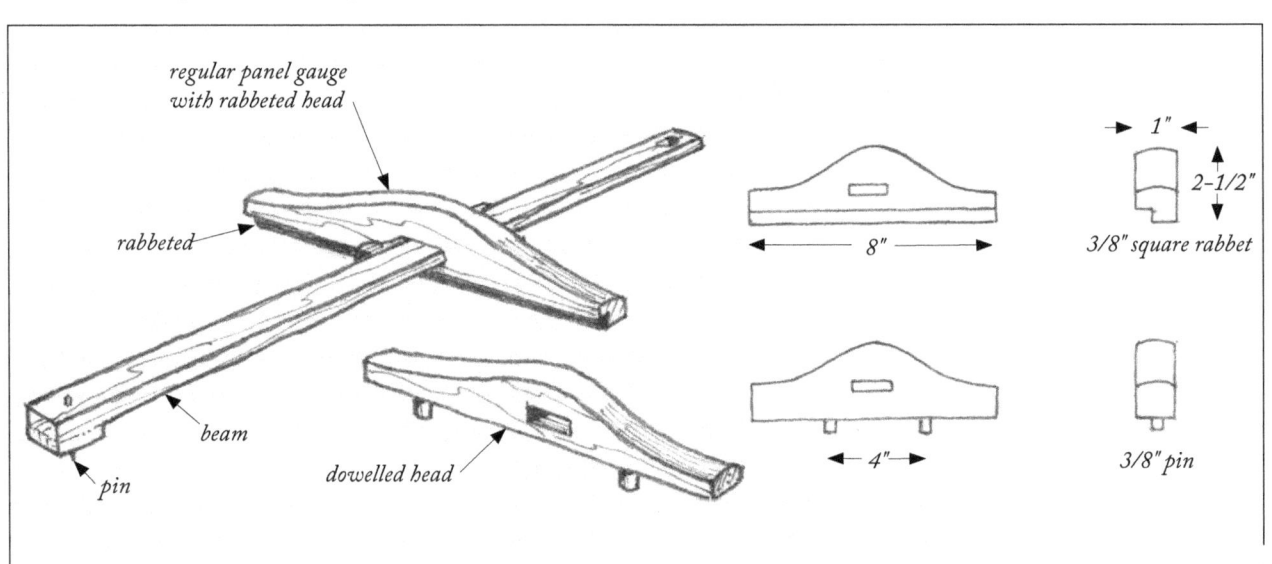

FIG. 45 PANEL & DOWELLED CURVE-GAUGE

TRADITIONAL JIGS & FIXTURES

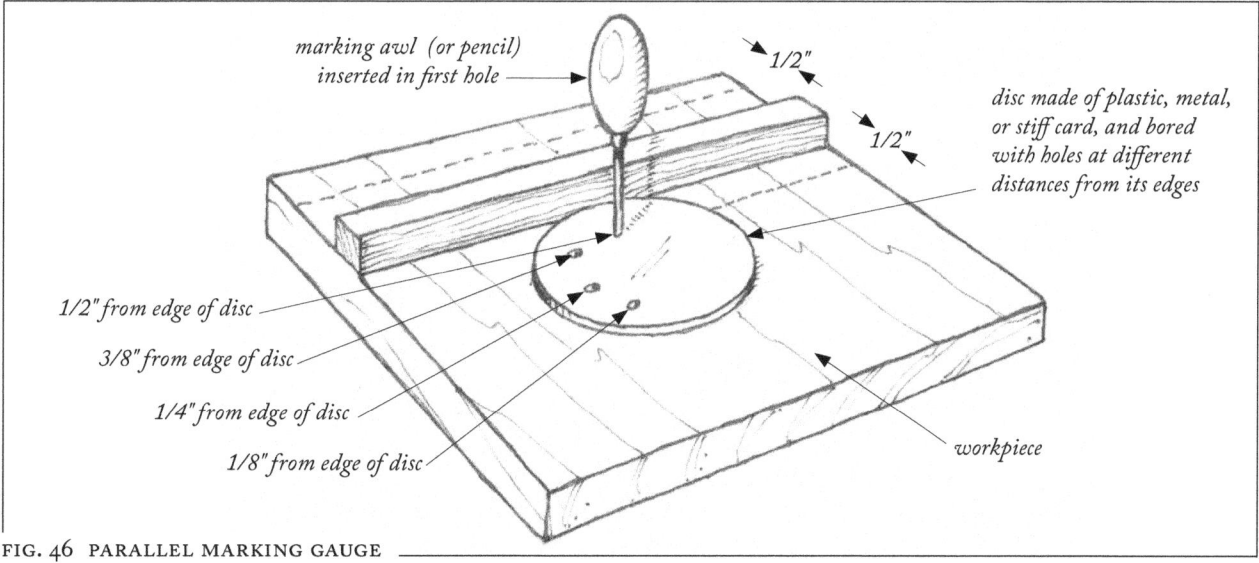

FIG. 46 PARALLEL MARKING GAUGE

PARALLEL MARKING GAUGE

THE STANDARD MARKING GAUGE NEEDS AN edge to work against. As a result, marking a series of parallel lines at a consistent distance apart requires resetting the gauge for every line. An easier method is to use a circular disc bored with a hole the required distance from its circumference through which you can use a marking awl or pencil point. By running the disc along a straightedge accurately clamped to each succeeding line, consistency can be achieved without having to reset the tool. Of course, there is no reason why such a disc may not be bored with a series of holes, each a different distance from the circumference, providing the different measurements are clearly marked.

PRESET GAUGES:

NOTCHED PRESET GAUGES

ANOTHER WAY OF AVOIDING HAVING TO RESET the standard marking gauge, especially useful when having to mark standard dimensions such as common lumber sizes, is to use a gauge with a fixed flat head notched at these measurements so as to receive an awl or pencil.

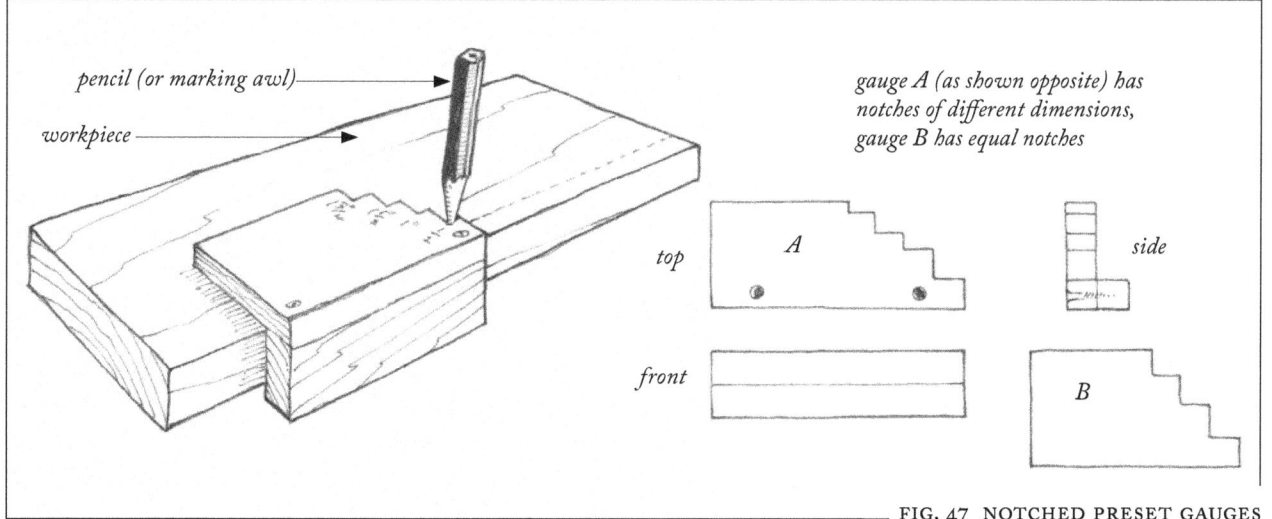

FIG. 47 NOTCHED PRESET GAUGES

MEASURING & MARKING

TRADITIONAL JIGS & FIXTURES

All that is needed is a flat head cut with a series of steps corresponding to standard milled lumber dimensions, and to which is attached a narrow lip that will bear against the edge of the workpiece. Note that if, instead of being notched as just described, the notches are all spaced equidistant from each other this jig becomes another method for marking equidistant parallel lines.

RABBETED PRESET GAUGE

AN EVEN MORE SIMPLE ALTERNATIVE TO THE preset gauge with a flat notched head illustrated on the previous page is a simple flat block of wood with one or more edges, each rabbeted to particular given widths.

By holding a pencil, marking knife, or even just a simple awl against its outer edge while sliding the rabbeted edge along the edge of a workpiece, layout lines can be easily and consistently marked without having to measure anything.

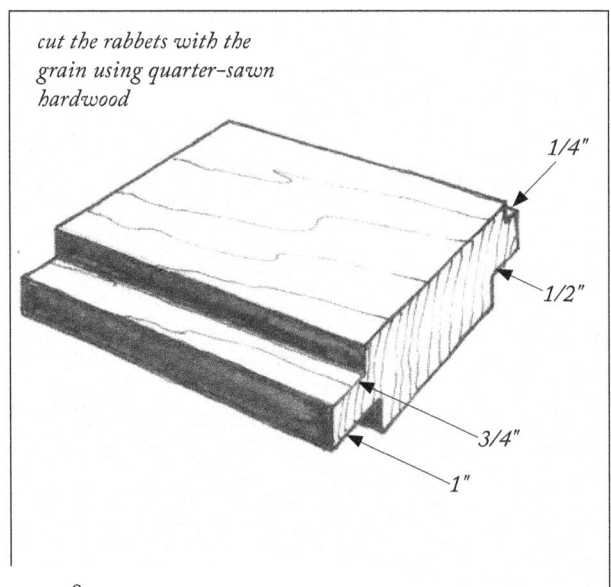

FIG. 48 NOTCHED PRESET GAUGE

BORED TRYSQUARE

ALTHOUGH AS PREVIOUSLY MENTIONED THE TIME was when every self-respecting woodworker made his or her own trysquare from wood, many woodworkers now use store-bought trysquares,

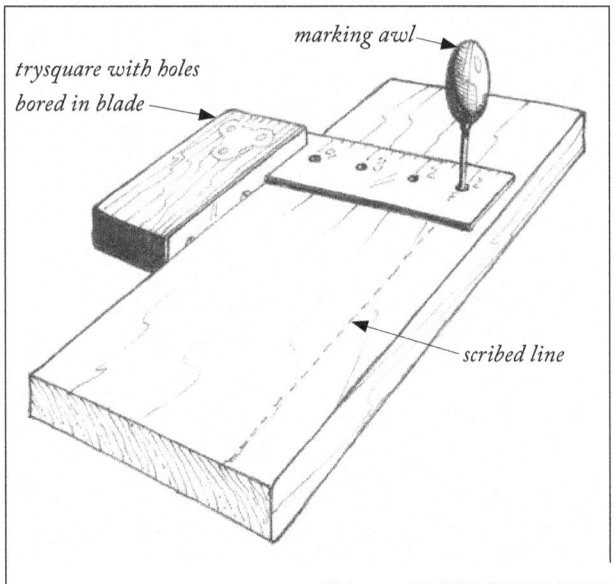

FIG. 49 BORED TRYSQUARE

some of which have graduated edges. The graduations can be useful for locating a series of bored holes in the blade, through which a marking awl or pencil point can be inserted, thereby turning the trysquare into another form of preset marking gauge.

DRAWER-PULL GUIDE

IT IS FAR SAFER WHEN HAVING TO MAKE THE SAME layout mark multiple times to lay out the marks from an exact guide rather than repeat measuring operations. This is particularly true in the case of drawer pulls, especially if you are dealing with many drawers, as in the case of kitchen cabinetry or even one chest of drawers with a single bank of perhaps six or more drawers. Each pull may require a measurement from the top of the drawer, a measurement from the side of the drawer, as well as a measurement between two possible screw attachments. A single guide with exactly marked and pre-bored holes will guarantee uniformity.

This guide is designed only for marking, perhaps with a sharp marking or scratch awl or even with a pencil or other fine marker. A stiff piece of card will suffice, or even a piece of thin plywood or even some brass or aluminum sheet stock. The width of this piece does not need to be much greater than the width of the drawer pulls whose position is to

TRADITIONAL JIGS & FIXTURES

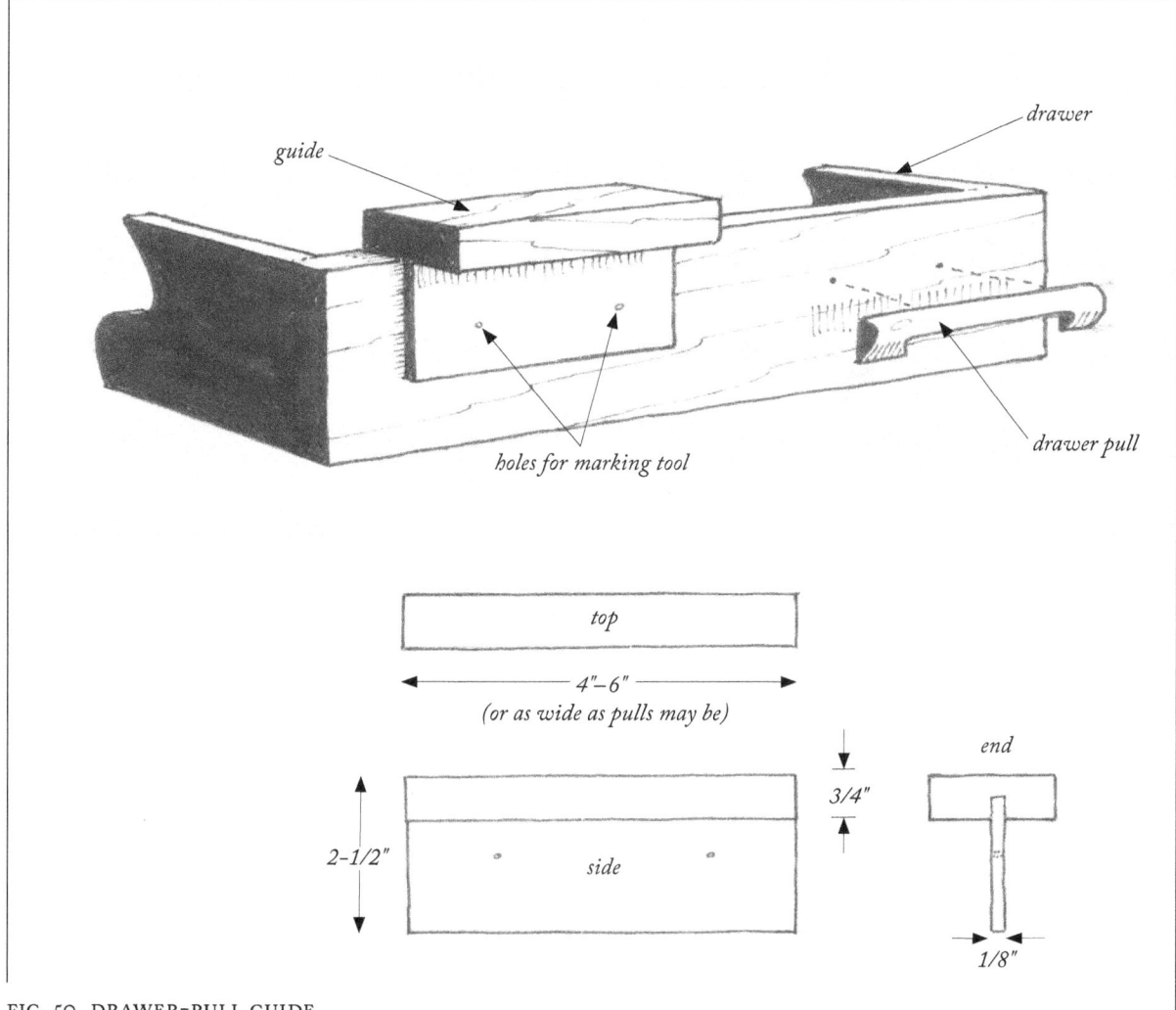

FIG. 50 DRAWER-PULL GUIDE

be marked. Four inches to 6 in. wide may be typical. The pull is positioned on the drawer front by being hooked over the top of the drawer from a piece of scrap into which the card has been inserted.

Assuming that the drawer pulls are to be regularly installed at the same distance from the top edge of the drawer, the depth of the card should be of a size great enough to reflect this. This lip further serves the purpose of ensuring that a two-screw drawer pull will have both screws aligned perfectly horizontally.

Once you have determined the size needed for the card, it may be fixed in the lip piece simply by a tight pressure fit alone. This is a useful method if you want to use different cards to mark different pulls that are to be attached at different heights — something you might want to do if you are constructing a series of graduated drawers. However, a piece of plywood permanently glued into the lip will ensure continued accuracy.

Since the guide is intended only for light positional marking, the holes (that should be very carefully laid out on the card) need only be large enough to admit the end of an awl or the tip of a pencil. Note that it is sometimes useful to locate more than a single pair of holes in the same card, for two different width pulls.

DRAWER-PULL CENTERING POSITIONER

A SLIGHTLY MORE ADVANCED FORM OF THE draw-pull guide which comes in handy when having to position pairs of drawer pulls on any number of

MEASURING & MARKING

TRADITIONAL JIGS & FIXTURES

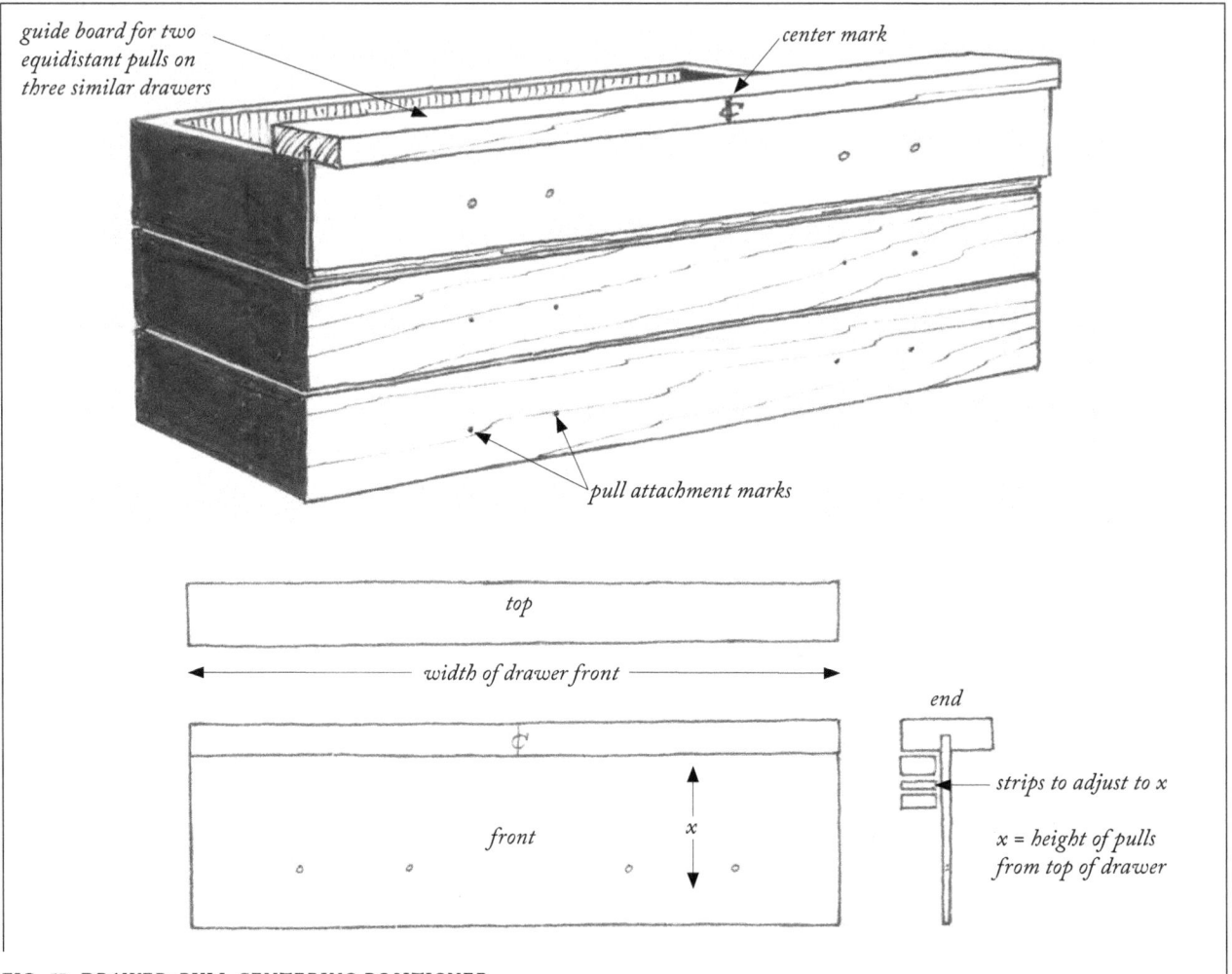

FIG. 51 DRAWER-PULL CENTERING POSITIONER

similar-width drawers is the centering positioner. It consists of a perforated thin board cut either to exactly the same width as the drawers to which the pulls are to be attached or to an unmatched piece divided clearly at its center into two equal halves. Matched pairs of guide holes (for awls or pencils) can be made equidistant from the centerline so that when the guide is positioned properly on the drawer front the left and right pulls can be marked accurately and consistently.

The guide itself may be made from 1/4 in. thick plywood or stiff card inserted into a straight lip or fence as for the drawer-pull guide above. In order to increase the utility of the guide, extra strips of varying thicknesses may be provided to adjust the depth from the bottom of the fence to the actual drawer-pull position for drawers of different heights.

CABINET DOOR-HANDLE GUIDE

A GUIDE SIMILAR TO THE DRAWER-PULL GUIDE may be made to locate door handles or pulls consistently, without having to measure the location of every handle, whether attached by one or two screws. This guide is used simply by being placed over the top opening corner of the door, for which reason it has two lips at right-angles to each other.

Since door pulls are typically located close to the top and opening edge of the door, the cabinet door-handle guide is constructed with two lips designed to fit over the top corner of the door. It is perhaps easiest to make a slot in the center of a single piece of lipping, and then saw this piece in half in the center of its length to guarantee that the card or thin board in which the guide holes are located fits evenly in both pieces when they are joined at right angles.

TRADITIONAL JIGS & FIXTURES

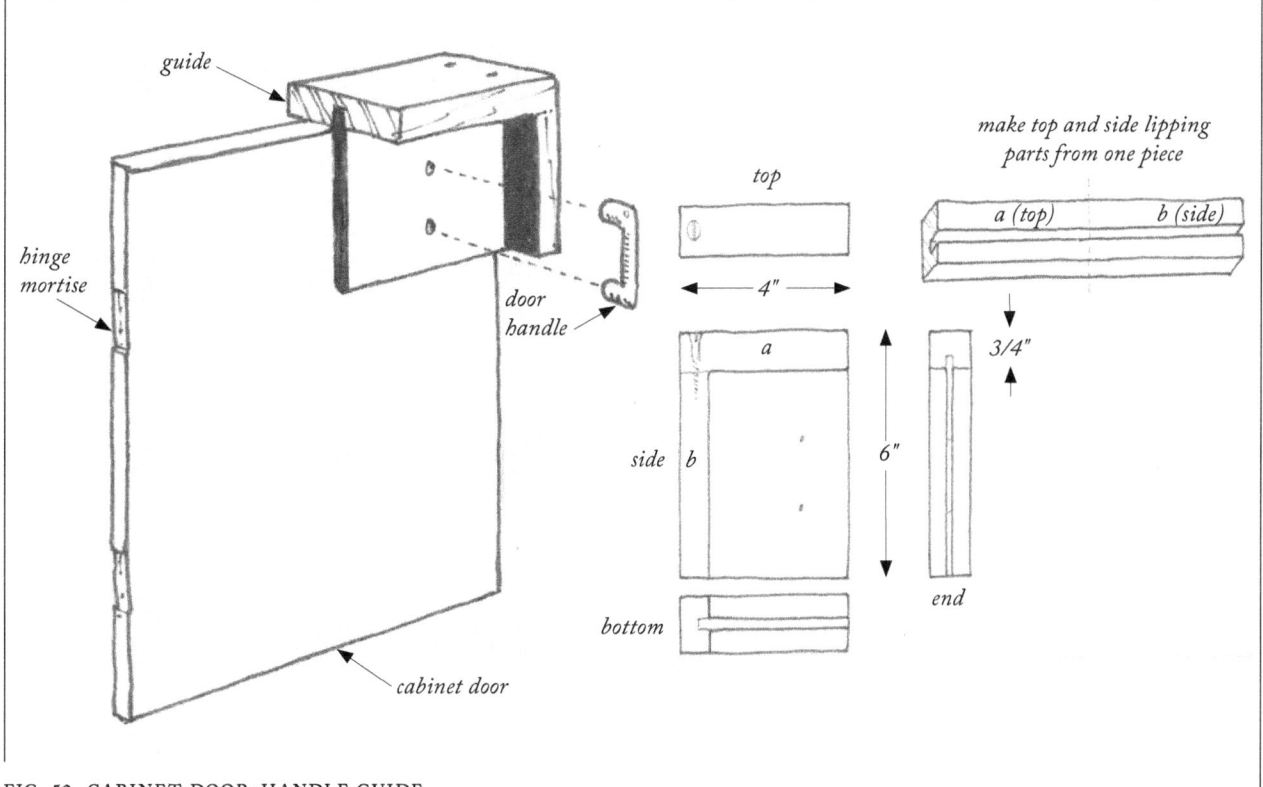

FIG. 52 CABINET DOOR-HANDLE GUIDE

SHELF-SUPPORT LAYOUT GUIDE

OF MOST IMPORTANCE WHEN LAYING OUT THE locations for boring the holes for shelf supports is to ensure that all four holes (there typically being two holes needed at each end of every shelf) lie in exactly the same plane, otherwise the shelf will rock. This can be guaranteed by using a perforated layout guide with parallel columns of holes. Such a guide need not be made each time this operation is needed if one is prepared with columns of holes no more than 1in. vertically apart — thus providing the opportunity to choose only those pairs necessary for the particular project in hand. Similarly, while two parallel columns may be most generally useful, there is no reason why a guide provided with a third, or even a fourth column cannot be made, and even with the outside columns located at different distances from the edges of the guide (which, of course, can be flipped over if necessary) thereby making more choices available for shelving sides of various widths to be accurately marked.

(A simpler version is the single strip used as a spaced hole guide shown in Chapter 6.)

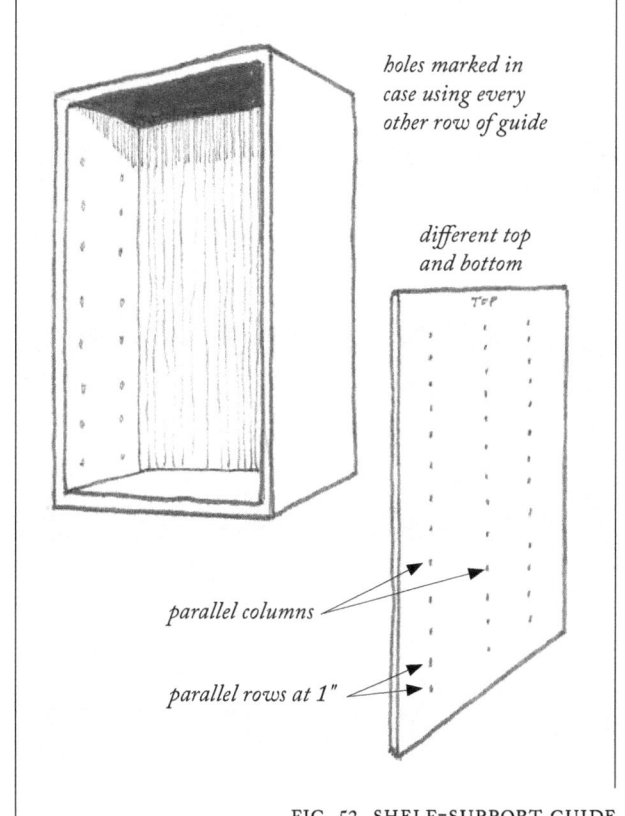

FIG. 53 SHELF-SUPPORT GUIDE

MEASURING & MARKING

TRADITIONAL JIGS & FIXTURES

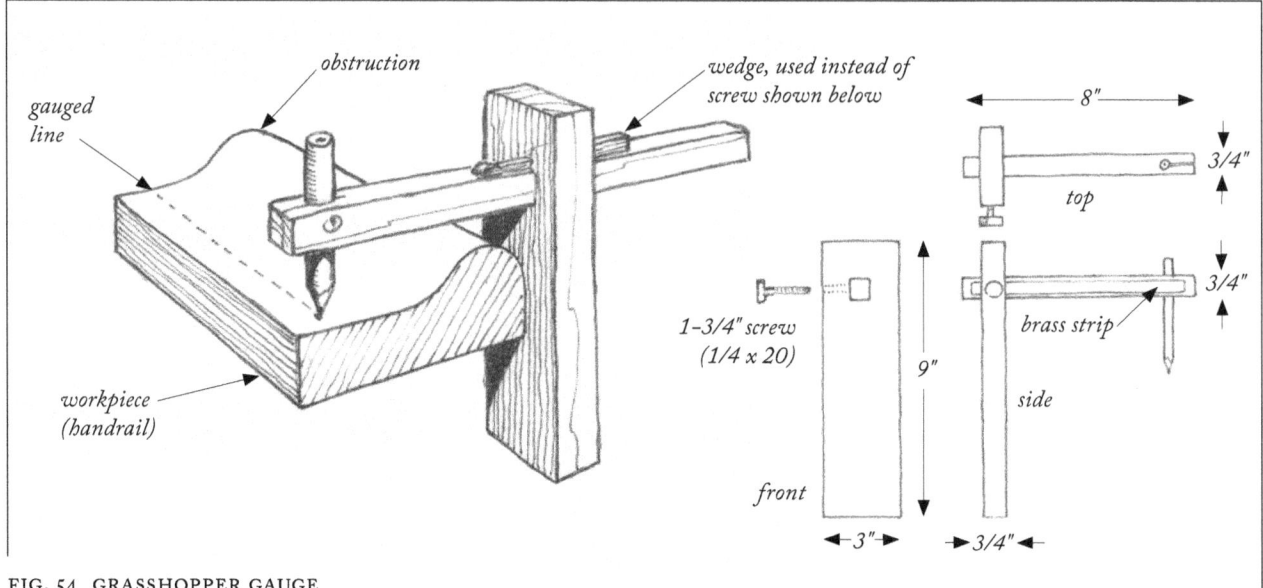

FIG. 54 GRASSHOPPER GAUGE

GRASSHOPPER GAUGE (HANDRAIL GAUGE)

A REALLY SURPRISING OMISSION FROM THE RANGE of today's available manufactured marking gauges is something traditionally known as a grasshopper gauge. Also occasionally referred to as a handrail gauge (since this was a particularly common use for this device) it is designed to mark a workpiece when there is something obstructive between the bearing surface of the head and where the mark is needed.

Its chief feature is an extra deep head that — sometimes with the help of a spacer block — allows the workpiece to be marked at a consistent distance from an edge that is not immediately adjacent to the area needing to be marked.

The head, however high it needs to be to enable the beam to clear any given obstruction, should be made wide enough to present a firm bearing surface to the workpiece. The traditional way of securing the beam in the required position in the head is by means of a narrow wedge, although a screw or wingnut tapped into the side of the head works equally well. A narrow strip of metal (sheet brass looks particularly fine) fixed to the side of the beam provides a longer lasting bearing surface for the machine screw. Depending on how high the vertical obstruction may be, an at least equally long pencil inserted in a hole bored in the end of the beam and secured by a screw is generally more useful than a pin.

CYLINDER GAUGING CRADLE

WHILE WITH CARE IT MAY BE POSSIBLE TO USE a standard marking gauge to mark cylinders or round workpieces (such as chair legs), a more secure method is to place the object to be marked in a V-block or cradle and use a grasshopper gauge as shown opposite in FIG. 55.

The cradle can be made by beveling one corner of a length of wood, sawing it in half, and fixing the two halves together as shown. Attaching a small lip to one side of the bottom of the cradle allows it to be held against the front of the workbench and remain in position when a grasshopper gauge is brought to bear against it and then slid along its face.

CORNER SCRIBE

IT IS IMPORTANT TO MAINTAIN A CONSISTENT angle with whatever marking tool is being used to scribe an irregular profile on any given workpiece if a good fit is to be guaranteed. The corner scribe is a simple device designed to hold such a marking tool (be this a marking awl, or more typically a pencil) at a precise angle while being held at a consistent

TRADITIONAL JIGS & FIXTURES

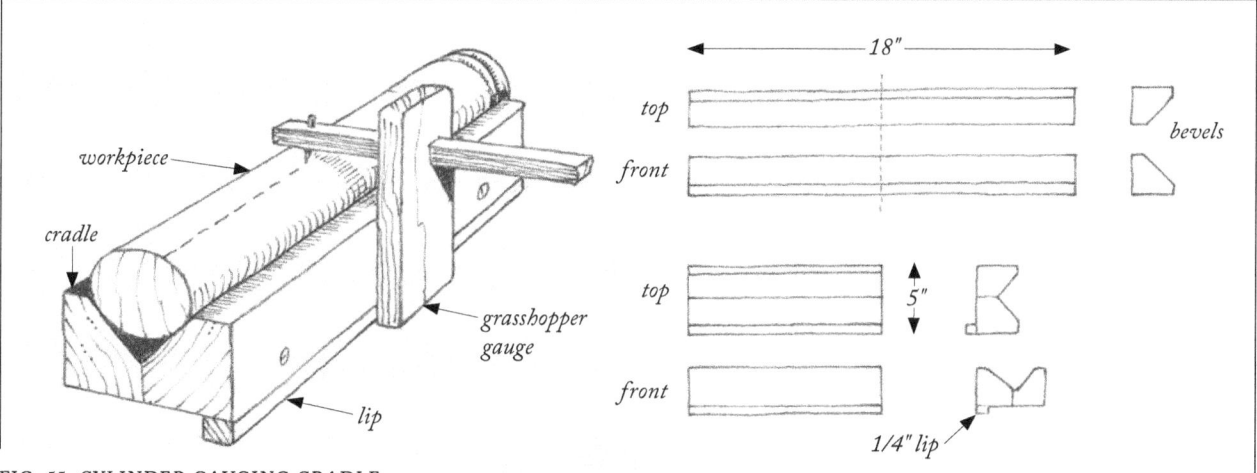

FIG. 55 CYLINDER GAUGING CRADLE

distance from the scribe's origin as a result of the built-in fence formed by the thickness of the jig. This fence also guarantees that the scribe will mark the precise location of the required cut without the marking tool being allowed to intrude into the gap should the workpiece being scribed not meet completely the pattern from which the scribe is being taken. Any block of wood thick enough to hold the marker securely will do, especially if the end is pointed — in order to allow it to follow particularly sharply angled profiles. But be sure to make the back of the scribe block wide enough to be comfortably held. Bore the hole for the marker at approximately 45°, and so that the tip of the marker is exactly in line with the bearing surface of the fence portion of the scribe.

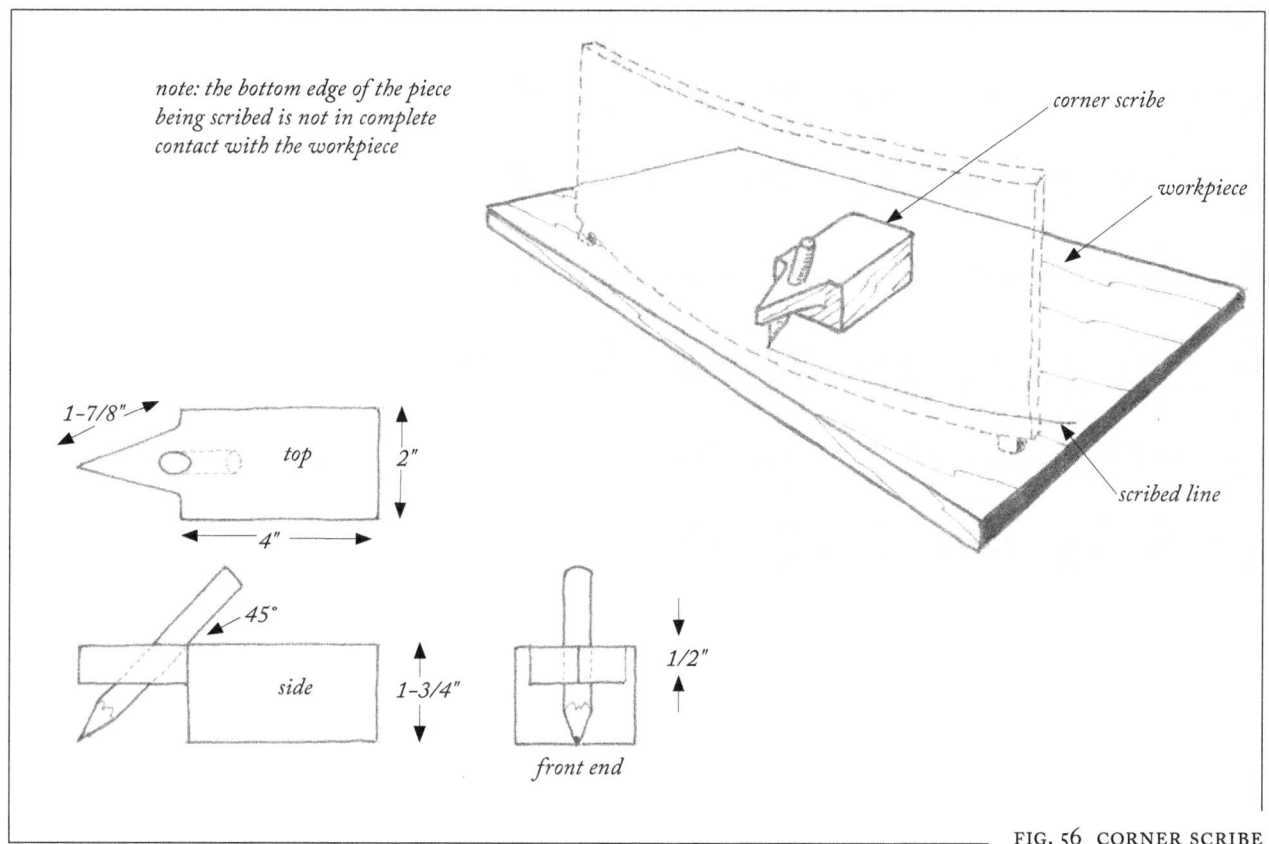

FIG. 56 CORNER SCRIBE

MEASURING & MARKING

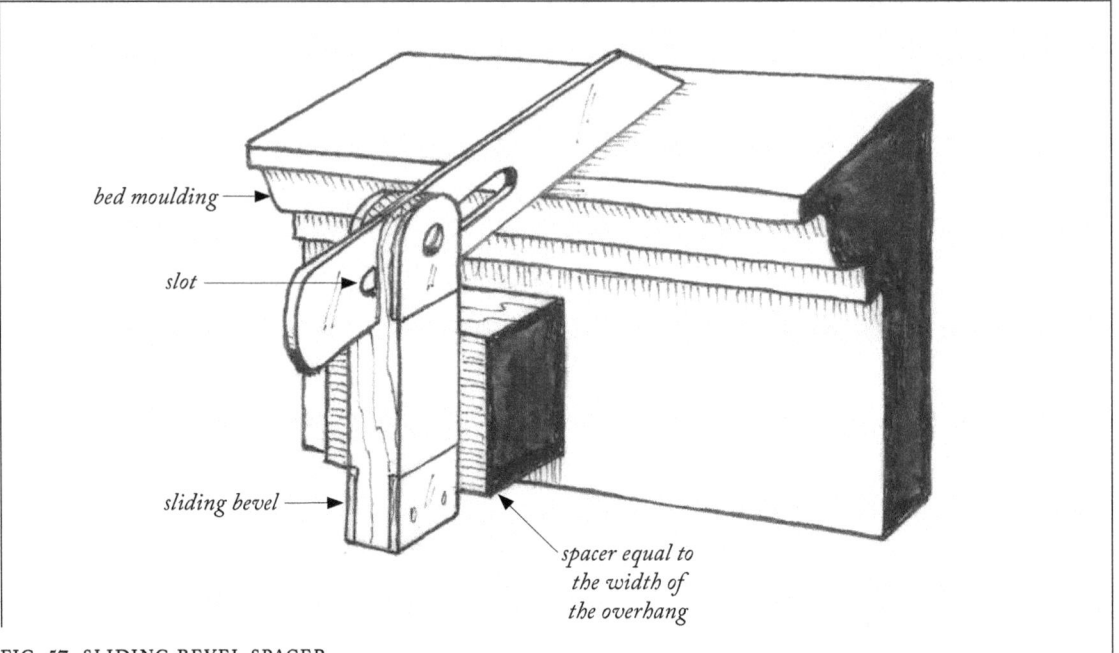

FIG. 57 SLIDING BEVEL SPACER

SLIDING BEVEL SPACER

THE PROBLEM SOMETIMES ENCOUNTERED WHEN trying to measure or mark a protruding slope with a bevel can be solved by adding a spacer block equal to the amount of the obstruction to the stock of the bevel. The spacer can either be held by hand against the stock of the bevel or temporarily attached with double-sided tape.

If the bevel being used is of the so-called sliding variety the exact width of the required spacer block (which might be difficult to measure from an angled overhang, especially if further obstructed by bed mouldings as shown above) need only be approximated since fine adjustments can be made by taking advantage of the slot in the bevel's blade. Therefore start by estimating the width required with the bevel's blade in its mid-position, and then slide the blade in or out to fit.

DOVETAIL GUIDES:

THE EXPERIENCED WOODWORKER CAN OFTEN place the workpiece to be dovetailed in the bench vise, tilt it to the correct angle for hardwood or softwood as the case may be, so that the ensuing sawcut can be made vertically, and saw without further ado. The beginner or more cautious worker will first mark out the tails and then tilt the workpiece so that these lines are aligned with a square held on the bench. In either case tilting the workpiece takes advantage of the fact that verticality is far easier to judge and maintain by eye when sawing than are other angles.

The problem for the tyro lies mainly in how to lay out the required angle. This can be done by setting a sliding bevel to the angle and ratios shown in FIG. 58, and then balancing this tool on the edge of the workpiece, but a more surefire method is to lay out the required cuts with either one of the two following guides.

DOVETAIL MARKING GUIDE

THE FIRST IS A DOVETAIL MARKER PROVIDED WITH a lip that can be held firmly against the workpiece with little fear of slipping.

All that is required is a small rabbeted block of wood a little longer from top to bottom than the proposed dovetails, with both sides cut to the appropriate angles for softwood or hardwood as shown in FIG. 58, so that the guide can be used equally on either side as well as at both ends of the workpiece.

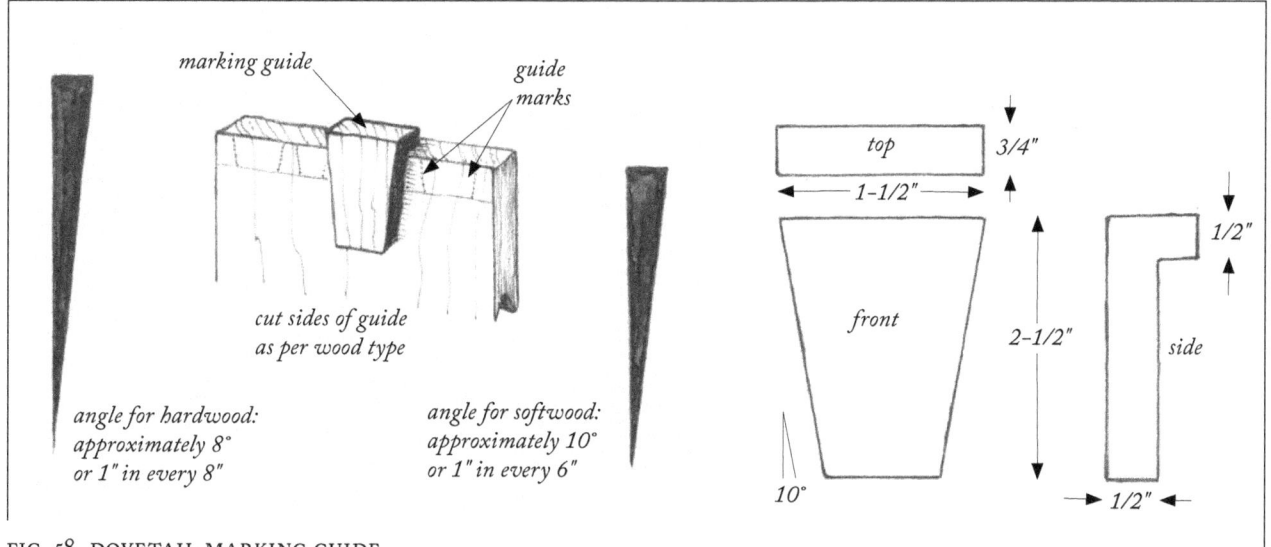

FIG. 58 DOVETAIL MARKING GUIDE

SIDE DOVETAIL GUIDE

A REGULAR DOVETAIL MARKING GUIDE IS NOT so easily used when laying out dovetails in the end of a framing member that is to be dovetailed or lap-dovetailed into another workpiece as it is when being used as shown in FIG. 58 since there is little bearing area for the guide's lip. A better item for this purpose is the side dovetail guide shown below in FIG. 59 since this offers more bearing surface.

The side dovetail marking guide can be made from a small rectangular block, one side of which has been grooved to accept a thin angled piece of wood, metal, or even stiff card cut to the appropriate angle. By cutting the groove in the center of the block the guide can be used on both sides of the workpiece.

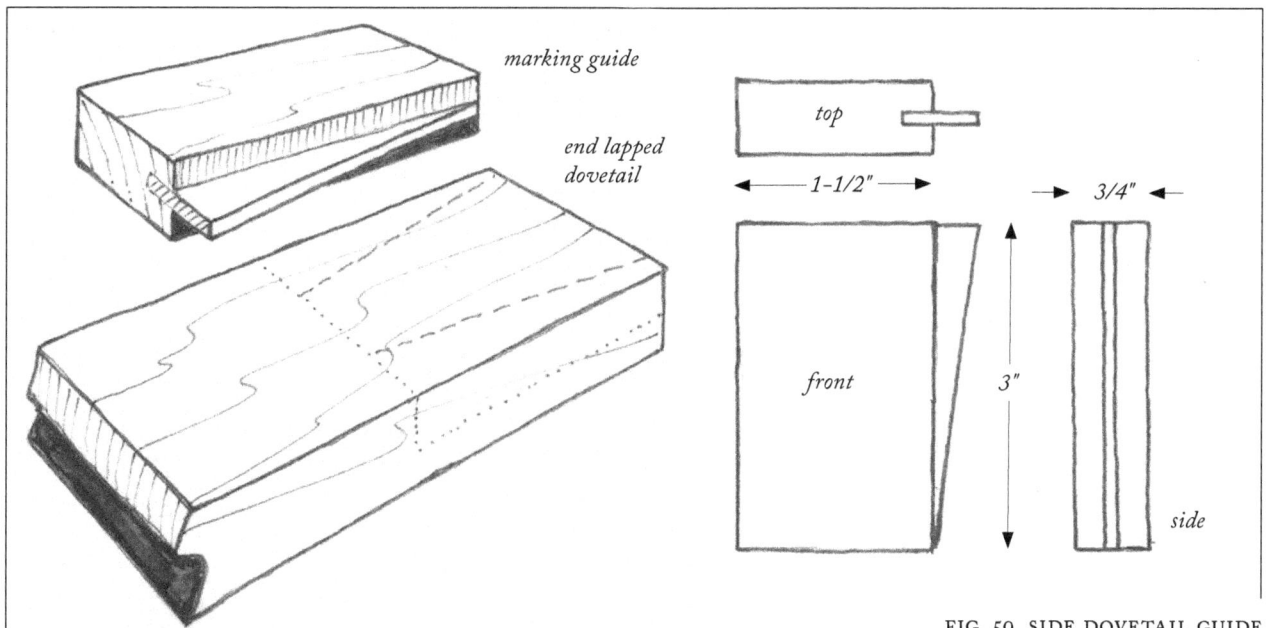

FIG. 59 SIDE DOVETAIL GUIDE

MEASURING & MARKING

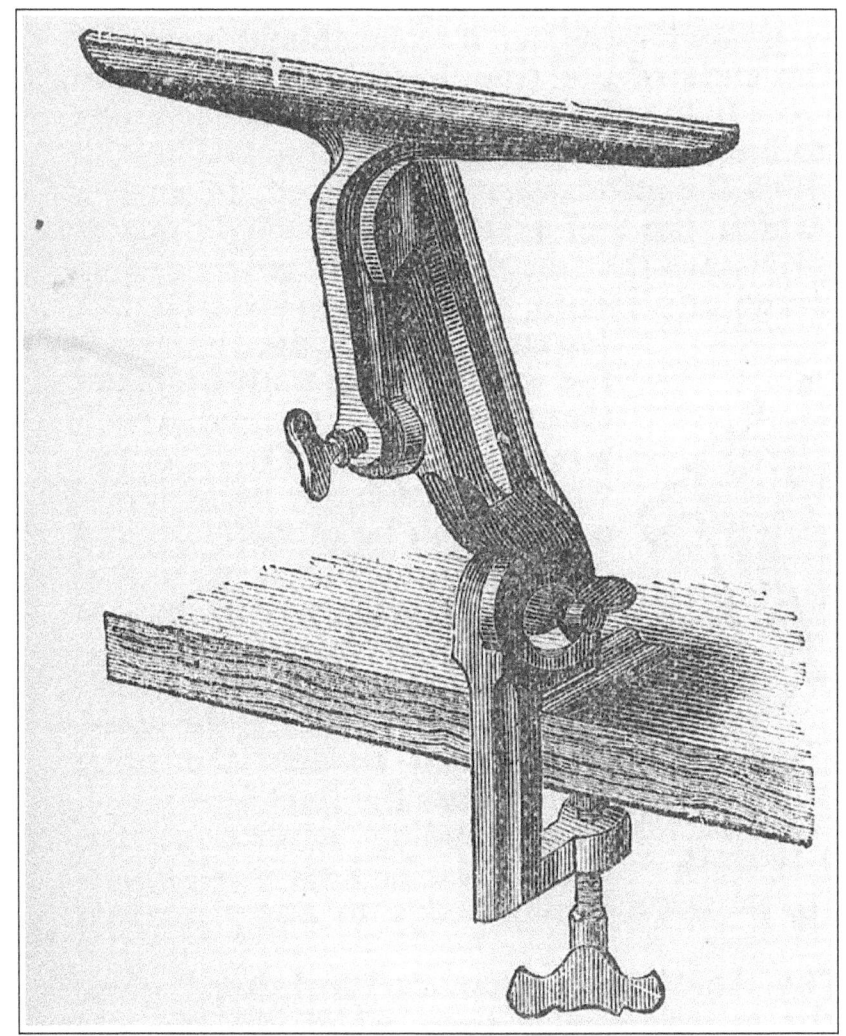

Saw Filer's Vise (from Elementary Carpentry and Joinery, c.1900)

3

JIGS & FIXTURES FOR SAWING

THE MODERN TABLESAW WITH A POWERFUL MOTOR, A PERFECTLY FLAT TABLE AND ACCURATE FENCE, PLUS ACCESSORIES SUCH AS OUTFEED TABLES AND A VARIETY OF JIGS DESIGNED TO MAKE THE SAW CAPABLE OF VARIOUS OPERATIONS THAT IT WAS NOT originally designed for (such as cutting tenons, tapers, and dadoes), is become the virtual icon of contemporary woodworking — the sine qua non of any respectable woodworking shop. Nevertheless, as any experienced woodworker ultimately discovers, a certain amount of handsaw use remains essential. What is become less discoverable, however, is that handsaws, like their bigger cousin the tablesaw, also depend on a variety of jigs and fixtures if their use is to be exact and efficient. In fact, equipped with such items, the handsaw — in all its varied forms (and there are almost as many different types of handsaw as there are planes) — is, especially in a one-person shop, often faster and more versatile than the tablesaw — and certainly safer and often more pleasant to use.

One item that shops totally dependent on tablesaw and chopsaw frequently lack is a place where handsaws can be used. The traditional woodworker makes much use of handsaws, whose use often compares favorably with contemporary machines. It can be just as quick to rip a 2 ft. long board by hand if provided with a properly sharpened ripsaw, a place to use it, and a little knowledge of the correct method as it is to set up and use a tablesaw.

SAW BENCH

A SAW BENCH IS ONE PLACE WHERE THIS CAN BE done (saw horses and benches being two others). The saw bench provides support and security, and is always ready for use. Its utility is based on the fact

TRADITIONAL JIGS & FIXTURES

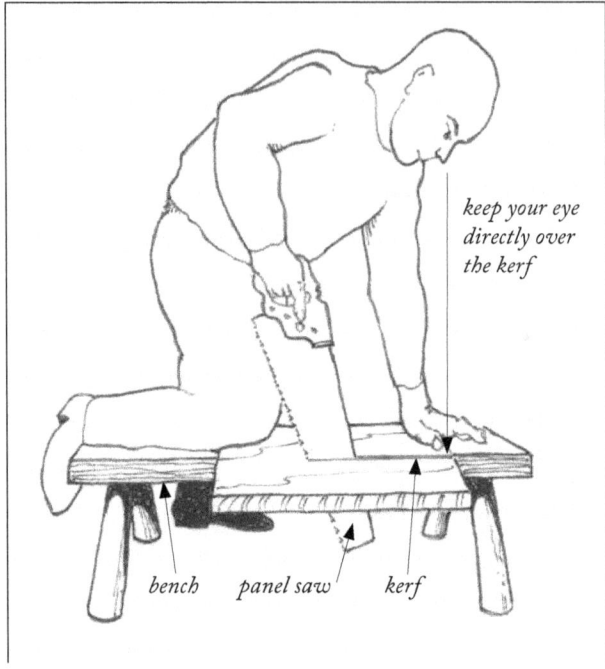

FIG. 60 SAW BENCH

A substantial board such as a length of two-by-ten or even a rough-sawn board surfaced on one side only is better than regular three-quarter or even five-quarter milled lumber obtainable at the local lumber yard or home-supply store. Equally important are legs stout enough to provide stability — to which end splayed legs are ideal. It should be low enough to kneel on while supporting the workpiece and at the same to time keep an eye above the saw when working, but also high enough to permit a full stroke of a 24 in. handsaw.

SAW HORSE

SAW HORSES ARE TYPICALLY HIGHER THAN SAW benches, and moreover used most commonly in pairs. Carpenters often make them all from lengths of two-by-four, but more useful in a general woodworking shop are sawhorses made from stock 5/4 in. thick by 6 in. wide tops and 4 in. wide legs. This construction provides a more useful flat working surface. Their use in pairs makes working long boards easy, whether cross-cutting or ripping.

The standard length is about 3 ft., the standard height about 2 ft. Notching the legs in the ends

that it is sturdy enough for vigorous use. Another part of its convenience comes from its height: it is easier and more accurate to saw with one's eye immediately above the saw cut, the better to saw perfectly vertically.

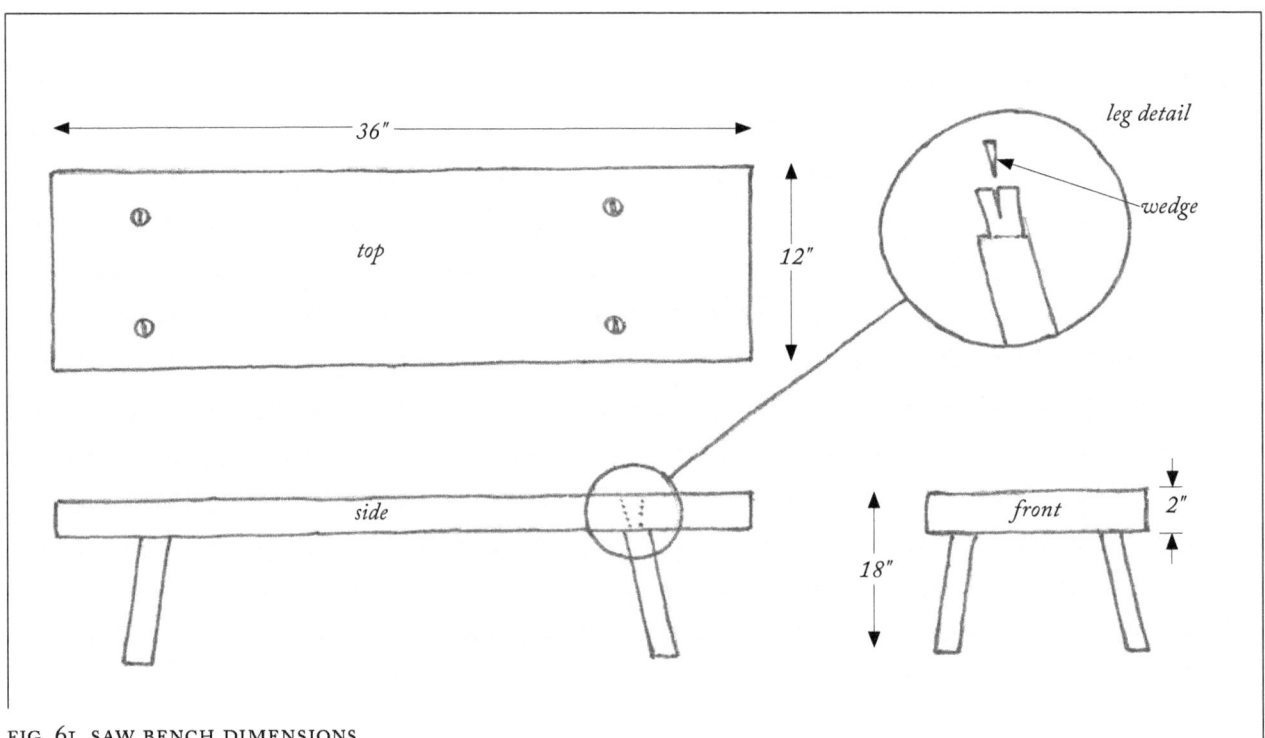

FIG. 61 SAW BENCH DIMENSIONS

TRADITIONAL JIGS & FIXTURES

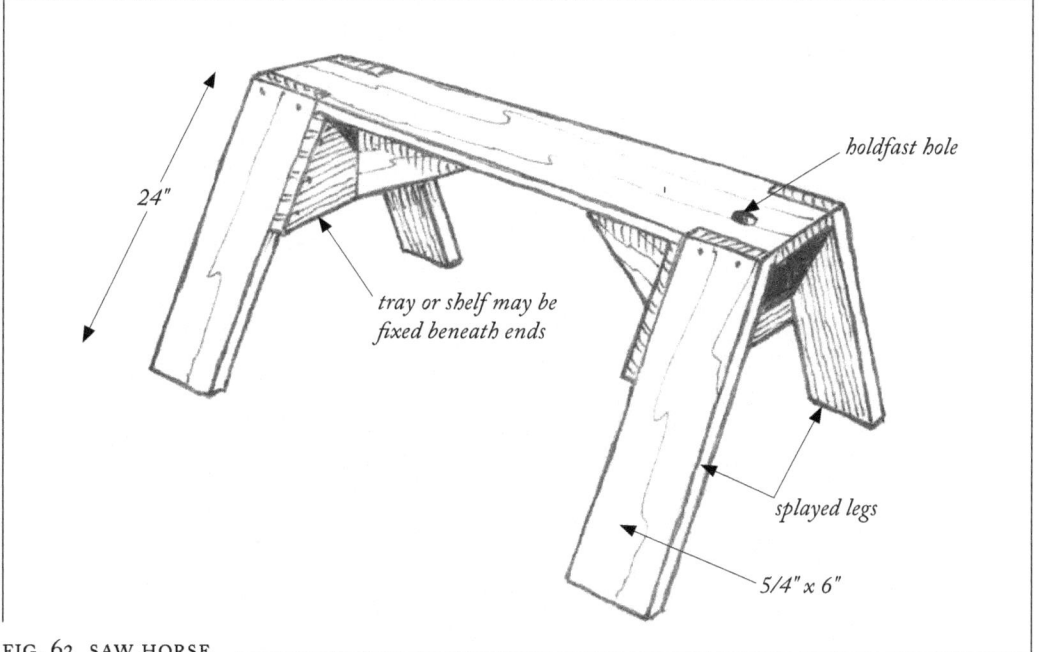

FIG. 62 SAW HORSE

of the top, providing each pair with a connecting brace on the inside, and finally bracketing each brace to the underneath of the top makes the horse very stable longitudinally and laterally, and in addition easily stackable. Locating the connecting brace on the inside of the legs rather than on the outside makes it possible to use the extreme ends of the tops as a place to attach clamps and bore holes for such purposes as making glue-escapes in dowelling or providing for holdfasts. If the bottoms of the connecting braces are kept level then it also become possible to attach a tool shelf here. Giving the legs a 15° splay from vertical will provide sufficient stability.

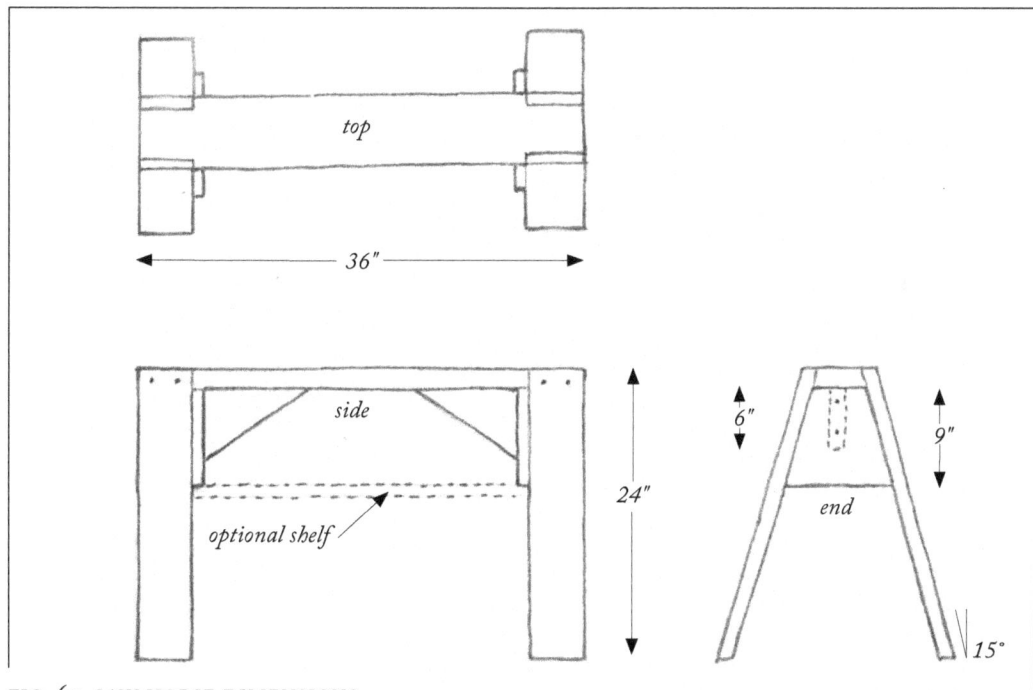

FIG. 63 SAW HORSE DIMENSIONS

SAWING

TRADITIONAL JIGS & FIXTURES

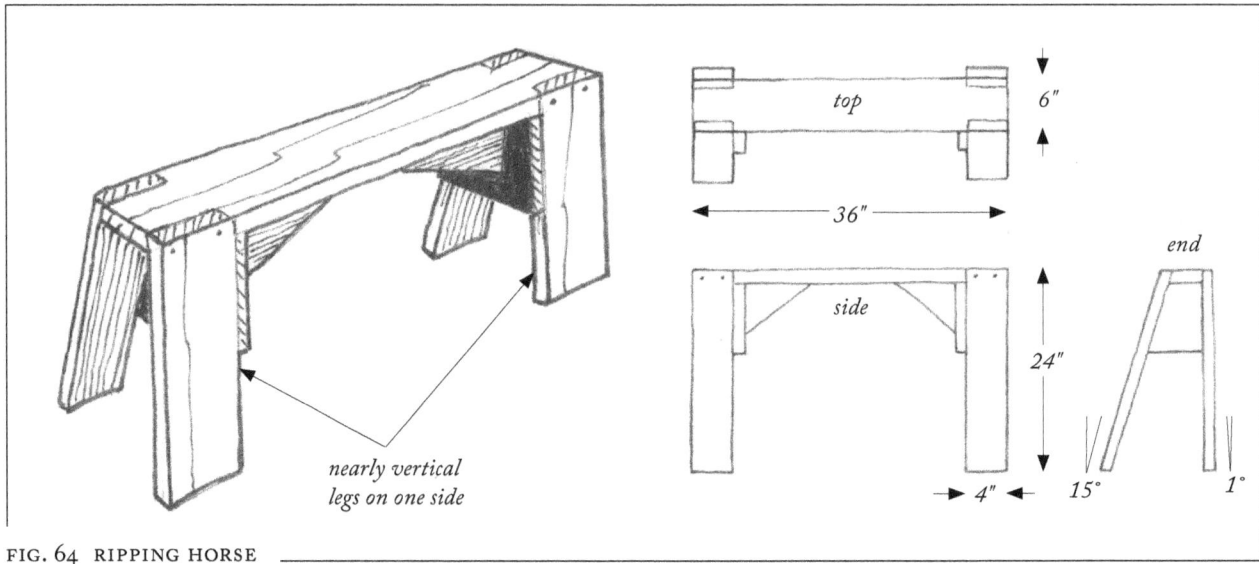

FIG. 64 RIPPING HORSE

RIPPING HORSE

ALTHOUGH RIPPING A BOARD WITH A HAND RIPSAW can often be comfortably undertaken at the standard bench by securing the workpiece vertically in a vise and sawing in an essentially horizontal position, it is sometimes easier to rip by hand using a pair of horses with the board to be ripped resting perpendicularly to the horses and one's knee resting on the workpiece. This, of course, requires that the board be periodically moved in order for its whole length to be cut. A better solution is to use a horse whose legs on one side are vertical rather than splayed. This enables the workpiece to be secured (by a knee or a clamp) longitudinally, leaving the sawcut accessible throughout its length, and if it is not too long, without the aid of a second horse.

A ripping horse can be made the same way as the saw horse described above but with the difference that the legs on one side are not splayed — or at least by not more than 5°. The slight loss in stability is compensated for by the fact that when used for ripping the sawyer is typically standing on the splayed-legs side and kneeling on the workpiece.

SAWBUCK (SAW-GOAT)

THE MODERN SAWBUCK IS A FORM OF SAW HORSE used for sawing shorter lengths off logs. It is characterized by legs that extend above its table, thereby preventing the workpiece (or log) from rolling off. Originally made from convenient forked

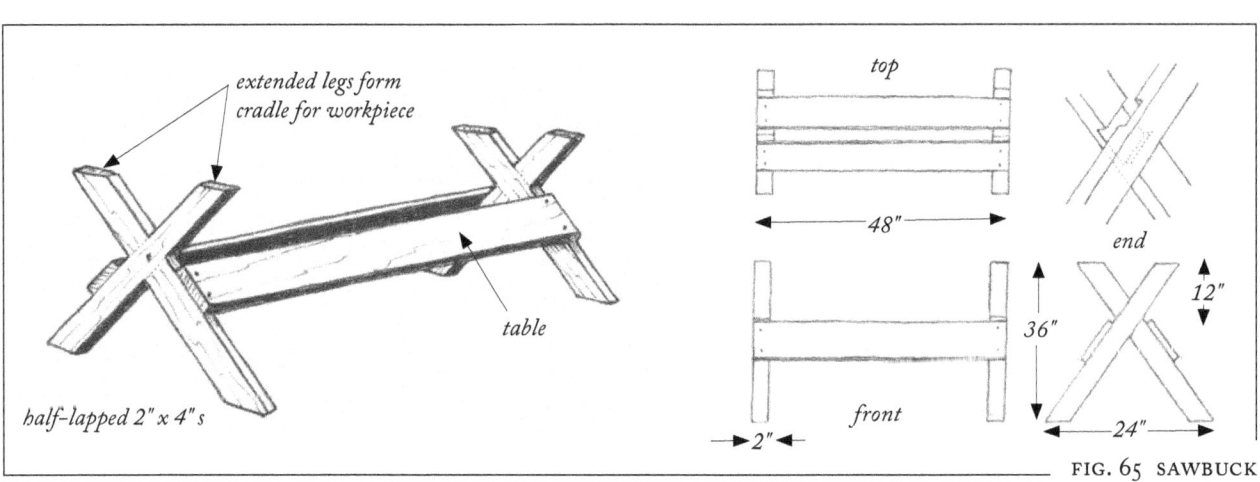

FIG. 65 SAWBUCK

TRADITIONAL JIGS & FIXTURES

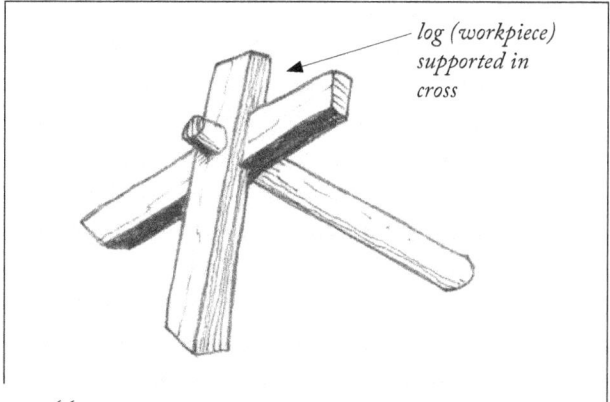

FIG. 66 DUTCH ZAAG-BOC

FIG. 67 BENCH STOP DAMAGE

sections of tree, and, indeed originally only having one end (the unsupported end of the workpiece resting on the ground), its name derives from the Dutch word *zaag-boc*, which literally translates to 'saw-goat'.

While it is not very important how the two ends are connected — other than ensuring some kind of longitudinal bracing — care should be taken in constructing the ends if the fixture is to have any longevity. Integral extensions are best; legs that are half-lapped at the point where they cross will last longer than legs nailed or screwed together. Unlike a shop saw-horse that is best constructed from more finished material, rough-sawn two-by-fours or similar material (maybe even actual undressed logs of small diameter) will be perfectly adequate.

BENCH AIDS:

FOR WORKPIECES MUCH SMALLER THAN THOSE requiring saw horses for support there exist several fixtures designed to keep workpieces secure while being sawed on the bench top. The simplest of these is the bench stop already described in Chapter 1. This, in whatever form and while convenient, has the disadvantage of risking damage to the bench top.

PIVOTING SAW-STOP

SOMETHING THAT WAS COMMON MANY YEARS AGO on my school benches is a pivoting stop that can be added to the end of any bench not having a tail vise (which would get in the way of such a device). It makes possible sawing off-the-bench rather than on-the-bench, since the workpiece braced against it overhangs the end of the bench Such a stop is a quicker method of providing for something against which to brace the workpiece than clamping the workpiece to the bench top, although very often the holdfast as shown in Chapter 1 will be found to be more than adequate.

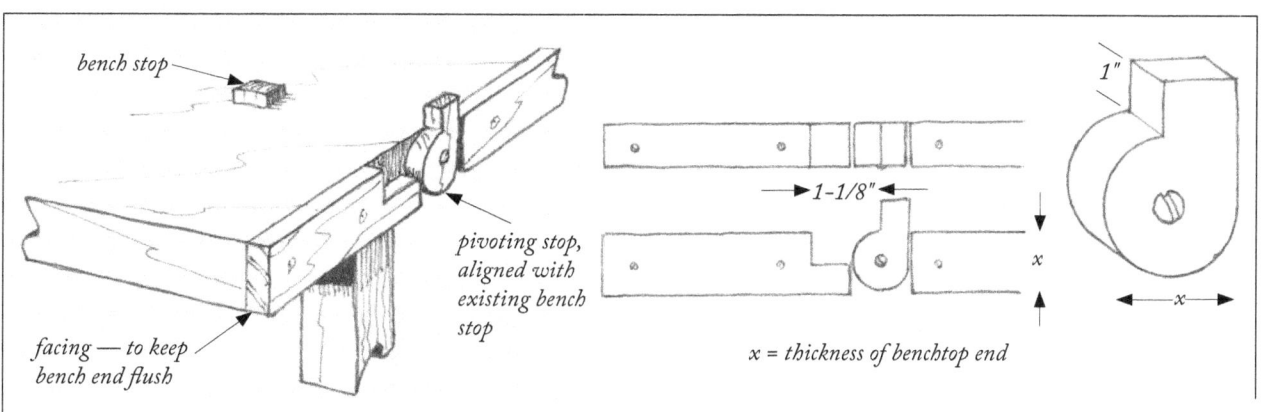

FIG. 68 PIVOTING SAW STOP

SAWING

Use hardwood and make sure that the end of the bench is thick enough — by adding extra material if necessary — to locate a pivot point so that the stop can rise high enough to be useful (at least 1 in.) and when returned become flush with the bench top. Both to protect the pivot and preserve a smooth bench-top end, adding a facing as shown on both sides of the actual pivoting stop is recommended.

KERFED BENCH HOOK

BY FAR THE BEST DEVICE FOR ACCURATE, SECURE, and safe bench-top sawing is a bench hook designed specifically for sawing. Such a bench hook will have a shortened back hook so that the bench top itself is in no danger of being gashed by the saw. It may also be kerfed — typically at 90°, and often at 45°, both left and right — by the same saw (usually a backsaw, either tenon or dovetail) that will be used in said kerf in order to guide the saw accurately. It should be apparent, however, that guide kerfs may be made at any angle that may be required. This will be especially useful when sawing compound angles or the sloping sides of end-dovetails.

This particular fixture is one which with use will eventually wear out, but although inherently disposable should still be made with care if you are to get worthwhile results.

It is most important to realize that any bench hook intended to be kerfed for saw slots should have the hooks affixed with glue and wooden dowels rather than with metal fasteners such as nails or screws, for otherwise it is inevitable that you will one day damage any saw you use to produce a fresh guide slot by inadvertently sawing into the fastener.

By planing a small bevel on the bottom inside edge of the hook you will not only avoid the danger of any dust build-up forcing the workpiece away from the hook, but you will also make the holding of small diameter round stock such as dowels more secure. Although you may kerf your hook anywhere you believe is convenient, it often pays to do so — especially with right-angled kerfs designed to produce perfectly square cuts — at a specified distance from the end of the hook so that you also have a built-in form of length guide.

Although MDF or other forms of particleboard have the advantage of flatness, I prefer to use a piece of hardwood for my bench hook's table since it wears better. But it is very important for maximum accuracy to make sure that this is flat, and that both hooks are affixed true and square. The width of the table may be anything from 6 in. to 1 ft. If a piece of scrap the same thickness as the table is kept handy this can be used to prevent long workpieces from sagging and being sawed at less than a perfect 90° vertical angle.

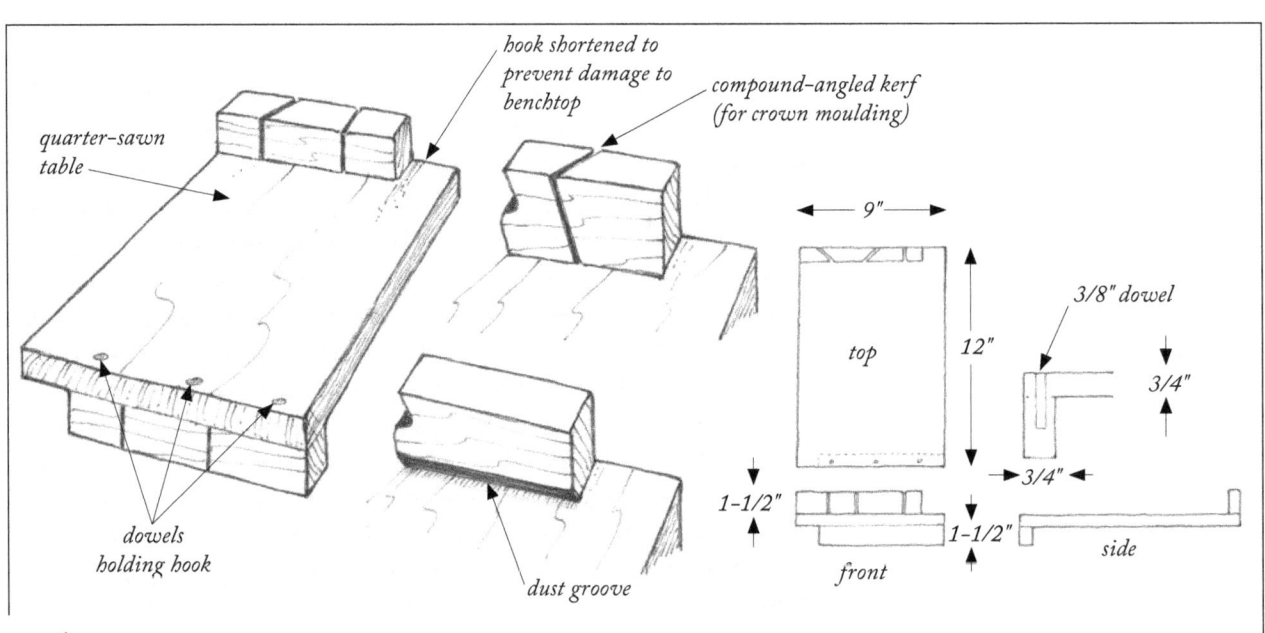

FIG. 69 KERFED BENCH HOOK

TRADITIONAL JIGS & FIXTURES

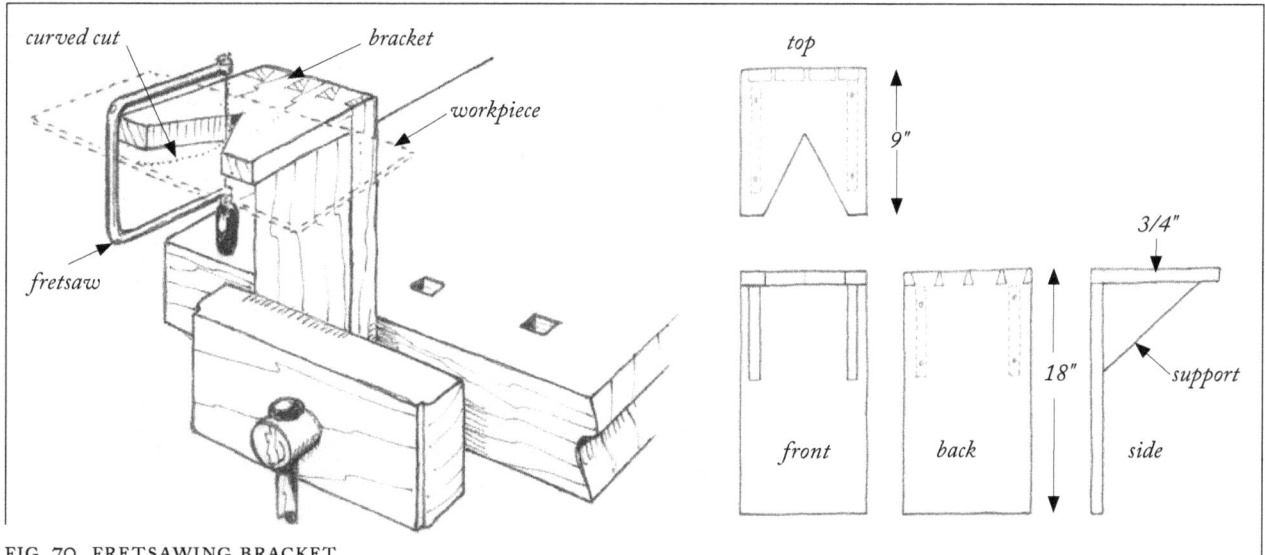

FIG. 70 FRETSAWING BRACKET

FRETSAWING BRACKET

A FRETSAWING BRACKET IS A FIXTURE DESIGNED to be held in a bench vise, raising the workpiece to eye level for a seated worker, and which most importantly has a deeply notched table that allows the fretsaw to work in the center of the table so that the workpiece enjoys maximum support.

A bracket whose table is exactly perpendicular to its support makes sawing easy, especially when attempting to make perpendicular cuts. Ideally the table should be dovetailed into the vertical support, but providing a right-angled support — off-center so as not to interfere with the notch — will both guarantee perpendicularity and provide additional strength.

FRETSAWING BLOCK

A MUCH FIRMER BASE THAN A FRETSAWING bracket, useful for smaller work, although perhaps not so convenient since the work height cannot be adjusted, can be made by clamping a substantial

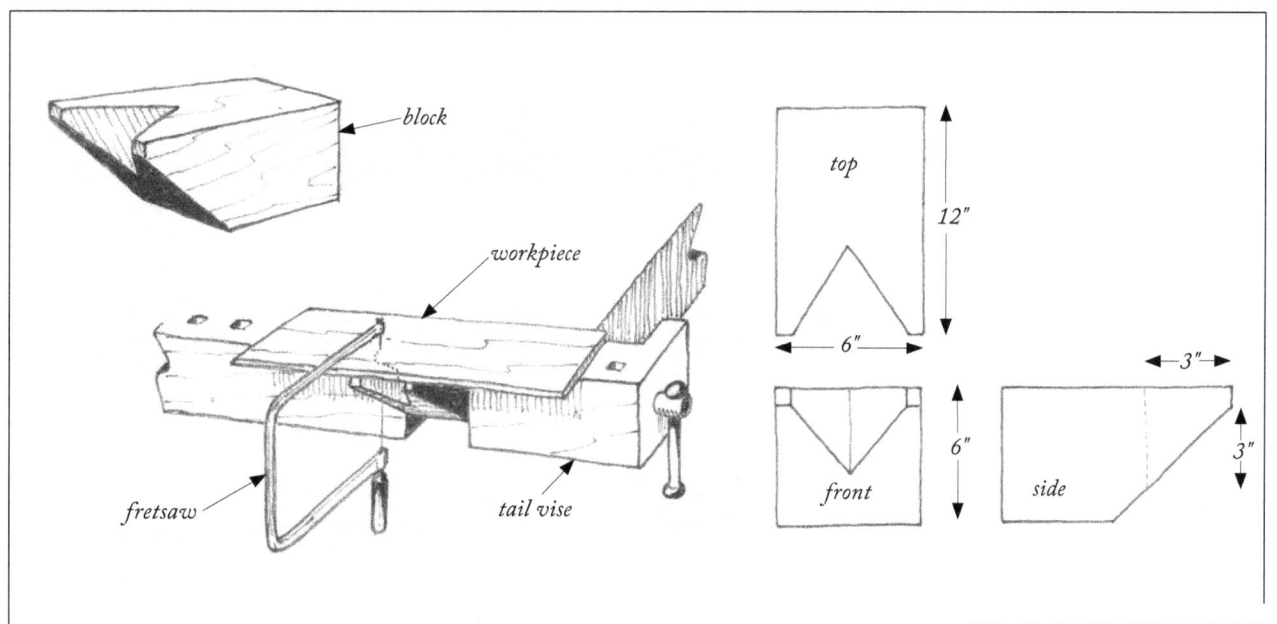

FIG. 71 FRETSAWING BLOCK

SAWING

V-shaped block in a tail vise — if your bench is so equipped. Cut one end of a 6 in.-thick block (or two thinner pieces glued together) at 45°, and into this beveled end cut a V-shaped notch. If the block is positioned in a tail vise so that its top is flush with the bench top it does not have to be much wider than the notch since the workpiece will be supported by the bench.

SAWING GUIDES:

THE NEXT GROUP OF JIGS AND FIXTURES IS designed more particularly for ensuring accuracy when making specific cuts, and assumes that securing the workpiece has already been attended to. There is, of course, a certain element of 'Catch 22' about such jigs, since they must usually be made without any jig to ensure their own accuracy. Therefore very careful layout is essential, together with good sawing habits, such as preparing a groove with trysquare and marking knife for the saw's initial cuts to run in, and positioning the workpiece so that wherever possible you can saw vertically, with your eye immediately over the saw.

DEPTH STOP

MUCH HAND WOODWORKING, ESPECIALLY SAWING, depends on working carefully to accurately laid out lines, penciled or scribed, but this advice is useless if layout marks cannot be seen. Such is often the case when sawing to a specified depth. Rather than attempting to see the impossible, limiting the saw's travel is a better idea. The simplest solution is a stop block fixed to the side of the saw, whether this be a 26 in.-long crosscut saw or a small, fine-toothed dovetail saw.

The simplest depth stop for almost any kind of saw is simply a straight scrap clamped to the side of the sawblade with any convenient clamp. More useful is a broader piece of wood slotted so as to be attached to nuts (preferably wingnuts) and bolts inserted through the sawblade. If you bore through the sawblade halfway between the teeth and the back, and make a long enough slot in the stop you will maximize the possible adjustment range. While you may not want to bore through the blade of every saw you own, keeping at least one backsaw thus equipped will prove very useful for repetitive jobs such as sawing tenons.

DOWEL LENGTH-STOP

DOWELS ARE COMMONLY USED IN GROUPS, ALL OF which may need to be cut to the same length.

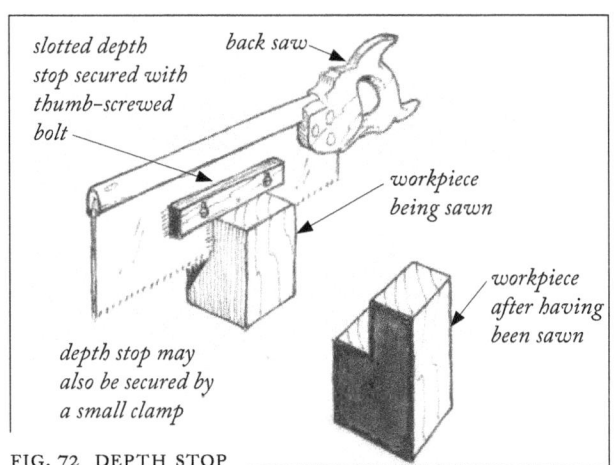

FIG. 72 DEPTH STOP

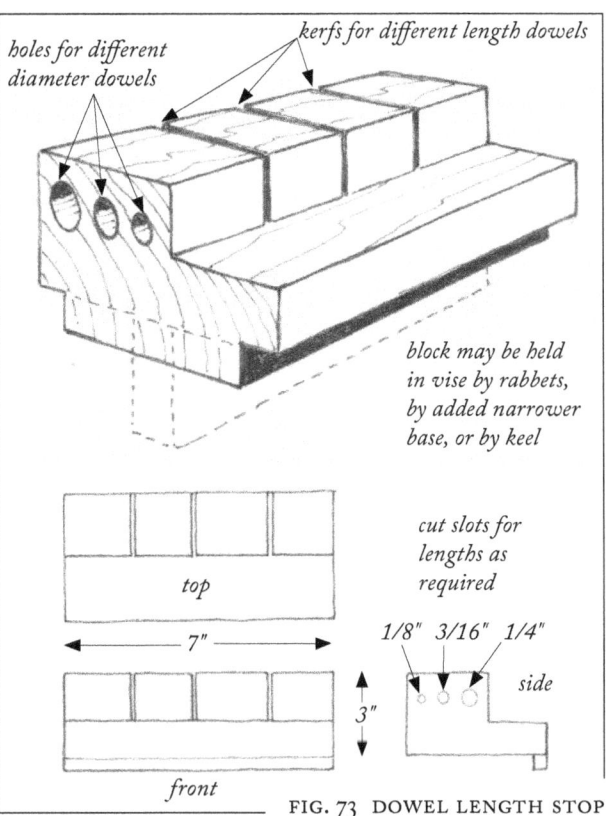

FIG. 73 DOWEL LENGTH STOP

Rather than measure each length individually the most efficient method is to use some form of pre-measured length stop. It is not difficult to clamp a stop block to the back hook of a bench hook, but an even easier method is to use a stop block bored with several holes, each slightly larger than the most common diameters you may need for dowels. By kerfing this block at various lengths you may slide in a dowel rod into one of these holes until its end is flush with the opposite end of the block and then use the appropriately marked kerf to produce the required length dowel.

More than three or four different diameter holes into which dowel rod may be inserted, and more than a length of stop block longer than is necessary to include three or four kerfs will prove too many and too much for convenience (even though another dowel rod of the same diameter as that being sawn can be used to push a reduced length into position). The block can be held in the bench hook, rabbeted to be held in a vise, or provided with its own lip or keel.

SHOULDER GUIDE

A KERFED BENCH HOOK IS GOOD FOR ANGLE-SAWING relatively narrow workpieces, but wider workpieces such as the sides of shelving or cabinet carcases cannot be brought to the bench hook. Instead, a guide may be temporarily fixed to the workpiece against which the saw can be held to ensure that it enters the workpiece perfectly perpendicularly.

Assuming that the workpiece and the guide are secured so that you have a hand free, using the thumb of your other hand to keep the blade pressed lightly against the guide block will help guarantee accuracy. This is much more reliable than the commonly recommended practice of attempting to sight the perpendicularity of the saw to the work by holding a trysquare against the saw.

ANGLE GUIDE

ONLY SLIGHTLY MORE ADVANCED THAN THE shoulder guide is an angle guide, the most common example of which is a block of wood whose end,

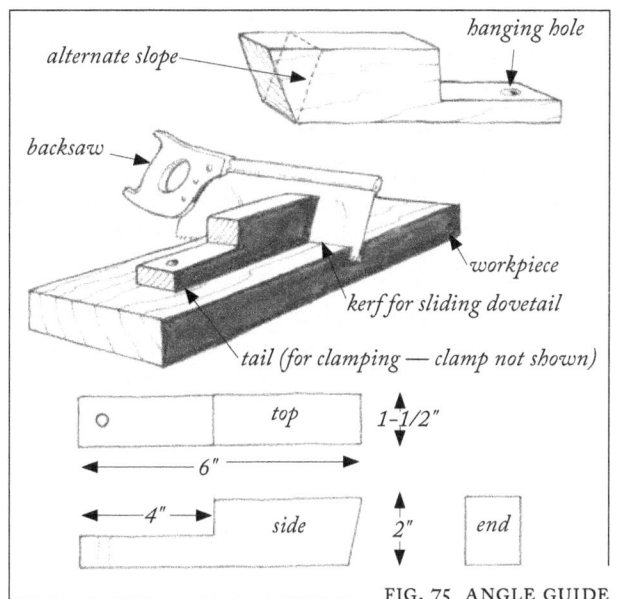

FIG. 75 ANGLE GUIDE

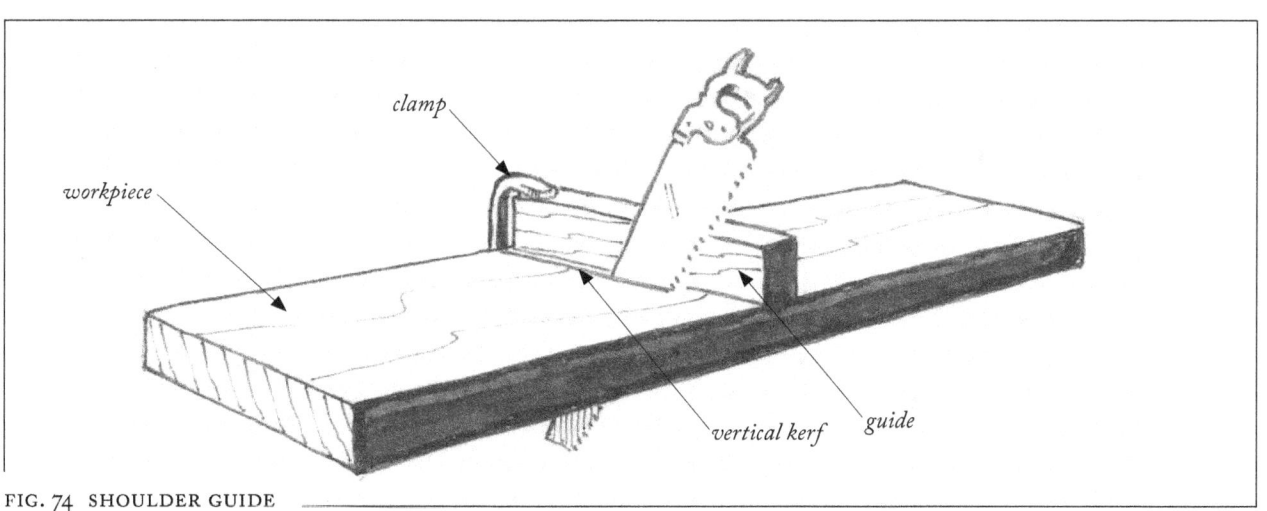

FIG. 74 SHOULDER GUIDE

against which the saw is held, is cut to an appropriate angle, such as that required to cut dovetails. Such a block may be held to the workpiece with the aid of a holdfast. Several variations are possible, each of which may be more convenient in a particular situation. One is to provide the angle block with a tail for easier clamping. Another is to cut the angle up or down, as shown. Yet a third is to use two identical blocks clamped together or spaced apart across the width of wider boards, or when using a larger saw.

MITERING AIDS:

MITER BLOCK (MITRE BLOCK)

THE SO-CALLED MITER BLOCK IS IN ESSENCE little more than a specific kind of bench hook intended solely for sawing miters. The hook is usually higher and wider than that belonging to a regular bench hook, the better to guide the saw. Although the kerf should be very carefully cut with the same saw as will be used to cut miters on the block, it is still liable to wear with use and become less than perfectly accurate. If hardwood strips are attached to the top of the block, close against the sides of an inserted saw, the jig's useful life will be greatly extended — provided that the saw is always inserted into the block through the front of its kerf and not from the top down, which practice would eventually wear the strips.

Similar to a kerfed bench hook, the miter block is much wider, thereby providing more guidance to the sawblade. Another fundamental difference is that the block itself should be let into its hooked table so that the various kerfs cut in it do not completely cut it into separate pieces.

MITER BOX (MITRE BOX)

ALTHOUGH A MITER BOX IS ONE OF THE FEW JIGS and fixtures readily available as a manufactured

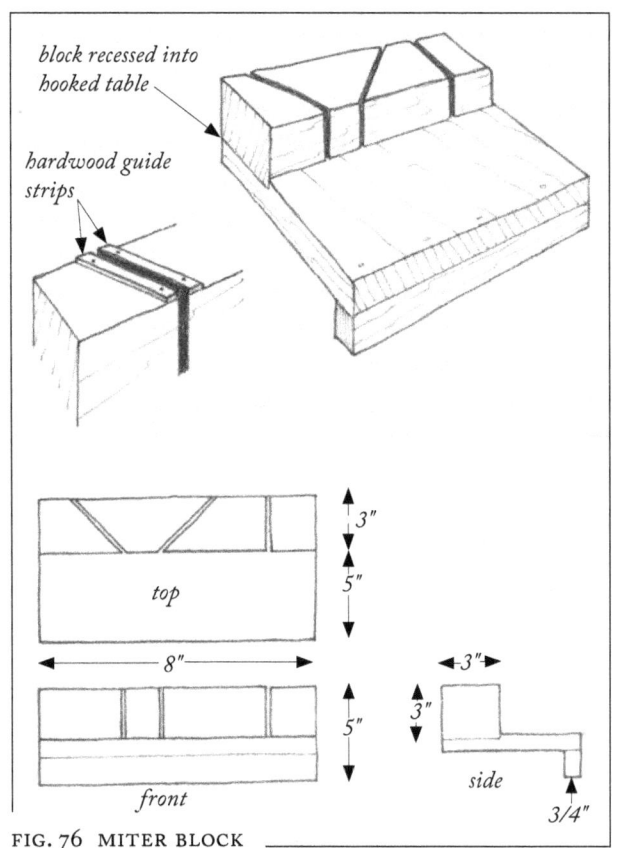

FIG. 76 MITER BLOCK

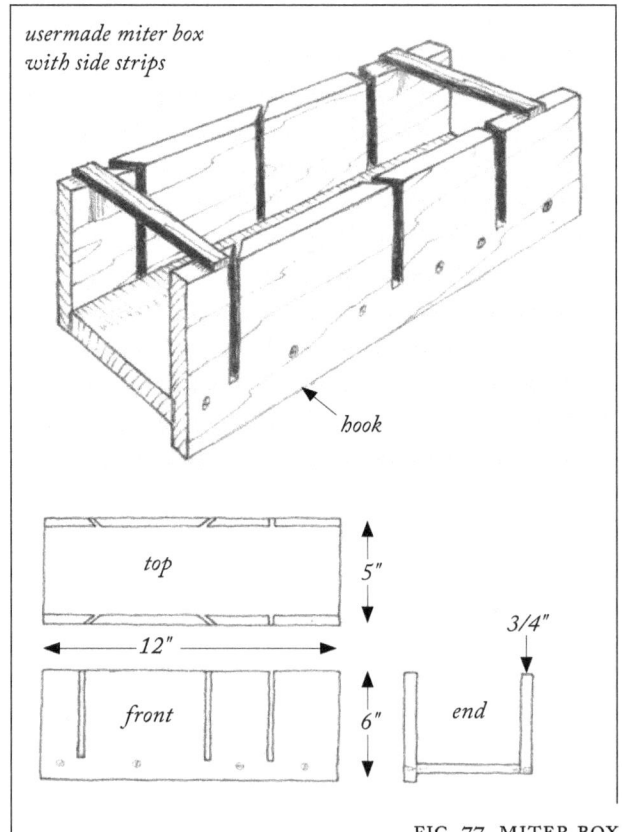

FIG. 77 MITER BOX

TRADITIONAL JIGS & FIXTURES

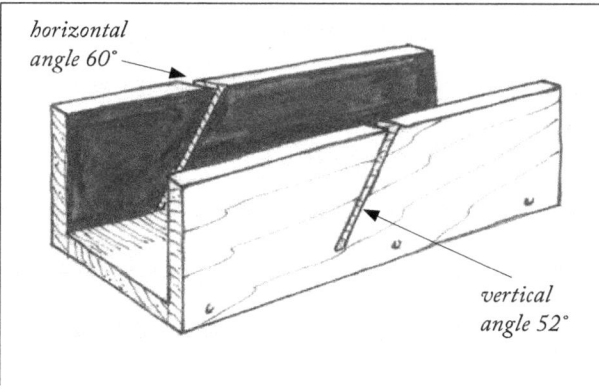

FIG. 78 COMPOUND MITER BOX

MITERED-DOVETAIL BLOCK

THE SIDES OF CHEST CARCASES AND OTHER CASE pieces that are dovetailed together are often finished at an exposed upper end with a miter. Such a miter cannot be sawed in a regular miter box because the workpiece is invariably too large. The solution is to attach a mitered block to a fence that can be clamped to the workpiece as shown in FIG. 79. This is also an operation where a depth stop may be usefully affixed to the saw.

While this little jig does not have to be very large it is important not to make it so small, or to cut the angled kerfs so close together, that the guide block parts cannot be fixed securely enough to the fence. Gluing and fixing each part with at least two nails or screws is recommended.

MITER-SAWING SADDLE

MITERED JOINTS, BEING FUNDAMENTALLY POOR candidates for a secure glue joint, are often strengthened with keys or feathers inserted across the miter. The kerfs for these keys can be easily cut if the two mitered pieces are clamped to a sawing saddle — essentially the opposite of a cradle.

Make the saddle as wide as the mitered pieces to be feathered so that they can be easily clamped to the saddle. Take care to make a perfect right-angled joint, and fix a backboard to one end of the saddle so that it can be held in the vise.

item, a miter box that is usermade will often be necessary for workpieces too large to be introduced into a store-bought model. Furthermore, although some manufactured miter boxes are adjustable, and have movable saw guides that allow mitering the workpiece at any angle from 0° to 90°, they cannot cut miters that slope perpendicularly (as, for example, might be necessary for slope-sided hoppers and knife boxes). Such a usermade miter box, however, is easily made, provided that it is carefully laid out. A worthwhile addition to any usermade miter box is a deeper front that can act either as a hook against the front of the bench or as a keel to be held in the vise.

As with the miter block described opposite, strips attached to the two sides at the top of the box either side of the kerfs will serve not only to prevent the kerfs from wearing wide too fast, but also to keep the front and back aligned.

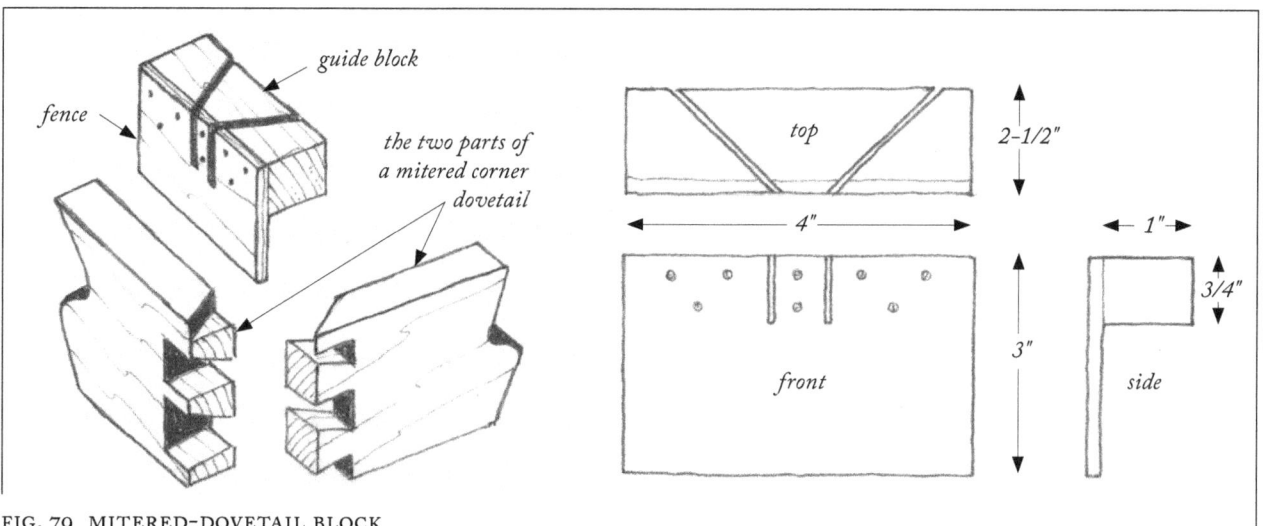

FIG. 79 MITERED-DOVETAIL BLOCK

SAWING

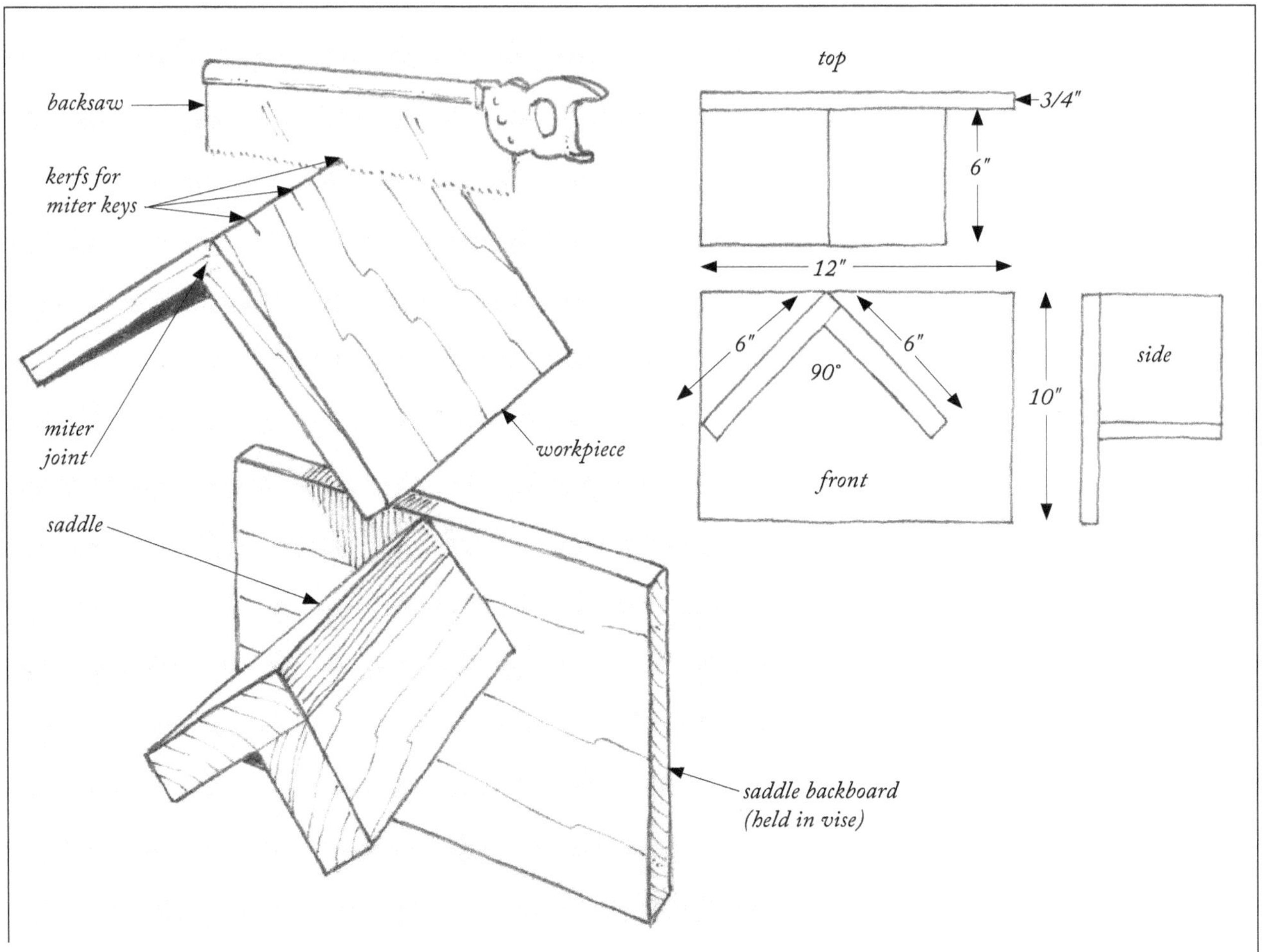

TRADITIONAL JIGS & FIXTURES

FIG. 80 MITER-SAWING SADDLE

Glue the horizontal pieces together in order to eliminate any possibility of damaging whatever tool is used to cut the feathers. It will, however be most easy to fix these horizontal pieces to the back board simply by inserting screws from the backside the backboard.

MITER-SAWING SADDLE

4

JIGS & FIXTURES FOR PLANING

FOR MANY CONTEMPORARY WOODWORKERS THE PLANE'S POSITION AS THE ICONIC TOOL OF WOODWORKING HAS LONG SINCE BEEN REPLACED BY THE TABLESAW, BUT FOR THE TRADITIONAL WOODWORKER THE PLANE REMAINS THE MOST IMPORTANT AND MOST VARIED TOOL. ONE special advantage — apart from the pleasure and safety in using a plane rather than a machine — is that many of the jigs and fixtures needed by woodworkers primarily dependent on tablesaws and routers are unnecessary. Rather than spend time jigging the machine to make a particular operation possible, the traditional woodworker equipped with a selection of bench planes — such as jack, smoother, and jointer, special-purpose joining planes such as tongue-and-groove planes and table planes, not to mention the inumerable selection of moulding planes still readily avaiable both second-hand and new — can simply reach for a particular plane already capable of performing the required operation with no further ado.

Nevertheless there are a number of jigs and fixtures that can make planing both faster and more accurate regardless of how many or how few planes you might have — old or new, wooden or metal. This chapter include jigs and fixtures for securing the work to be planed as well as jigs and fixtures for ensuring accuracy.

Many holding jigs and fixtures that are also useful for planing have already been mentioned in Chapter 1. What follows here are jigs and fixtures designed specifically and solely for planing.

FACE-PLANING STOP

FASTER TO SET UP THAN USING A PAIR OF REGULAR bench stops *(q.v.)* — which in any event presupposes a tail vise that not all benches may have — is a single wide stop held by a keel in the face vise. The work

TRADITIONAL JIGS & FIXTURES

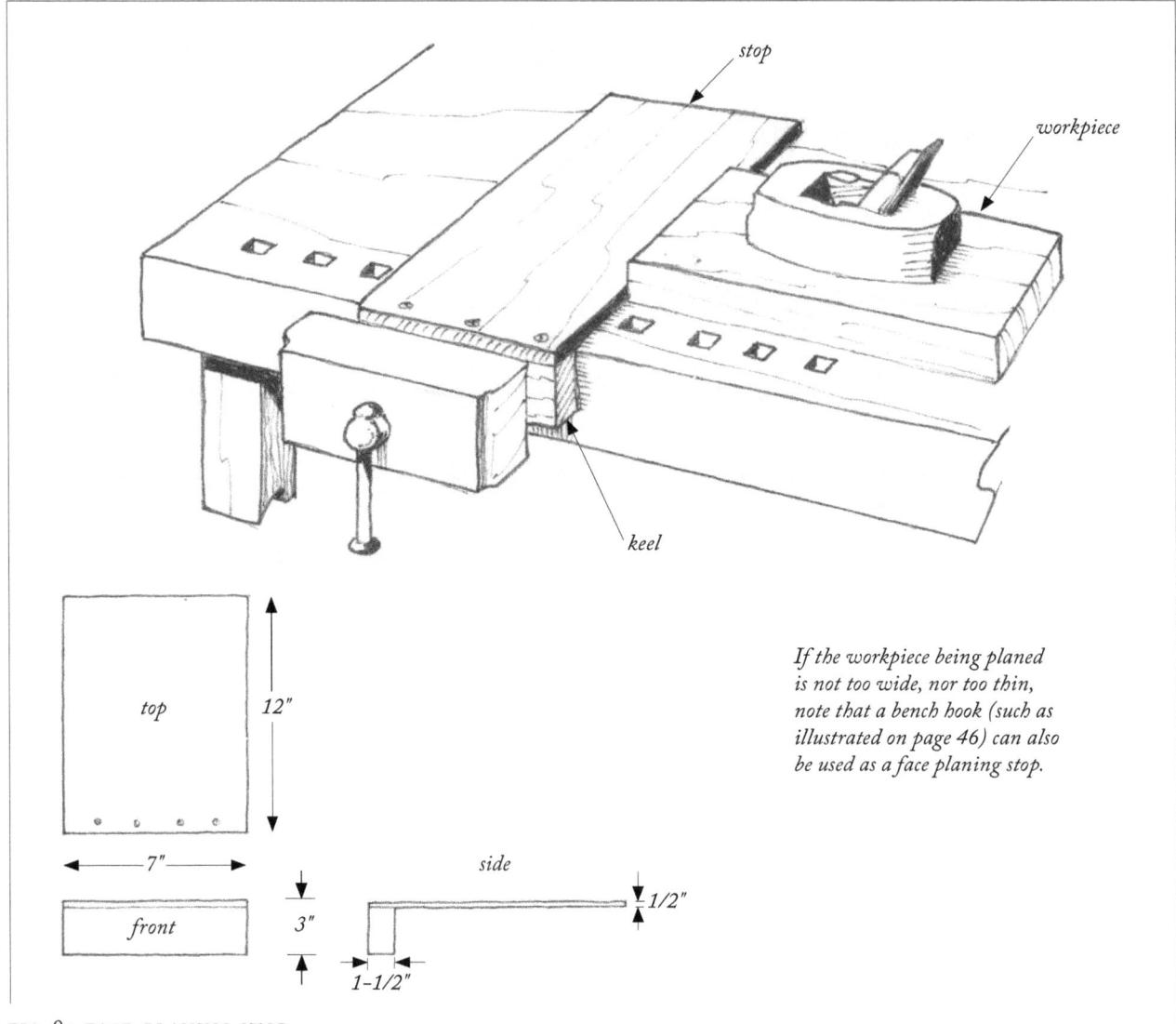

FIG. 81 FACE-PLANING STOP

If the workpiece being planed is not too wide, nor too thin, note that a bench hook (such as illustrated on page 46) can also be used as a face planing stop.

is simply butted up against the stop, and provided there is no cross-planing involved (in which case see the planing board described on page 56) planing can proceed with confidence.

The actual stop can be quite thin — assuming your bench is as flat as it should be, and further assuming that the workpiece has already been made flat, something no thicker than 1/2 in. will work well. Note that for maximum utility the stop should not be thicker than the workpiece or you will need constantly to turn the workpiece end-for-end. Attach the stop to a keel more substantial and note that the longer the keel the wider the stop will be, and the wider the stop the less it will deflect under pressure.

EDGE-PLANING FIXTURES:

IF YOUR FACE VISE IS IN GOOD CONDITION WITH parallel and level jaws many workpieces can be secured for planing with many of the various fixtures illustrated in Chapter 1. The following three edge-planing fixtures, however, deserve special mention since they are intended exclusively for planing.

ROMAN PEGS

THE FIRST FIXTURE DATES BACK TO ROMAN times when boards were held on a planing table by being wedged between two upright pegs fixed

EDGE-PLANING FIXTURES

TRADITIONAL JIGS & FIXTURES

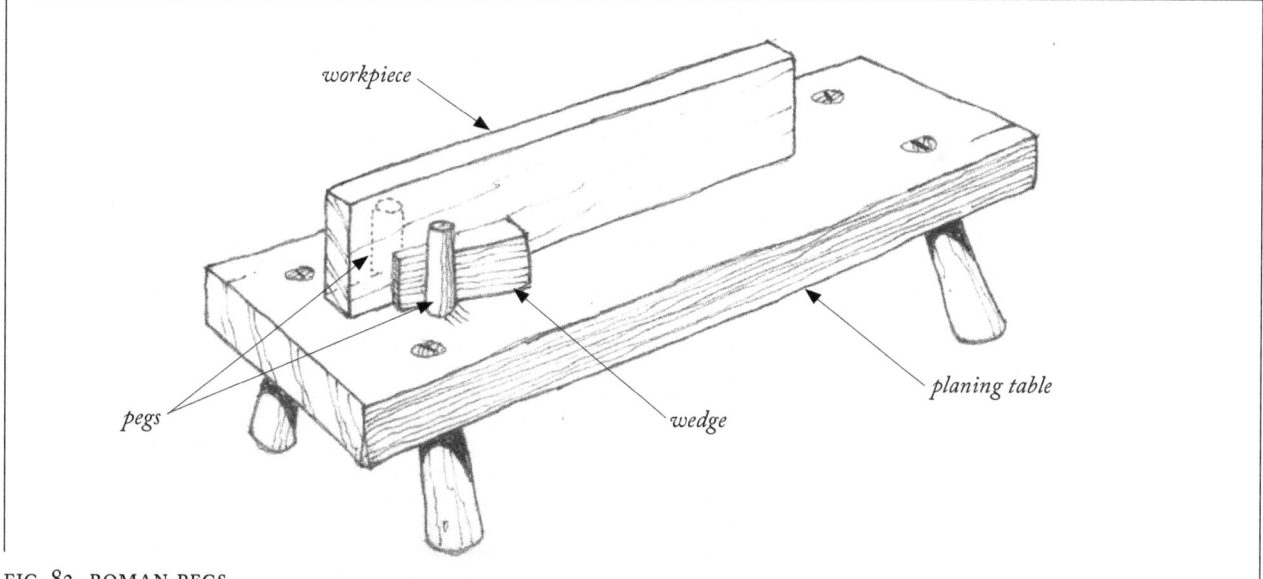

FIG. 82 ROMAN PEGS

in the surface of the bench. Modern woodworkers will probably find this peg system more useful on a higher bench or sawhorse.

STRIP CLAMP

THE SECOND FIXTURE IS THE STRIP CLAMP, perhaps most useful in a shop that lacks a regular bench equipped with vises and bench dogs, but which may nevertheless possess a flat work space. Roman pegs are replaced by angled short strips fixed to the worksurface between which the workpiece is secured by wedges.

Two 6in.-long strips being securely fixed in V-formation, no more than 2in. apart at their narrow end, each at an angle approximately 15° from the center line, form the clamp. Two wedges, cut with matching angles, are then used to hold the work.

By making the wedges thicker than the strips it will be easy to knock them out when the work is completed — a better technique than knocking the workpiece itself out.

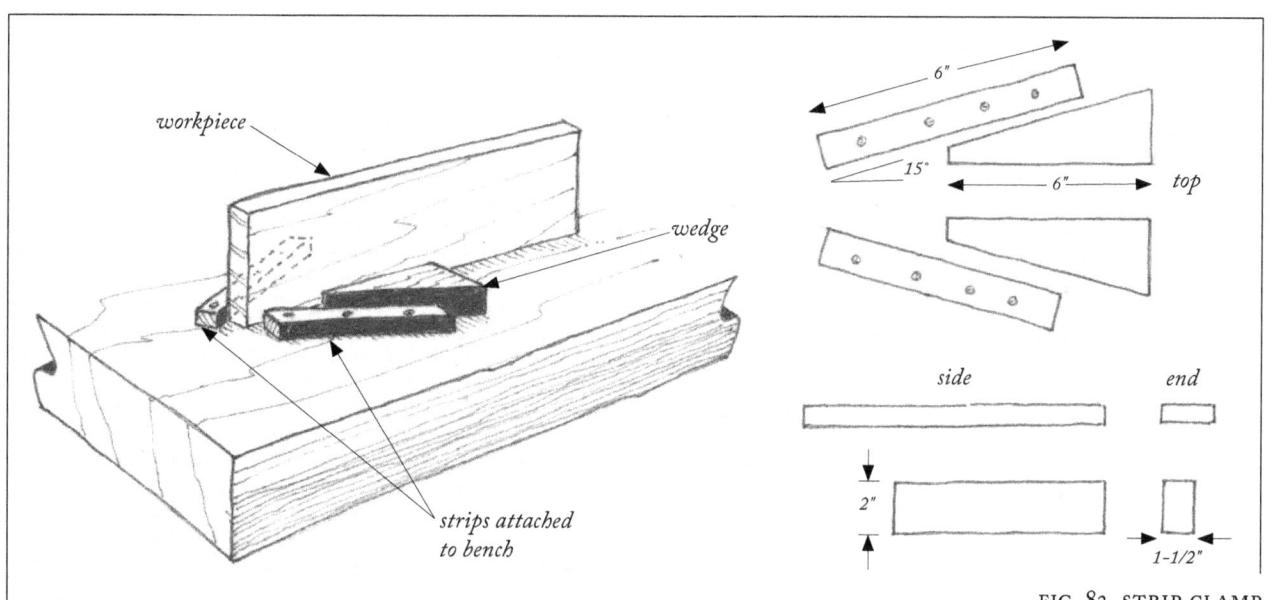

FIG. 83 STRIP CLAMP

PLANING

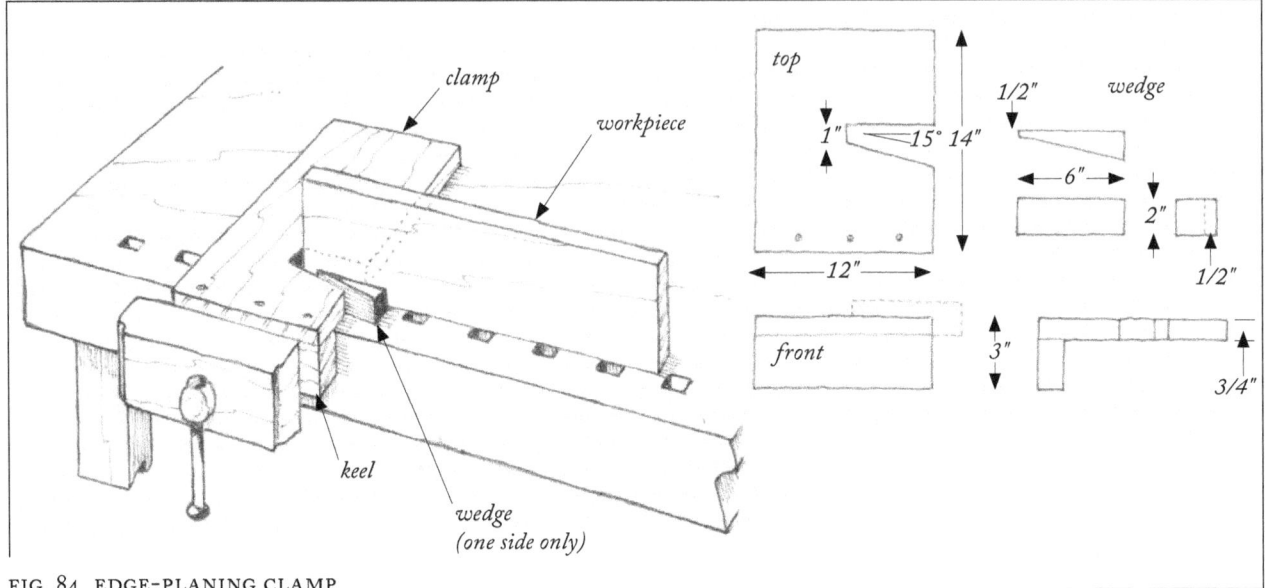

FIG. 84 EDGE-PLANING CLAMP

EDGE-PLANING CLAMP

THE THIRD EDGE-PLANING FIXTURE IS AN improvement on the V-block bench stop shown in FIG. 7, Chapter 1.

One side of the clamp is straight, and the other is angled to accept a matching wedge. The great advantage here is that the workpiece is afforded sideways support as well as being held vertically in place, and unlike strip clamps nothing need be attached to the bench since the clamp is held in the vise by a keel.

The board that forms the clamp should be at least 3/4 in thick, and the wedge that secures the workpiece even thicker (for the same reason as just given above.) It is the thickness of the clamp that makes two wedges unnecessary. For maximum strength cut the notch for the workpiece and wedge in the center of the clamp's length, and no more than halfway across its width.

PLANING BOARD

SHOULD YOUR BENCH TOP NOT BE PERFECTLY flat, or if the board being planed is slightly bowed, when you attempt to plane the high side the pressure of the plane on the high spot of the workpiece may cause the end of the board held against the stop to rise — and no longer be held in place. The solution

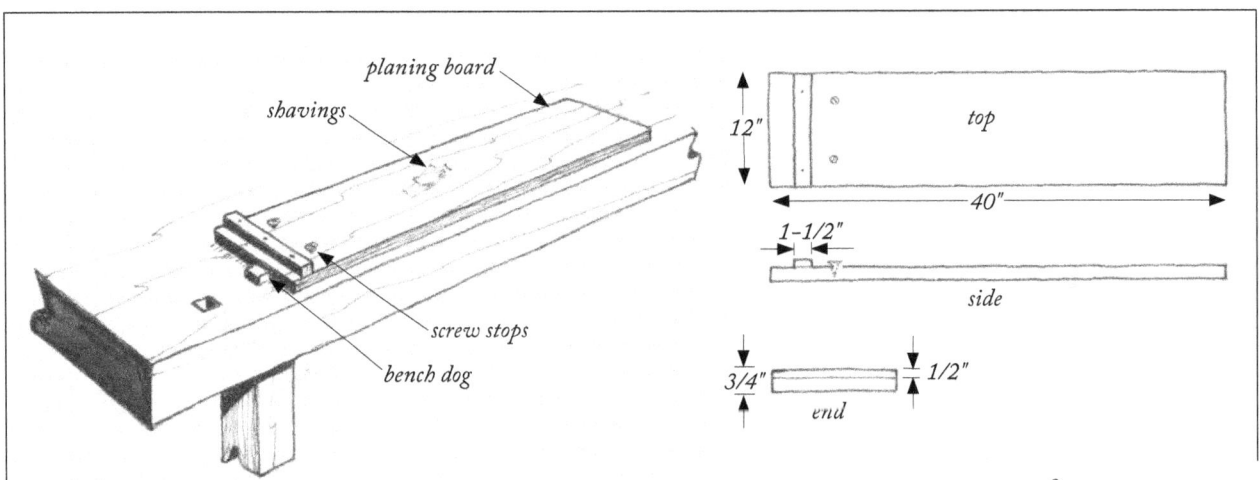

FIG. 85 PLANING BOARD

is to use a specially prepared, perfectly flat board — at least as big as the workpiece to be planed — which board can be more easily held against the stop. A couple of flathead woodscrews (which may be raised or lowered according to the thickness of the workpiece) will act as stops. If there is any concern about the screws damaging the end of the workpiece, fix a small strip at this end of the board. As a further precaution against the workpiece lifting clear of the stop (or of any screws that may have been used) when pressure is applied to the center of the board, place a shaving or two under this spot.

The planing board jig is one example where the use of medium density fiberboard (MDF) is perhaps the best choice since it is less likely to warp. The use of a thin stop strip rather than screws is a better idea with MDF since constant adjustment of the screws will eventually cause them to fall out.

CAMMED PLANING BOARD

FOR VERY SMALL AND IRREGULARLY SHAPED workpieces, a special cammed planing board, fitted with a keel that may be held in the vise, should be made. A stop on one side and a boomerang-shaped cam on the other side will hold most pieces. The cam, which is attached to the board by a screw and a washer (the better to allow it to turn), presses

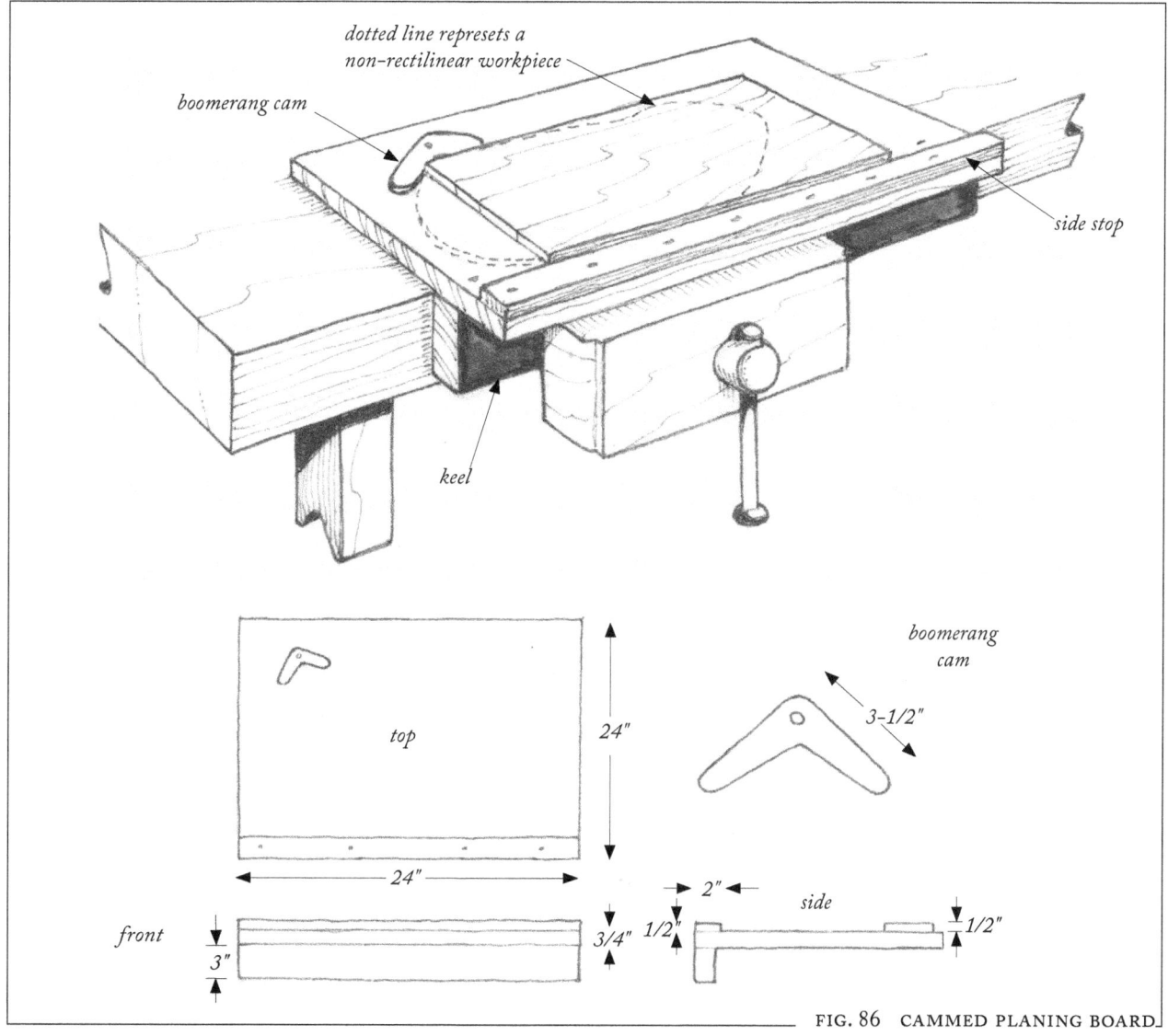

FIG. 86 CAMMED PLANING BOARD

more firmly against the workpiece the harder the workpiece is pressed against it.

On a base of plywood fix a long holding strip along one side, and either directly underneath or offset a little (in order that the edge of the board may rest on the top of the vise's outer jaw — assuming this is flush with the surface of the bench) attach a keel that may be held in the vise. On the opposite side and at the far corner attach a boomerang-shaped cam.

In order to avoid weak cross-grain, make the cam also out of plywood, and be sure to countersink the screw (and washer) holding the cam so that there is no danger of damaging the plane iron should this be inadvertently run across it, even though both the cam and the longitudinal stop should be made thinner than the workpiece. The exact location of the cam may, of course, be moved to accommodate differently shaped workpieces as required.

STICKING BOARD

STICKING BOARDS ARE ONE OF THE OLDEST fixtures used by traditional woodworkers, references to them being found in very old texts. Most useful for small narrow pieces that need to be plowed, moulded, or rabbeted, sticking boards may be made in various sizes ranging from 1 ft. to 2 ft. in length. They may be built-up or rabbeted, smaller ones being commonly furnished with a short nail or pin to hold the workpiece in place. Sticking boards may be held in the vise by a keel or simply fixed between bench stops.

The most common form consists of a single narrow rabbeted board with a stop at one end of the rabbet. There is, however, no definitive shape or form for a sticking board, for once the principle is grasped they maybe made in a variety of shapes and sizes depending on the precise form of the workpiece to be held.

DOWEL BOX (ROUNDING CRADLE)

FOR PLANING SMALL PIECES OF SQUARE OR octagonal stock to a round profile, whether for use as dowels or other rounded items, a V-shaped box fitted with a stop at one end will not only hold the workpiece securely but will also prevent it from rotating until it has been sufficiently faceted eight or sixteen times.

Since this is typically a relatively small fixture — common sizes are from 6 in. to 9 in. long — planing a 45° bevel on one side of a length of scrap is an easy task.

When the bevel is complete saw the scrap into two equal lengths and glue or screw the pieces together with the beveled sides facing each other. The stop may be simply nailed to one end, although for greater permanence cut a narrow slot across the bevels and glue it in at one end, making sure to level its top with the sides.

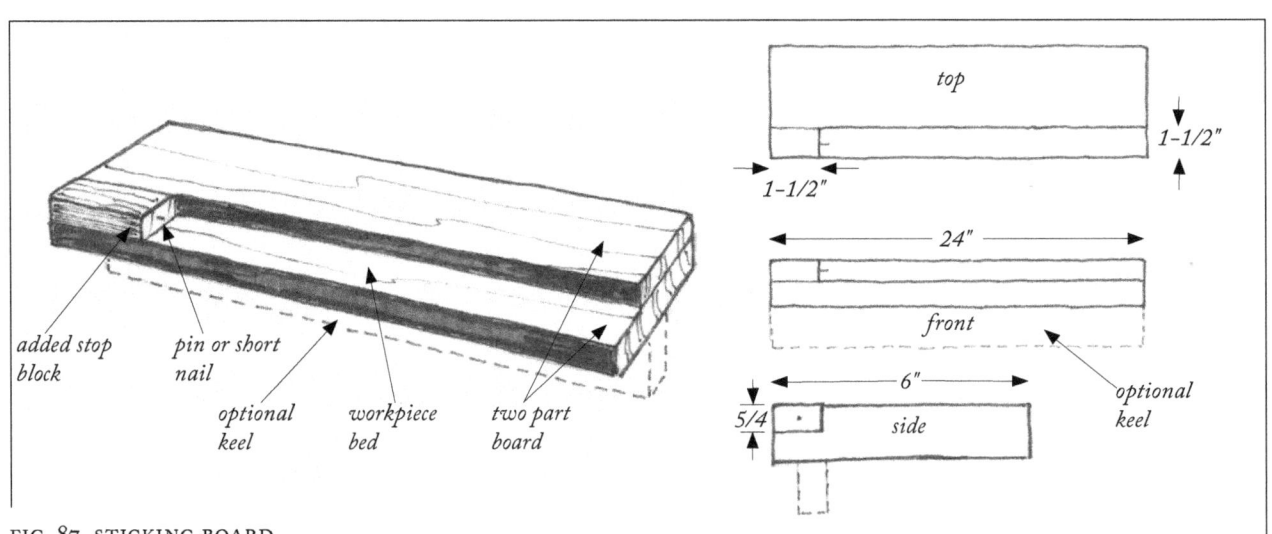

FIG. 87 STICKING BOARD

TRADITIONAL JIGS & FIXTURES

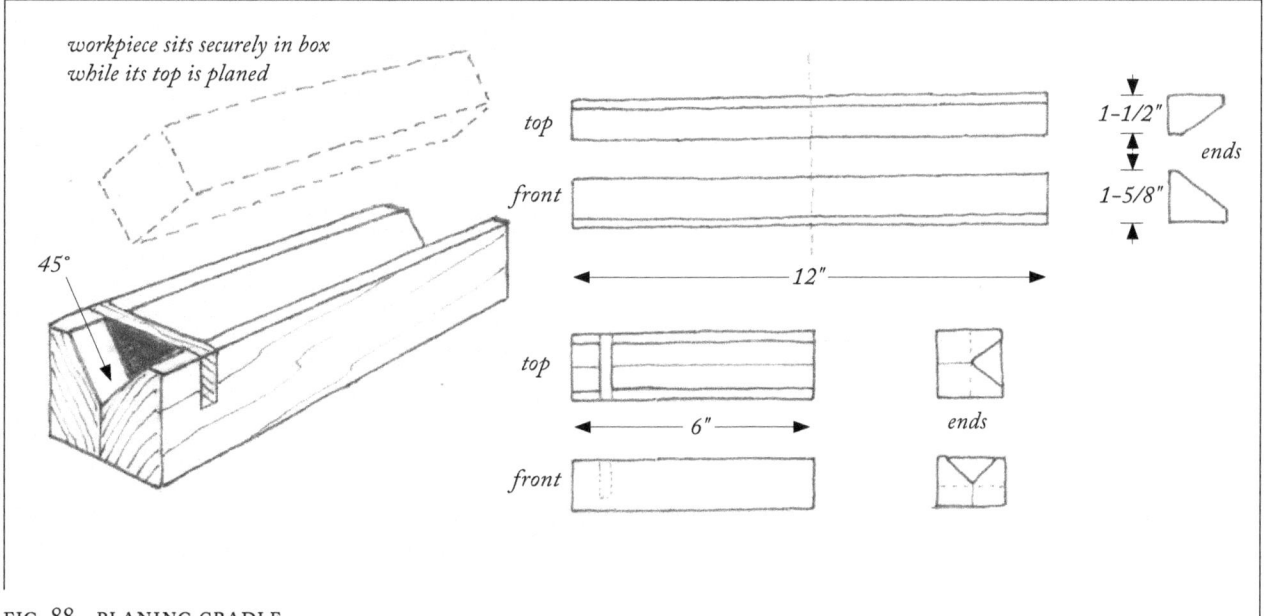

FIG. 88 PLANING CRADLE

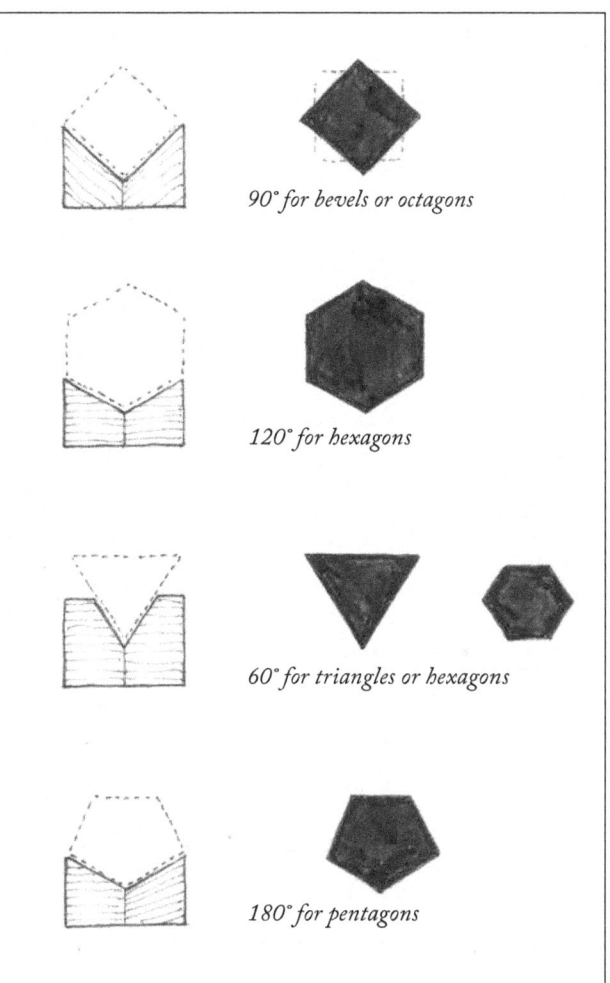

FIG. 89 CRADLE INTERNAL ANGLES

PLANING CRADLE

A QUICK CRADLE MAY BE IMPROVISED BY simply clamping a small piece of scrap, perhaps no more than 2 in. wide, in the vise and then resting the workpiece between the jaws so that one end bears against the stop and one corner is centered between the jaws like the workpiece indicated by dotted lines in FIG. 89 above. But for more exact work for larger workpieces that must be planed to specific profiles, such as beveled, octagonal, triangular, or any other regular, not-square shape, a stopped cradle made like the dowel box previously described above, but with sides corresponding to the required polygonal profile should be used. Depending on the length of the workpiece such a box may be anything from 1 ft. to 4 ft. long.

SHOOTING BOARDS (CHUTE BOARDS):

SHOOTING BOARDS ENSURE THAT EDGE OR SIDE planing is accomplished with the desired accuracy because they provide a consistent relationship between the tool and the workpiece. Most require that the sole and sides of the plane are at perfect right angles to one another. This presented little problem when planes were made of wood, for it was

PLANING

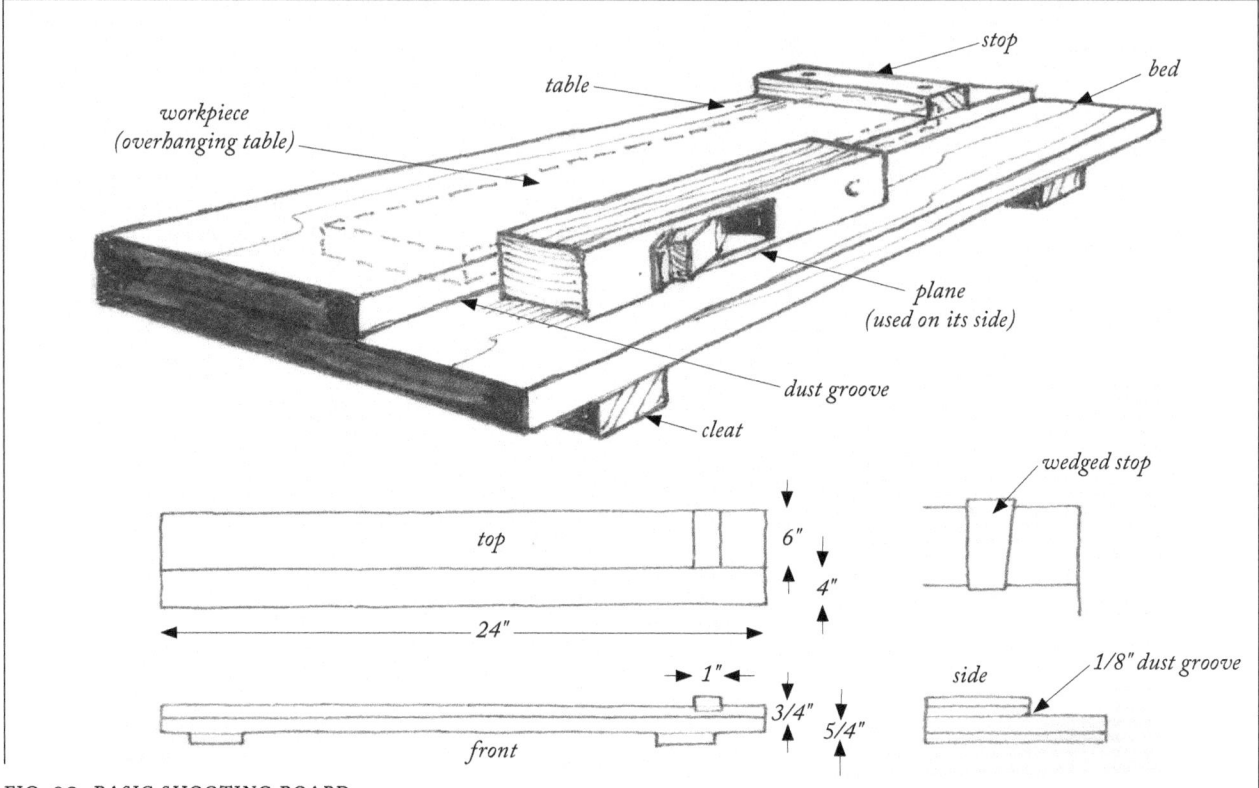

FIG. 90 BASIC SHOOTING BOARD

common practice periodically to shoot (plane) the sole of a plane with another plane to maintain truth and flatness. But poorly made metal planes whose sides are not exactly at 90° to their soles can be difficult to use with various shooting boards unless attention is paid to the relationship between the sole and the side, making allowance for anything less than perfection.

BASIC SHOOTING BOARD

THE BASIC SHOOTING BOARD IS LITTLE MORE than a stopped, two-part shelf, one level (the bed) for the workpiece to rest on and another level (the table) for the plane, used on its side, to ride on. If the boards are perfectly flat and if the plane body is perfectly square it is virtually impossible to plane anything other than a perfect right-angled edge by virtue of the fact that the plane, by being run on its side, meets the workpiece at exactly 90°— something that if attempted freehand can prove frustratingly difficult. Typically made with two boards about 24 in. long, the upper one 6 in. to 8 in. wide, and the lower one sufficiently wider to accommodate a plane resting on its side, the only critical aspect is that the boards be kept flat — usually by fixing a couple of transverse cleats to the bottom. With sufficient forethought these cleats may be positioned so that they also act as hooks to secure the shooting board transversely across the bench top. A stop (often wedge-shaped) to prevent the workpiece being pushed off the board is usually rabbeted into the top board, but this may also be screwed onto a flat surface, thereby allowing it to be fixed at an angle other than the usual 90° whenever this might be necessary.

If the stop is made a little longer than the width of the board into which it is rabbeted it can be used to back an end being trimmed as described below, and then be simply pushed further across as its end is worn, splintered, or planed off.

A dust groove cut on the bottom edge of the top board is helpful, but it should be realized that the plane is not run against this edge or it would soon be cut away, the workpiece being placed on the upper bed against the end stop but overhanging the edge slightly as shown in FIG. 90.

TRADITIONAL JIGS & FIXTURES

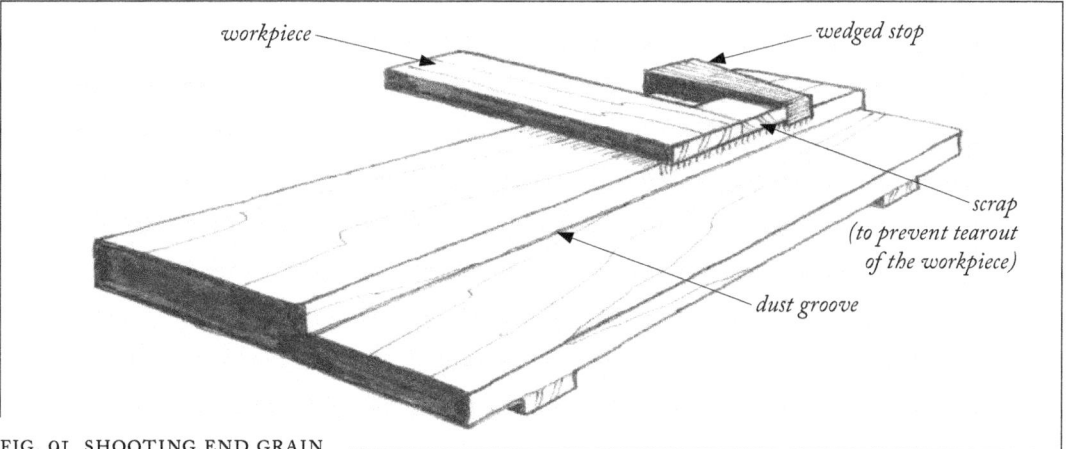

FIG. 91 SHOOTING END GRAIN

The basic shooting board is equally useful for trimming perfectly square the ends of workpieces when they are held against the stop — with the addition of a scrap piece between the stop and the workpiece in order to prevent the back corner of the workpiece being torn out.

WEDGED SHOOTING BOARD

EDGES OTHER THAN THOSE AT NINETY DEGREES to the face may also be accurately planed by the simple expedient of altering the angle of the bed on which the workpiece rests. This may be achieved simply by placing a wedge or wedges under the workpiece, or by making the bed adjustable with a longitudinal hinge.

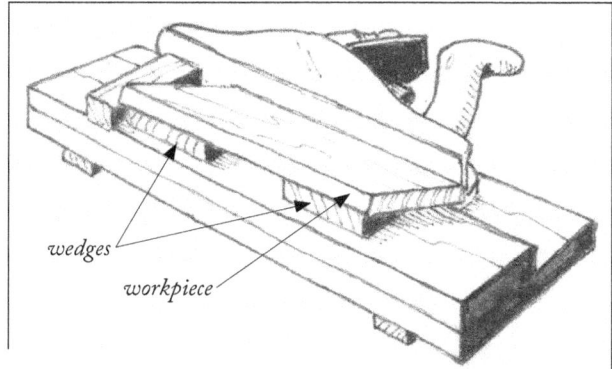

FIG. 92 WEDGED SHOOTING BOARD

COMPOUND ANGLE SHOOTING BOARD

BY USING A TILTED BED OR WEDGES TO support a transversely held workpiece, together with an angled stop, the accurate planing of compound angles (such as might be necessary for trimming splayed joints or angled crown-moulding) is made equally easy and accurate.

The work rests on block A, which is cut to match the thickness angle 'a'. Block B provides the width angle 'b'.

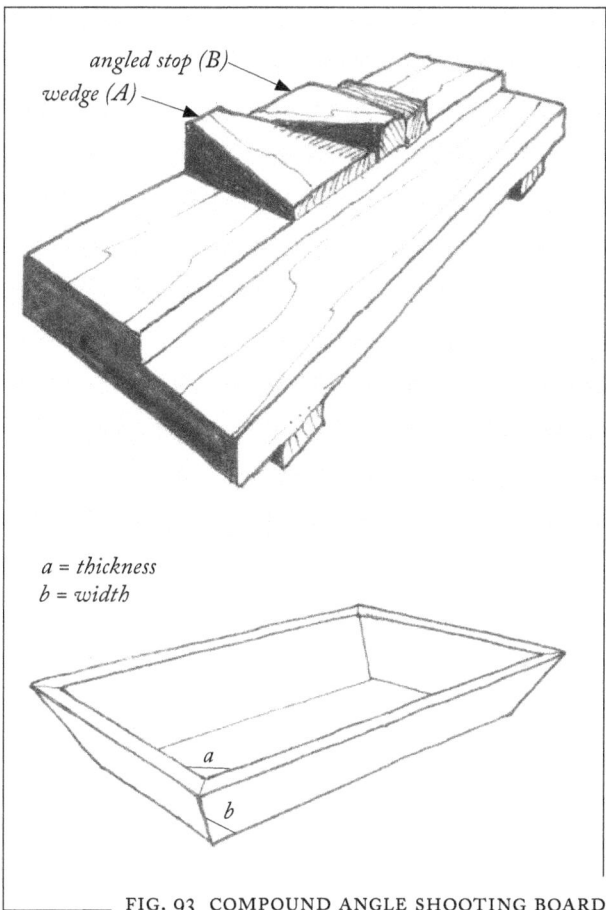

FIG. 93 COMPOUND ANGLE SHOOTING BOARD

PLANING

TRADITIONAL JIGS & FIXTURES

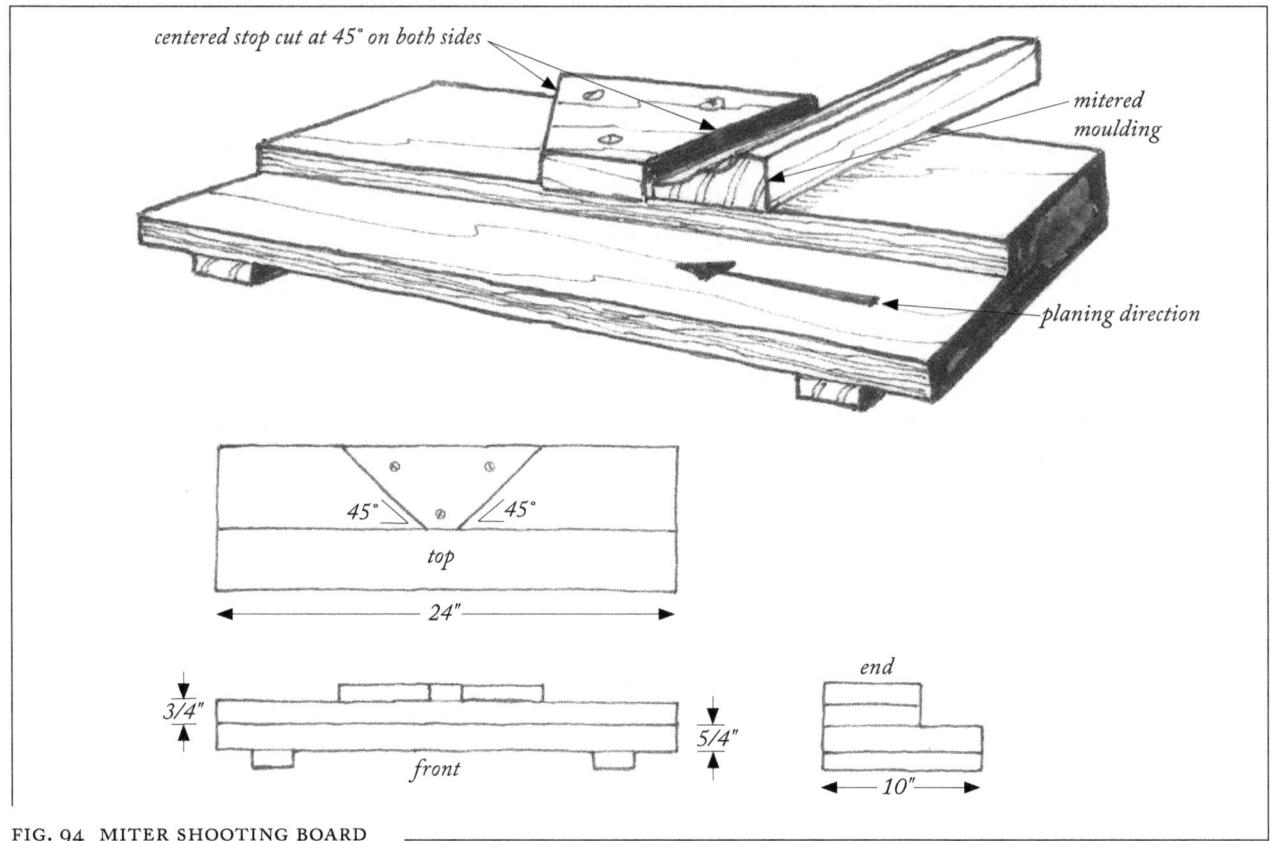

FIG. 94 MITER SHOOTING BOARD

MITER SHOOTING BOARD

A SPECIALIZED SHOOTING BOARD FOR TRIMMING miters accurately can be made by using a broad stop with sides cut at complementary 45° angles and locating it in the middle of the upper bed. Care should be taken always to plane 'uphill' into the sharp angle of the miter to avoid splitting the workpiece, for which reason both angles are necessary on the stop.

DONKEY'S EAR SHOOTING BOARD

FOR PLANING WIDE MITERS, SUCH AS ACROSS THE end of a wide board intended for baseboards or skirting, or along the edge of a board, the donkey's ear shooting board is especially useful. Its distinguishing feature is an upper bed built at a 45° angle to the bed on which the plane runs. The stop is most usefully located in the center of the bed rather than at one end in order to provide support for the

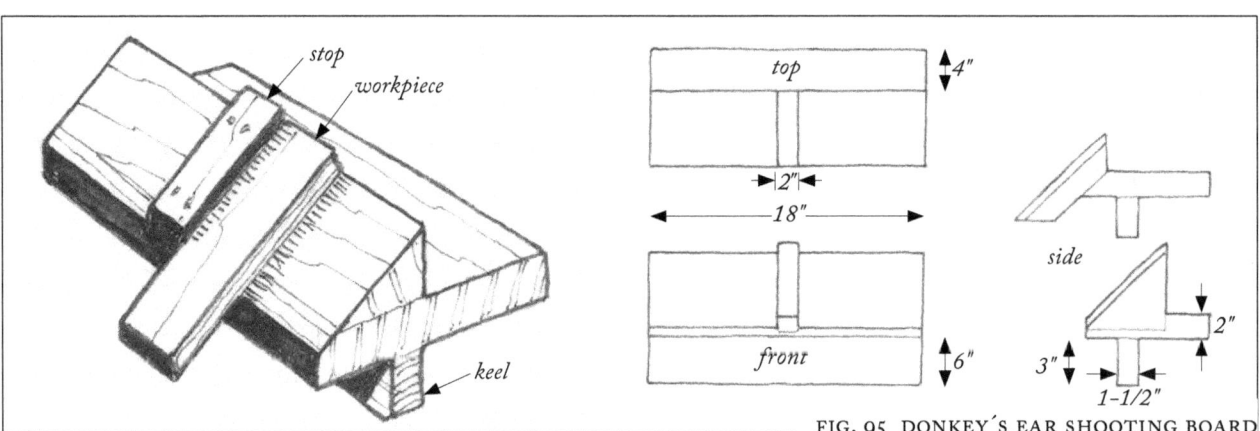

FIG. 95 DONKEY'S EAR SHOOTING BOARD

plane beyond the stop. It is also most conveniently held in the bench's vise by means of a keel, since the workpiece is often long, and using this shooting board transversely (like the basic shooting board mentioned opposite) with the end of the workpiece extending below the level of the bench top would be impossible.

Various methods can be employed to produce an upper bed at 45° to the plane bed: a single wide board can be fixed at a 45° angle to the plane bed, several boards can be used to produce a half-pyramid; or a square block can be diagonally cut along its length (as shown in FIG. 95). But whichever method is used note that although the upper bed should be wide enough to provide sufficient support for the workpiece, it should not be so great that it raises the end of the workpiece to be planed above the level that the plane's iron can reach, or additional pieces will have to be added to the plane bed.

SHOOTING BLOCK

A SHOOTING BLOCK IS USED FOR MITERS THAT are both long and wide since a greater area of referenced support for the plane is necessary. The most common form of shooting block was once one that was commonly manufactured. It consisted of two large jaws on which the plane's sole could run, shooting (trimming) the mitered end of the workpiece held between the two jaws.

Made left-handed and right-handed, depending on which end the adjustable jaw was found, it was typically secured by either a transverse or longitudinal keel. The surface of the jaws is usually

protected by thin card, even though these are intended only for the part of the plane's sole not containing the mouth, the plane being held askew so that only the cutting edge of the iron contacts the workpiece.

A simpler version of a shooting block can be made by fixing a bed for the plane to ride on to the bench top in front of the vise, and then clamping the workpiece to an 45°-angled stop which is itself held in the vise and whose angled upper end is flush with the planing bed. The plane is then run askewed, resting equally on the piece attached to the bench and the stop clamped in the vise, and cutting only the end of the workpiece. The only slight difficulty is in providing a stop exactly the same thickness as the workpiece so that the two may be equally securely held.

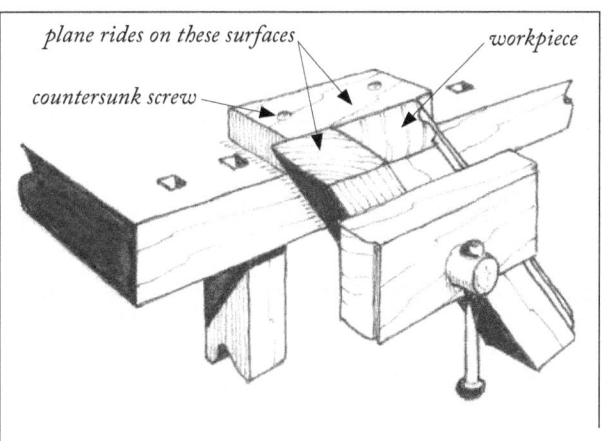

FIG. 97 USERMADE SHOOTING BLOCK

FIXTURES FOR ACCURACY:

THERE ARE A NUMBER OF EASILY-MADE FIXTURES that can be used to guarantee the accuracy of various planing procedures. These all work by limiting the amount that can be planed and by controlling how the plane is presented to the work. It might be argued that their chief advantage is that they make it unnecessary to buy more expensive tools already fitted with fences and depth stops, but these sometimes get in the way and often have to be removed anyway. Nevertheless, even if you do buy simpler tools, it is well to remember that most planing will be more accurate if not performed completely freehand but by using one of the following guides.

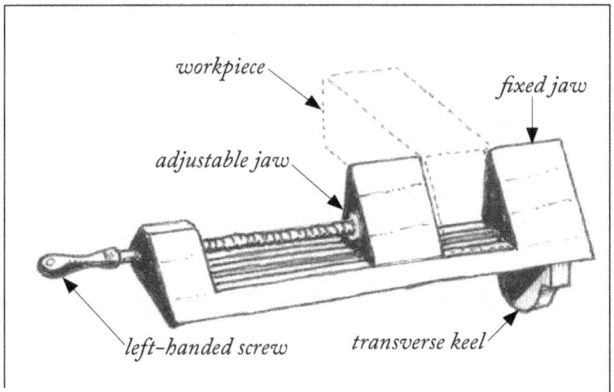

FIG. 96 SHOOTING BLOCK

TRADITIONAL JIGS & FIXTURES

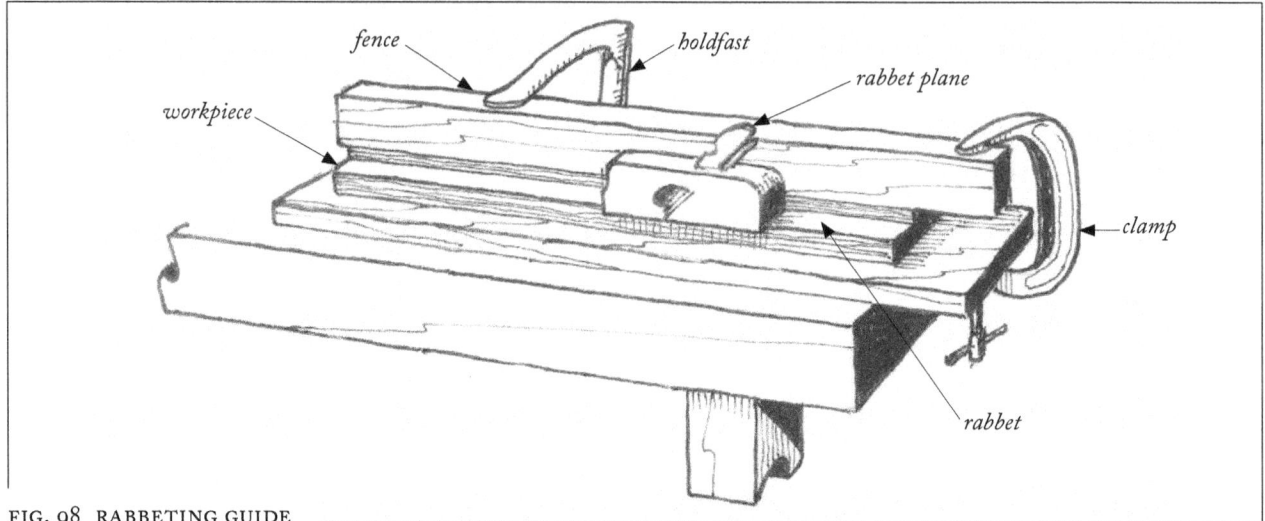

FIG. 98 RABBETING GUIDE

RABBETING GUIDE

THE SIMPLEST PLANE USED FOR FORMING A rabbet is one whose iron extends across the entire width of the sole — a so-called rabbet ('rebate' in British English) plane. Such a plane will require some form of fence if the rabbet is to be cut to a consistent width — at least at the start of the cut. Both fences and depth stops may be easily fixed to a wooden plane (holes in the sides and soles of old wooden rabbet planes bear witness to this), but such is not the case with metal-bodied planes, such as newer shoulder planes.

One solution is to fix a temporary guide to the workpiece itself, but if this is not possible because unsightly nail holes might be the result, try clamping the workpiece between two boards so that the upper piece may be used as a fence to guide the plane.

FIELDING GUIDES

A SIMILAR PROBLEM IN STARTING AN EXACTLY located cut is encountered when fielding panels if a fenced fielding plane (expensive and rare, and in any event only capable of a single profile that may not be desired) is unavailable. The usual method is to use any plane whose blade extends flush on at least one side, such as a badger plane or a regular jack rabbeting plane. Such a plane may be guided against a fence that is attached to a second piece held under the panel by bolts and wingnuts.

If fences are used in pairs, the panel may be kept level on the bench. If the bottom piece of one of the fence pairs is provided with a keel this may be held in the vise, and the entire assembly of workpiece and guides thus prevented from moving while being worked on.

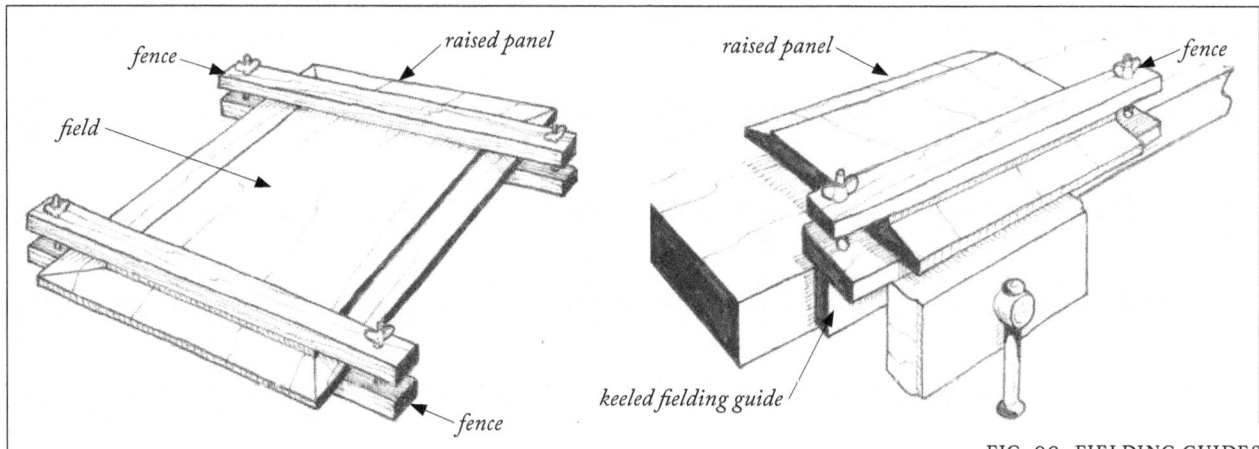

FIG. 99 FIELDING GUIDES

RABBETING GUIDE

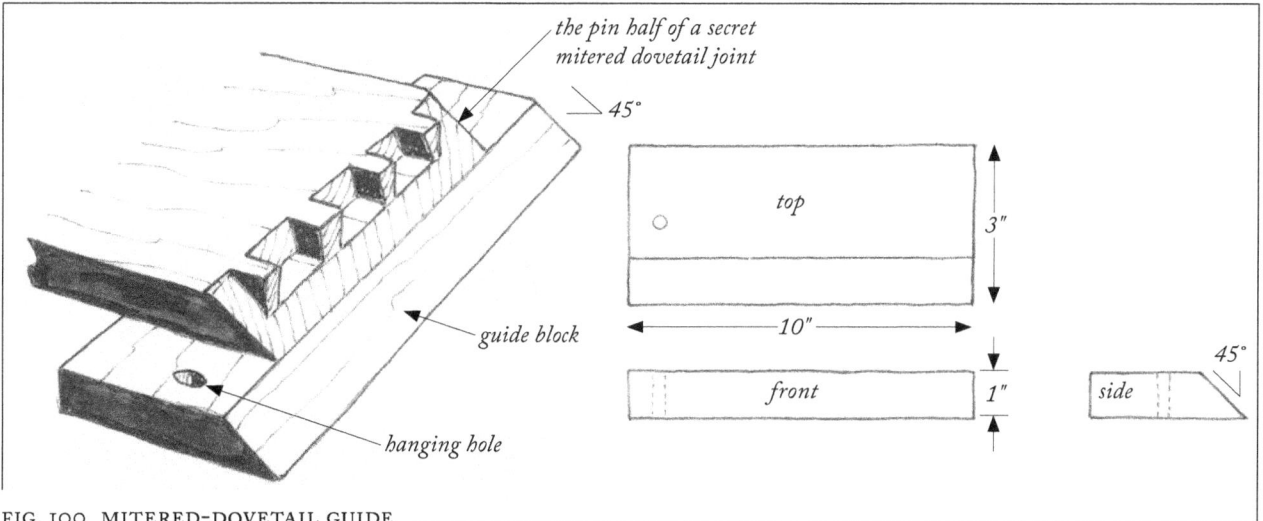

FIG. 100 MITERED-DOVETAIL GUIDE

MITERED-DOVETAIL GUIDE

THE SO-CALLED SECRET MITERED DOVETAIL actually contains two secrets. The first is that when assembled the dovetail portion of the joint is hidden. The second is that contrary to what the tyro might fear, this joint is easier to make than he or she might expect, because when assembled the accuracy of the dovetails is not observable. The only essential is that the mitered sections fit neatly, and this is made easy if a plane trimming these parts is run over a guide that has one edge cut at 45°.

One of the easiest jigs to make, a guide for trimming miters consists of nothing more than a length of wood equal to the length of the miter to be trimmed and of sufficient thickness so that when one side has been beveled to a 45° angle there is enough surface for whatever plane is used to do the trimming to run on.

DEPTH & WIDTH STOPS

SIMILAR TO THE DEPTH STOP THAT MAY BE FIXED to the side of a saw *(see Chapter 3)*, a simple strip fixed with screws (if it is a wooden-bodied plane, as the holes in many second-hand wooden planes will attest, or a small clamp if it is a metal-bodied plane) to the side or sole of any plane used for rabbeting (a plane whose iron extends across the entire width of its sole) is all that is needed to limit planing to the required amount, thereby relieving the operator of the necessity to peer constantly at a layout line that is often difficult to see.

One detail that should not be forgotten when fixing a width stop to the sole of any plane is to make a small groove in the stop beneath the cutting edge of the plane's iron, for otherwise it will prove impossible to extend the iron beneath the sole and cut anything. The exact location of such a groove is

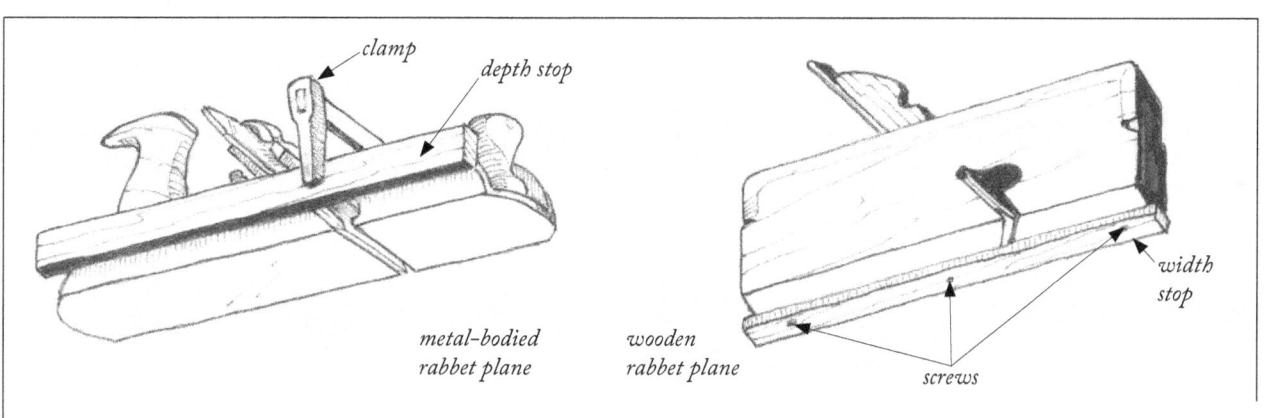

FIG. 101 DEPTH & WIDTH STOPS

PLANING

best determined by temporarily affixing the width stop and lightly tapping the iron to bite into it.

It is also important to ensure that the edge of the width stop is square and perfectly perpendicular to the sole of the plane for otherwise repeated passes of the plane (when held upright) will produce a sloping-sided rabbet. A corollary of this possibly unintended mistake is that a purposely beveled edge to the width stop can turn the plane into a guided beveling plane if the plane is held so that the beveled side of the width stop always bears against the square edge of the workpiece.

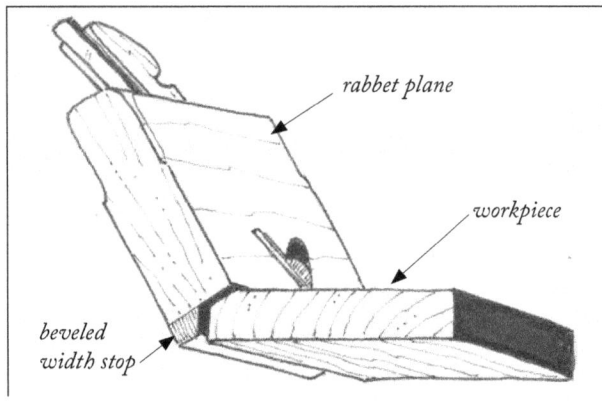

FIG. 102 BEVELED WIDTH STOP

SQUARE-EDGE GUIDE

FOR WORKPIECES THAT ARE TOO LARGE TO BE conveniently worked on a shooting board *(q.v.)* it is only necessary to remember the Muslim proverb: 'If the mountain won't come to Muhammad then Muhammad must go to the mountain.' Clamping a long straight strip to the side of whatever plane is being used, and holding the plane so that this strip bears securely against the side of the workpiece, effectively turns the plane and its guide strip into a moving shooting board, and will guarantee that the edge being planed will be perfectly square.

PLANING PUSH GUIDE

ALTHOUGH IT IS A DANGEROUS PRACTICE TO attempt to move very short pieces over a power jointer, this is precisely what should be done when planing very short pieces with a handplane. If a very small piece needs to be planed it is often safer and easier to push the workpiece over an upside-down plane held in the vise than it might be to attempt to secure the workpiece and plane over it. However, doing this with your fingers is risky, but moving the workpiece across the plane's blade while held under a stopped push-block is much better.

This is a relatively small jig, since most planes' soles are not very wide, but it is still worth while to include a handle in the center of the block in order to be able to apply an even pressure on the workpiece securely. The under side of the block should either be slightly rabbeted or have a thin strip, no more than 1/4 in. thick, preferably attached with glue rather than small nails which could damage the cutting edge of the plane iron.

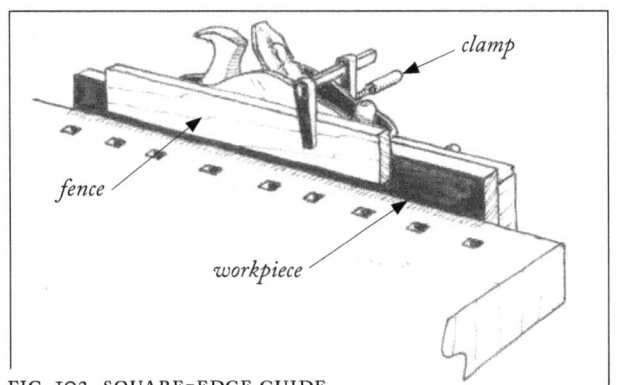

FIG. 103 SQUARE-EDGE GUIDE

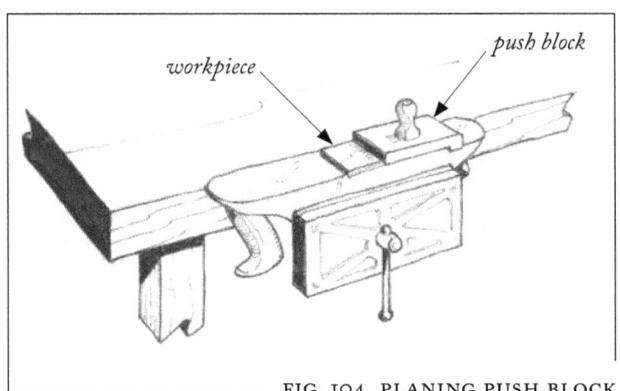

FIG. 104 PLANING PUSH BLOCK

5

JIGS & FIXTURES FOR JOINERY

THE TERM 'JOINERY' IS USED HERE IN THE AMERICAN SENSE OF SIMPLY MEANING THE MAKING OF ANY AND ALL JOINTS, WHETHER FOR FURNITUREMAKING, CABINETMAKING, BUILDING CONSTRUCTION, OR INDEED ANY OTHER BRANCH OF WOODWORKING. It should be noted, however, that in Britain, by contrast, the term refers specifically and only to what in America is referred to as 'finish carpentry' in the building trades.

Bearing this distinction in mind it remains true that at the heart of many projects (in whatever branch of woodworking on either side of the Atlantic, but perhaps mainly for fine woodworking such as furnituremaking) lies a number of joinery operations which typically involve cutting and shaping on a much smaller but more detailed and often more exacting scale than would have been necessary up to this point. This is where tools such as chisels, gouges, scrapers, and spokeshaves come into play. As with many, if not most other traditional handtools, using these items freehand can be a sure recipe for disappointment. The following jigs and fixtures are examples of ways to make this part of any project less faster and more accurate.

SIMPLE SCRATCH STOCK

BY FILING A SMALL PIECE OF THIN METAL SUCH AS a piece of old bandsaw blade to a required profile and then securing it between two matching shouldered pieces of scrap a jig can be made that will produce a moulded edge for which there may be no available moulding plane or even — should you be tempted for a moment to abandon traditional woodworking methods — a router or shaper bit.

One of the simplest forms for this typically user-made tool is a sideways L-shaped block about 3in. to 6in. long. Saw such a piece of scrap in half and

TRADITIONAL JIGS & FIXTURES

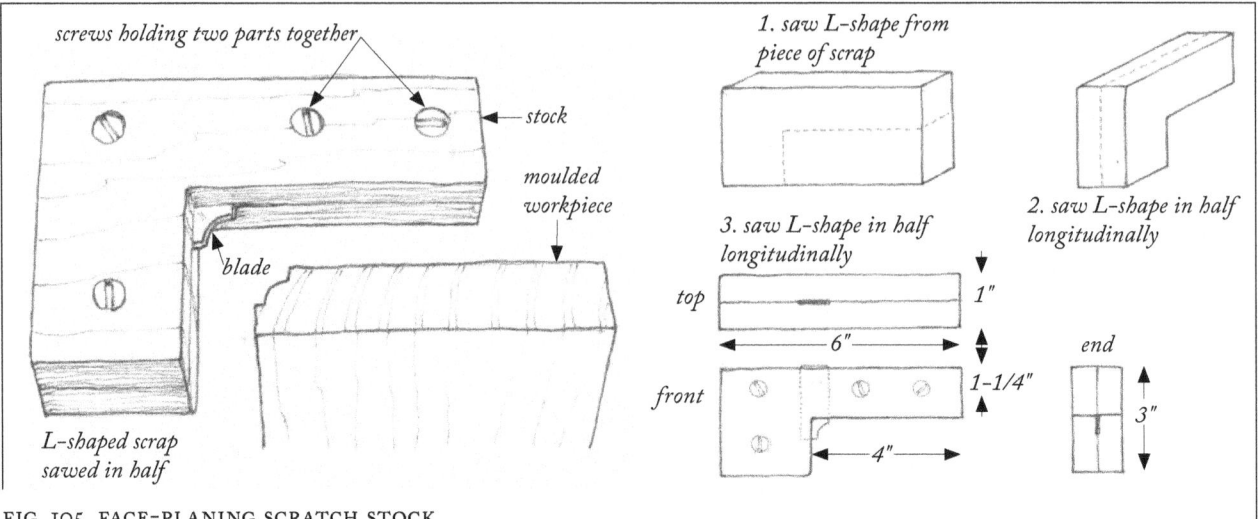

FIG. 105 FACE-PLANING SCRATCH STOCK

then screw the two halves back together with the filed metal 'blade' in position. Since a scratch stock is used by being dragged or pushed along the workpiece (hence the name) the blade does not need a bevel, and after having been filed to the required profile is simply stoned flat on both faces.

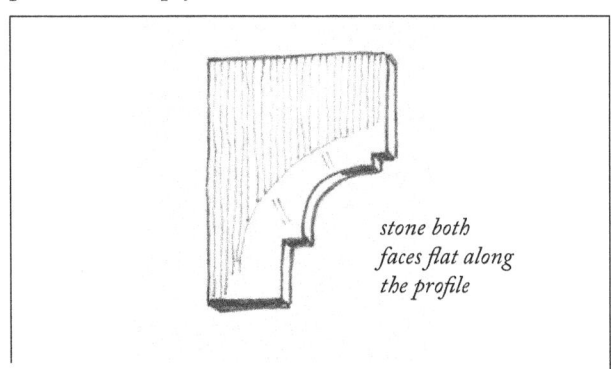

FIG. 106 SCRATCH STOCK BLADE

Although other patterns exist, by making the sock L-shaped a fence is formed that may be held against the workpiece so that the profile is scratched into it at a consistent location — either right on the edge or some distance away from it, depending on exactly where in the stock the blade is secured, against the fence or farther out along the stock portion.

ROUNDED-EDGE SCRATCH STOCK

IF THE FENCE PORTION OF THE STOCK IS ROUNDED it will better follow a horizontal curve; if the under portion of the stock is rounded it will better follow a vertical curve. The advantage of a scratch stock over an electric router is thus clearly demonstrated, for a router cannot safely or accurately follow rounded edges in two planes simultaneously.

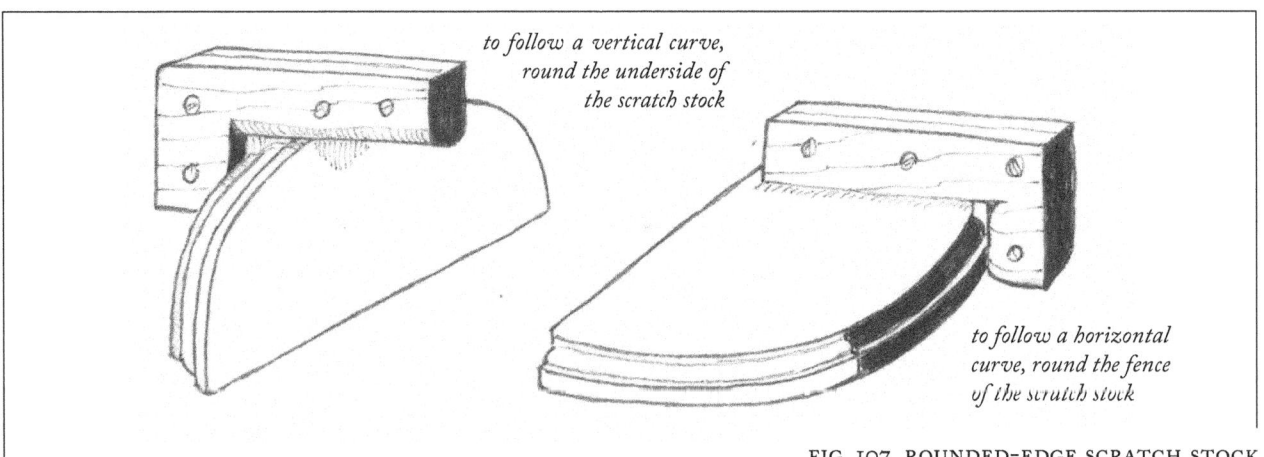

FIG. 107 ROUNDED-EDGE SCRATCH STOCK

While the primary purpose of a scratch stock may be to create or match a unique moulded profile, it should be realized that simple grooves or rebates can also be formed, by providing an appropriately shaped blade. This jig can therefore go a long way to substituting for older traditional tools such as hand routers, hand beaders, moulding routers, and quirk routers — tools that are invaluable for making items such as curved glazing bars or window sash.

DOWELLING:

DOWEL GROOVER

ALTHOUGH NOT ORDINARILY USED IN GOOD quality joinery where mortise-and-tenons, tongue-and-groove joints, and splines are normally preferred — except perhaps for aligning long edge-joints — dowels require a little attention for successful use. Apart from being slightly rounded at each end for trouble-free insertion, it is also good practice to provide them with longitudinal grooves so that excess glue may escape from the bottom of the hole into which they are inserted. The easiest way to provide these grooves is to drive the dowel through a matching hole in a piece of wood into the side of which a small nail has been inserted.

Although some woodworkers use holes for this purpose that have been bored in bench tops and other surfaces around the shop, a separate small hardwood block is preferable. This should be bored with two or three holes corresponding to the most common diameters used. One inch or 1-1/2 in. finishing nails may be driven into the side of the block so that their tips protrude enough to leave a small groove when the dowel stock is driven through the hole — usually with the help of another length of dowel that remains in the hole until the next dowel is needed. In order that the block may be held and not be knocked out of the vise when a dowel is being driven through it, cut a 1/2 in. rabbet on either side. The vise can then be closed against the sides of the rabbets so that the tops of the rabbets will rest on the tops of the vise jaws.

A once more common method of providing glue escapes in dowels was the practice of boring appropriately sized nail-pierced holes in one end of the shop saw horse.

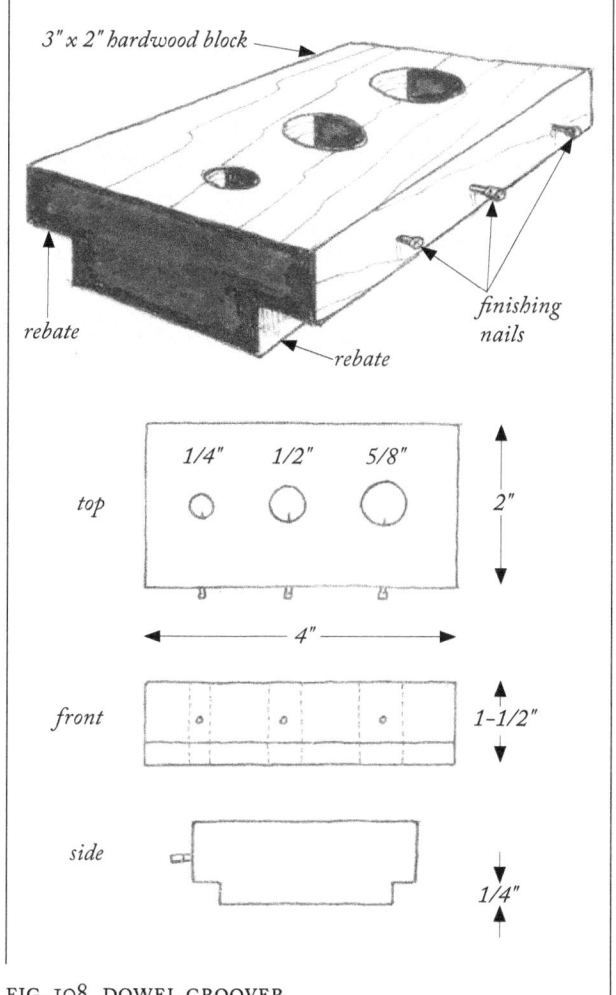

FIG. 108 DOWEL GROOVER

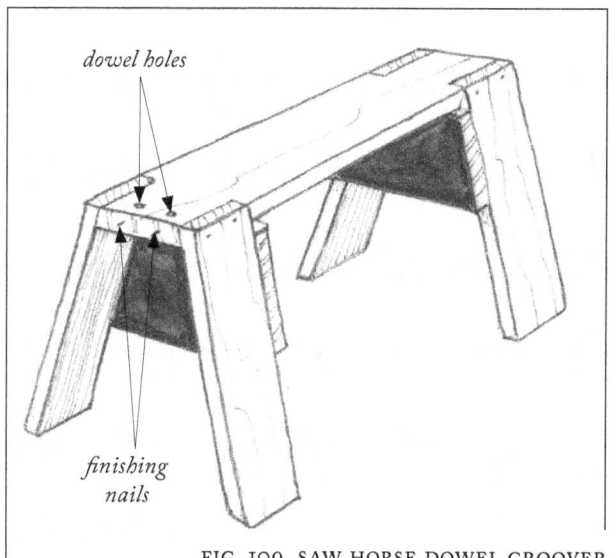

FIG. 109 SAW HORSE DOWEL GROOVER

TRADITIONAL JIGS & FIXTURES

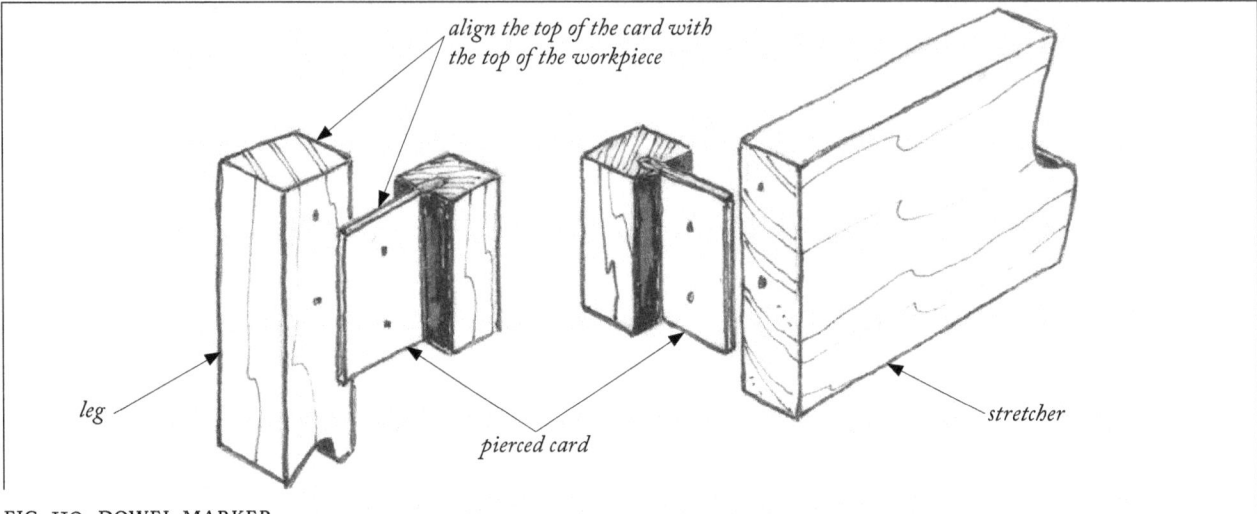

FIG. 110 DOWEL MARKER

DOWEL MARKER

AFTER HAVING DECIDED WHERE TO BORE HOLES for dowel joints, this particular jig (which might also be thought of as a layout fixture, except that it is usually specific for individual projects) can quickly be made both to save time and guarantee accuracy. A small piece of scrap is grooved on any flat surface to receive a piece of stiff card which is pierced at the point or points where dowel holes will be bored in the workpiece. The marker is particularly useful for items such as tables, chairs, or boxes where there will be several identical dowel joints. If the holes are pierced at the correct distance both from the edge of the block and the end of the card it is a simple matter to hold the jig on the matching parts of the workpiece with your thumb aligning the end of the card with the end of the workpiece and insert a marking awl through the pierced holes to locate where holes must be bored without having to measure every instance.

MITERS & DOVETAILS:

MITERED MOULDING GUIDE (MITER TEMPLATE)

THE MITERED MOULDING GUIDE IS USED TO guarantee that moulded profiles which form only part of the workpiece — such as the inner edge of frame-and-panel members made with integral moulding (such moulding being properly known as 'stuck' as opposed to 'applied') — and which have to be mitered, fit perfectly.

The guide is used by first clamping its fence to the work so that the angled part of the guide's fence lines up with the line of the desired miter. Then, while holding a paring chisel's back tightly to the sloping part of the guide, take light, paring cuts through the moulding until its surface becomes flush with the slope of the guide.

Cut a piece of scrap with two 45° angles, and then attach this piece (from the side or from the top, as shown in FIG. 112 opposite) to a fence which continues the slope of the angled ends. By making both ends 45° the guide can be used to trim miters at both ends of a framing member.

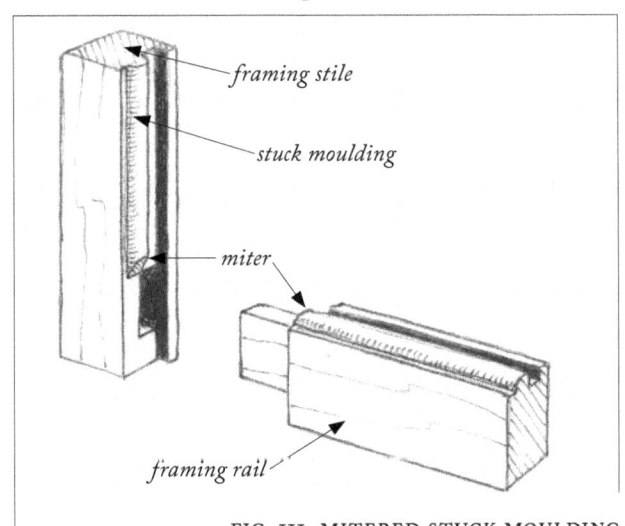

FIG. 111 MITERED STUCK MOULDING

TRADITIONAL JIGS & FIXTURES

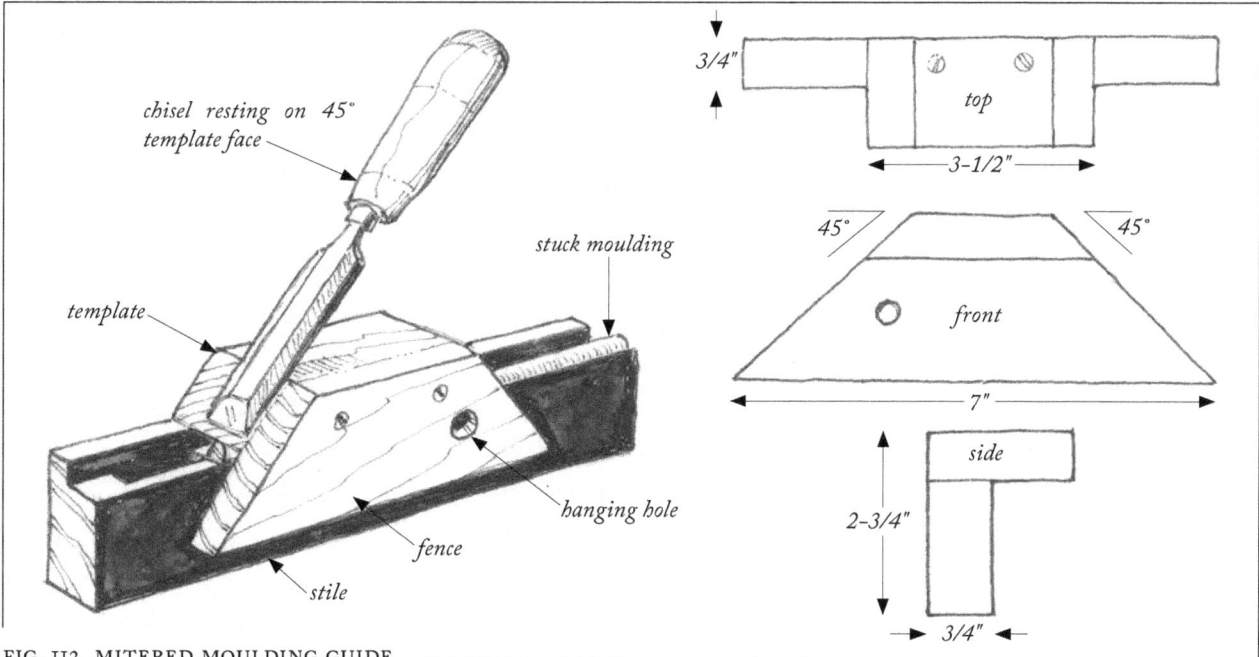

FIG. 112 MITERED MOULDING GUIDE

DOVETAIL PARING GUIDE

A LONGITUDINAL DOVETAILED HOUSING IS AN excellent joint for attaching shelving and carcase rails to uprights and sides, but the dovetails are difficult to trim. Stanley Tools once made a specialized plane for this purpose but it is now become an expensive collector's item, and is not strictly speaking 'traditional', especially if the joint is made tapered or stopped. The fundamental difficulty lies in maintaining the correct dovetail angle over the entire length of the joint, stopped or not. This can be made much easier, however, if the tail is formed by first cutting a simple rebate and then trimming to the correct angle using a wide guide block cut at this angle to support a wide paring chisel.

The guide should be wide enough to provide support for the back of your widest paring chisel and long enough to make it possible to pare at least a few inches at a time without having constantly to reposition the guide. The critical dimension is the low edge of the guide, which should match perfectly the high edge of the dovetail. This dimension may be arrived at differently depending on whether you cut the male portion or the female portion of the joint first, but in either event take care not to make the dimension marked as 'x' as shown below in FIG. 113, too small — it is much easier to remove a little more wood than it is to replace it. The slope of the guide should be cut at the same angle as is used for the dovetail.

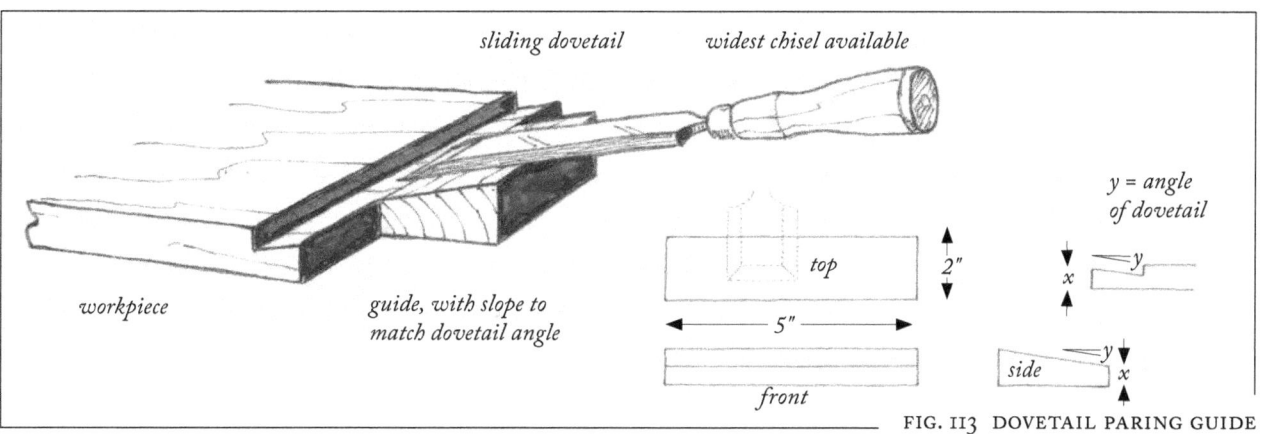

FIG. 113 DOVETAIL PARING GUIDE

JOINERY

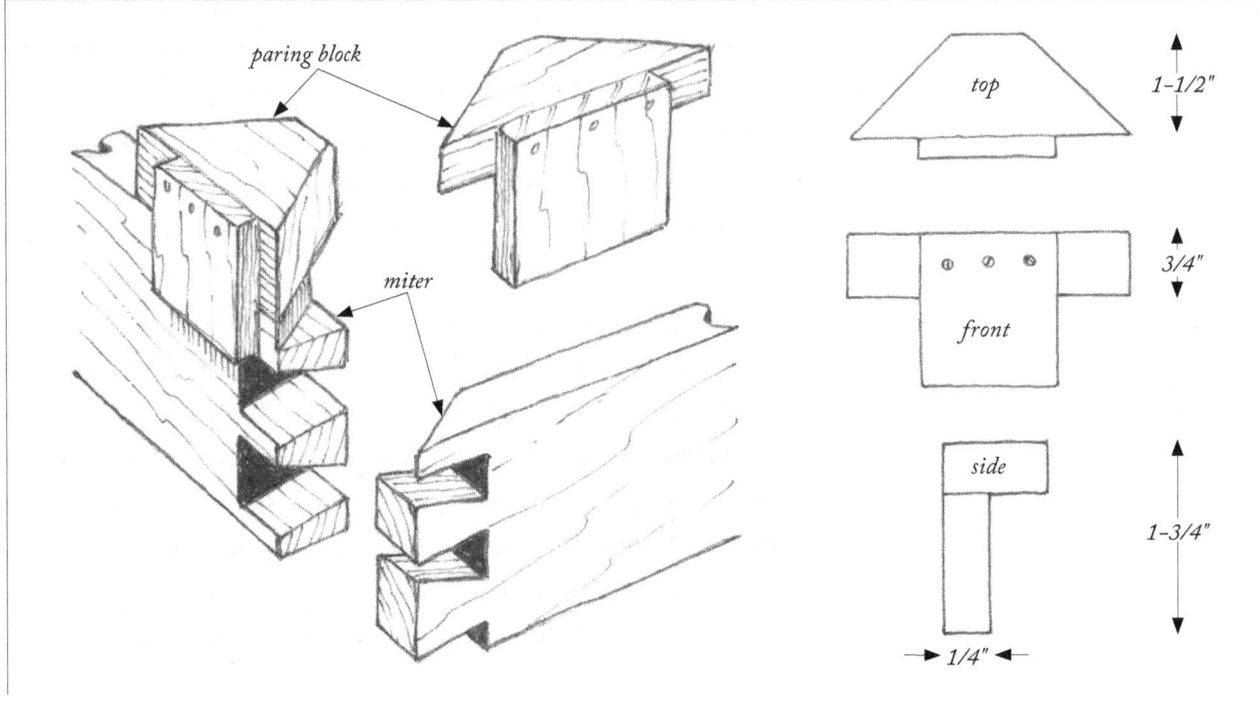

FIG. 114 MITERED DOVETAIL PARING BLOCK

MITERED-DOVETAIL PARING BLOCK

THE TOP ENDS OF CASE PIECES, SUCH AS TOOL chests, blanket chests, and trunks that have sides joined with various kinds of dovetails (lapped, half-lapped, full, or blind, etc.) are often finished with miters for a better, more even appearance, but cutting this miter can be a risky operation after having spent so much time on carefully cutting pins and tails. The usual method is to saw this part oversize then assemble the joint and resaw the miter in the hope that the new kerf will allow the two parts to fit perfectly. The better solution is to cut close to a carefully scribed layout line so that the joint will almost close and with no undue strain on the pins and tails, and then pare to perfection using a paring block that can be held or clamped to each side in turn.

While the previous jig — the dovetail paring guide — could be used for this operation, it will usually be found to be too large and clumsy; a smaller jig, made with a thinner fence and a shorter paring block will be easier to use. Cut a short length of one-by-two with 45° angles at each end, and attach a fence no greater than can be held with one hand against the side of the workpiece.

MORTISING:

MORTISING BLOCK

Chapter 1 describes various ways of securing a workpiece in order to perform different operations, including mortising, but depending on the size of the workpiece not all these may be ideal. For example, a holdfast, although capable of holding a workpiece securely, especially when being mortised, may have problems keeping a narrow workpiece perfectly vertical. Clamping something in the vise might preserve verticality, but it could prove somewhat difficult to prevent the workpiece from being knocked downwards between the jaws, with possible damage to the sides of the workpiece. A better solution is to clamp such a workpiece to a mortising block. The block's fence is held in the vise while the workpiece, the verticality of which is maintained by the block, rests on the bench.

Any square-sided block sufficiently large to offer substantial bearing surface to the workpiece should be used; just make sure to attach this block to a fence that is sufficiently deep to be securely held in the vise as shown in FIG. 115.

TRADITIONAL JIGS & FIXTURES

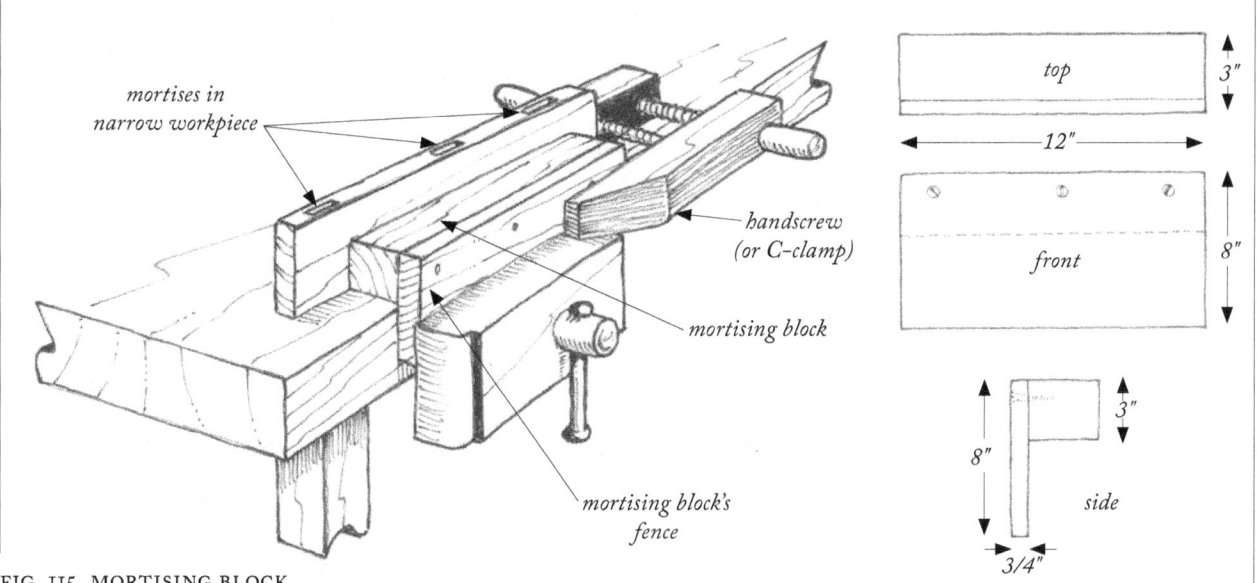

FIG. 115 MORTISING BLOCK

MORTISING HANDSCREW

CUTTING MORTISES BY HAND WITH SASH MORTISE chisels or registered mortise chisels near the ends of narrow workpieces — such as at the ends of stiles — often runs the risk of splitting the wood sideways, even if care is taken only to drive the chisel in perfectly vertically. While this danger can be minimized by first boring most of the waste away with a bit of a slightly smaller diameter than the width of the desired mortise, the danger can be effectively eliminated by clamping the mortise end with a handscrew, itself held to the bench by a holdfast or another clamp. If the workpiece to be mortised is taller than the jaws of the handscrew are wide, extra scrap pieces, as wide as the workpiece, can be used between it and the jaws of the handscrew.

A further advantage of this method is that by clamping the handscrew flat against the bench top the workpiece can be held perfectly vertical, which is just one more way to minimize splitting the mortise and at the same time guarantee a properly aligned joint.

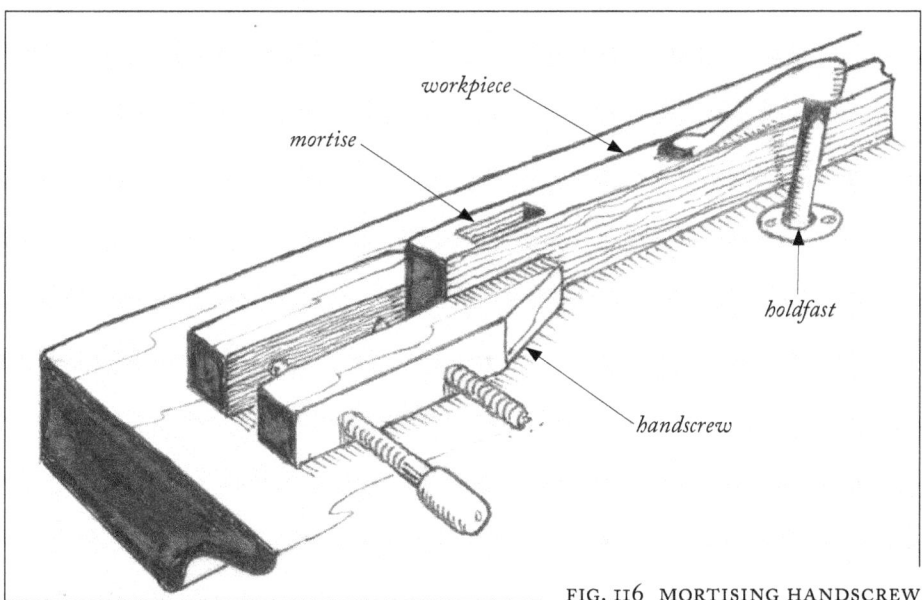

FIG. 116 MORTISING HANDSCREW

JOINERY

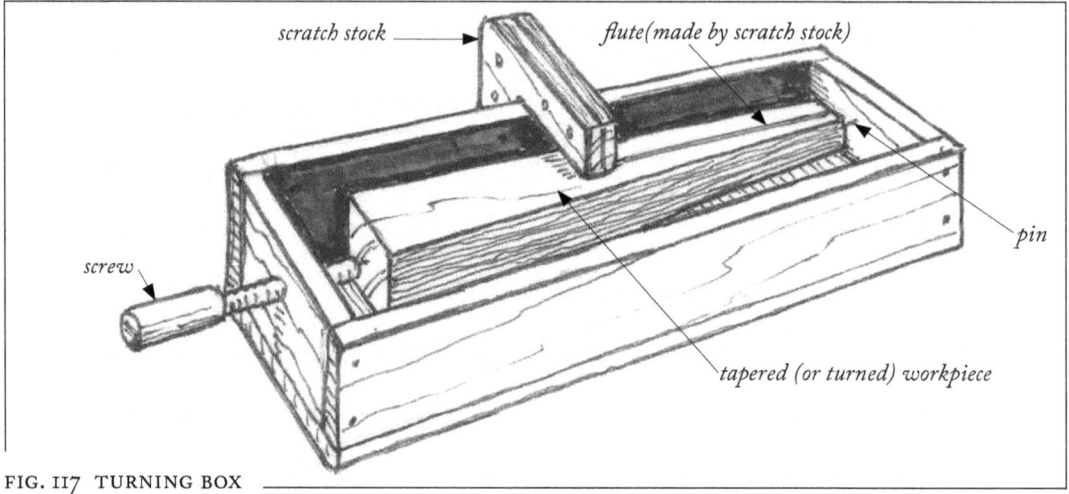

FIG. 117 TURNING BOX

TURNING BOX
(MOULDING BOX, FLUTING BOX)

CUTTING MOULDINGS ON NON-RECTILINEAR workpieces (such as round legs or turned sections of furniture) can be difficult even if the workpiece can be firmly held in vises or cradles, etc. A turning box makes this and other operations, such as fluting, planing, and even mortising, easy, since the box provides a method for securing the workpiece as well as a means of centering (or off-centering) the workpiece while other tools such as scratch stocks are used.

The box should be made not only large enough to contain the workpiece, but should also be provided with a screw at one end that can be tightened against the end of the workpiece in order to prevent it from rotating. It is usual to provide a pin or short nail at the other end against which the workpiece can be centered, and rotated when necessary.

A further refinement known as a clock can be added to function as an index plate. The purpose of this is to be able to rotate the workpiece either in regular increments or according to the number of finished faces it might have. The clock is a simple disk fixed to the end of the workpiece where it is pivoted at one end of the box, and whose circumference is bored with a number of equally-spaced holes corresponding to the number of facets required. The workpiece can then be rotated a controlled amount and held in place by a pin passing through the appropriate hole in the index plate into a receiving hole in the end of the box. In order to use a scratch stock (to make beads or reeds, or to produce a longitudinal moulding on the workpiece) the sides of the box should be made perfectly straight and parallel. For tapered workpieces, all that is necessary is to reposition the pin to which the end of the workpiece is fixed so that the sides of the workpiece are parallel to one side of the box.

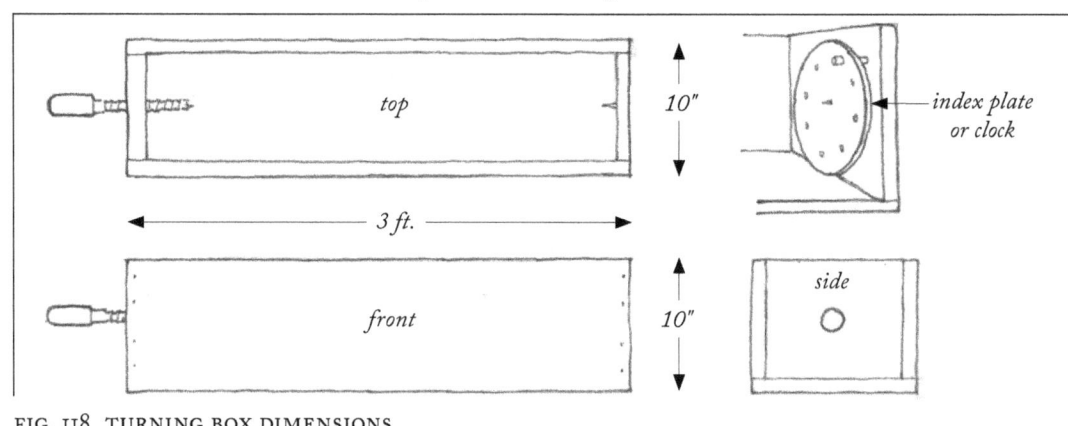

FIG. 118 TURNING BOX DIMENSIONS

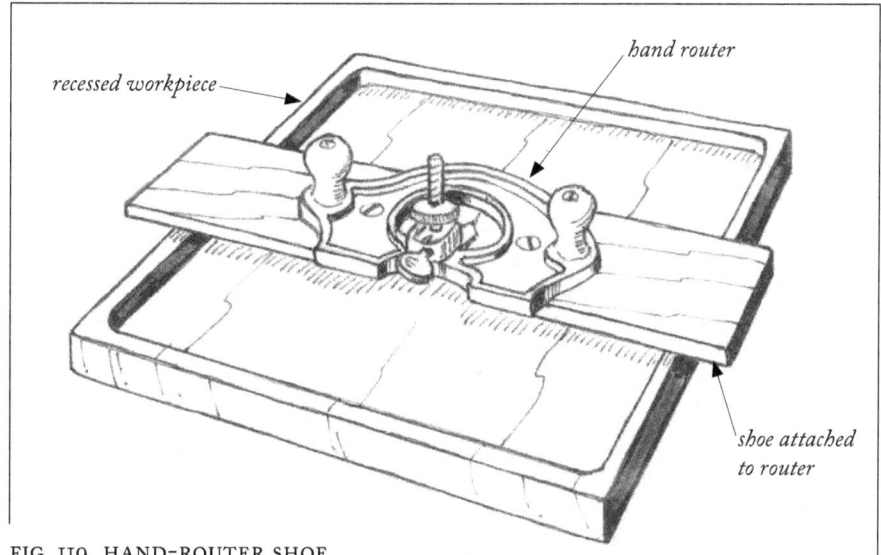

FIG. 119 HAND-ROUTER SHOE

HAND-ROUTER SHOE

TODAY´S ELECTRIC ROUTER HAVING USURPED THE name of the original handtool the latter must now be distinguished from the former by being called a hand router. The common metal versions which are made in several sizes are descended from a simpler wooden design (known as 'an old woman's tooth') and are usually provided with depth gauges, fences, and even variously-shaped irons. But one thing these modern tools all lack is the ability to work an area larger than the base that constitutes their sole. By attaching a wide wooden shoe with screws through holes often provided for this purpose in the tool's base the hand router becomes capable of flattening a recessed or sunken surface much wider than the width of the tool itself.

ANGLED CIRCLE-CUTTING GUIDE

TO CUT A CONSISTENTLY ANGLED-EDGE CIRCLE, either interior or exterior, partial or complete, by hand is extremely difficult if attempted freehand. But by fixing an angled block with a radius — the distance from the pivoting fixing point to the angled edge — equal to the radius of the circle, or part circle, required for the workpiece, and using the outer angled face as a guide for a keyhole saw the job is made much easier.

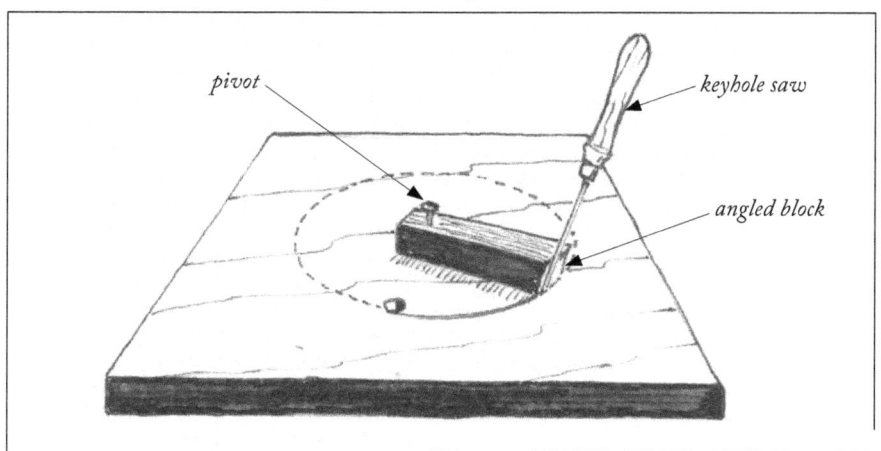

FIG. 120 ANGLED CIRCLE-CUTTING GUIDE

*16th cent. wagonwright enlarging an axle hole
(from Das Ständebuch by Jost Ammon)*

6

JIGS & FIXTURES FOR BORING

TRADITIONAL WOODWORKING, WHICH RELIES PRIMARILY ON THE BRACE, BOTH WOODEN AND METALLIC VERSIONS, AND THE HAND DRILL FOR MOST BORING OPERATIONS, MAKES USE OF A WIDE VARIETY OF BITS SUCH AS CENTER BITS, SPOON BITS, HALF-TWIST, SHELL BITS, AND AUGER bits. Since electric drills, both corded and cordless battery-run models, are now almost universally used by even the most diehard traditionalist, this is an area of woodworking less furnished with jigs and fixtures than most. Nevertheless, there remains a number of devices that can improve the accuracy if not necessarily the efficiency of certain boring operations, especially for the woodworker not possessed of a drill press, Many of these are equally useful for traditional tools such as push drills, hand drills, corner braces, and T-augers, as well as for electric drills.

Perhaps the first thing to be borne in mind, almost regardless of what boring tool or bit is being used, is the ability to bore a clean hole, especially if the hole being bored is a through-hole that penetrates the workpiece completely as opposed to a desired hole that penetrates the workpiece only partly. For this latter job there are specially designed bits, known as forstner bits, which are made for a variety of tools, both traditional handtools as well as modern electric tools both hand and stationery, which will bore a flat-bottomed hole. But for through-holes extra care must be taken to prevent the exit hole from splintering out.

When boring with drill bits such as auger bits that have small lead- screws, or center bits that have a sharp center, it is possible to bore from the reverse or exit side the moment the lead screw or center is seen exiting the hole, using its exit point as a guide to position the bit and bore back into the cavity, as shown in FIG. 121 on the next page.

TRADITIONAL JIGS & FIXTURES

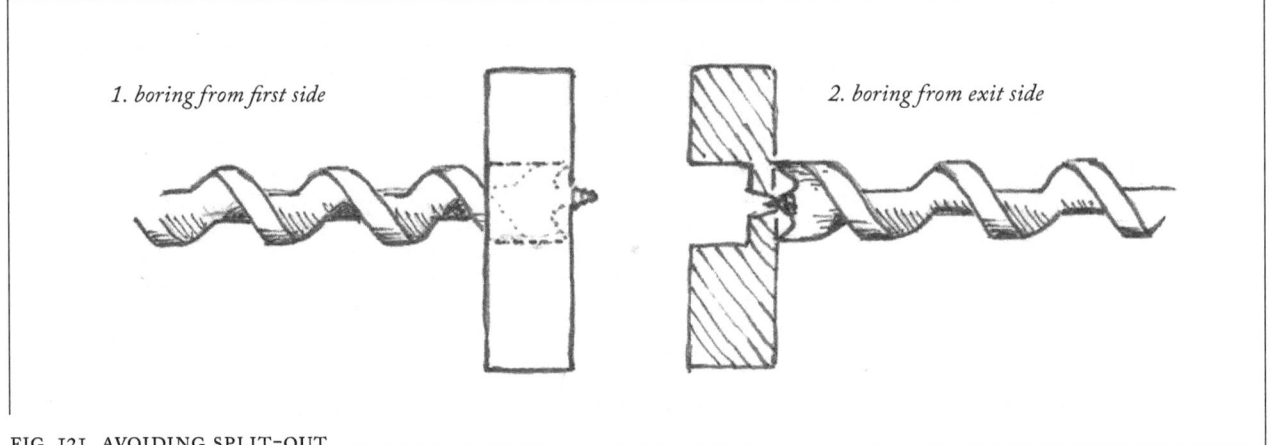

FIG. 121 AVOIDING SPLIT-OUT

SPLINTERING GUARD

IF, HOWEVER, BORING FROM BOTH SIDES IS NOT possible, or if it is simply more convenient just to bore all the way through the workpiece from one side, fix a sacrificial scrap piece tightly to the exit side of the hole by clamping or perhaps holding the two pieces together in the vise — neither method being shown in the illustration below for the sake of clarity).

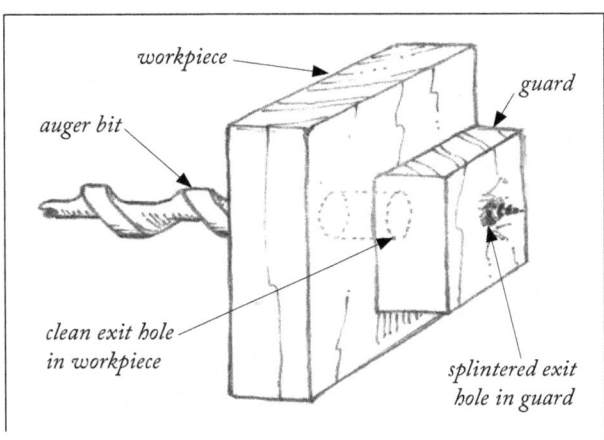

FIG. 122 SPLINTERING GUARD

STRAIGHT BORING GUIDES:

NO MATTER WHAT HANDTOOL YOU USE, BORING perfectly perpendicularly to any given workpiece can be difficult unless some form of guide, even if only visual rather than virtual, is used. The following four methods require little set-up but can go a long way to ensure accuracy depending on the lengh of the bit being used.

TRYSQUARE GUIDE

PERHAPS THE SIMPLEST TECHNIQUE IS TO USE a large or small trysquare stood on end next to the desired entry point as a useful visual guide.

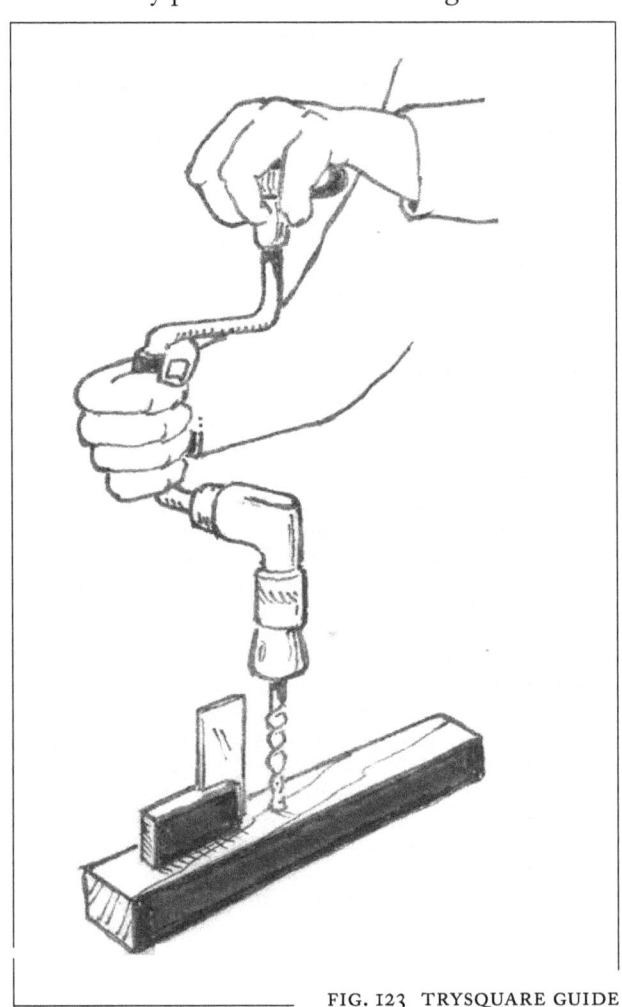

FIG. 123 TRYSQUARE GUIDE

TRADITIONAL JIGS & FIXTURES

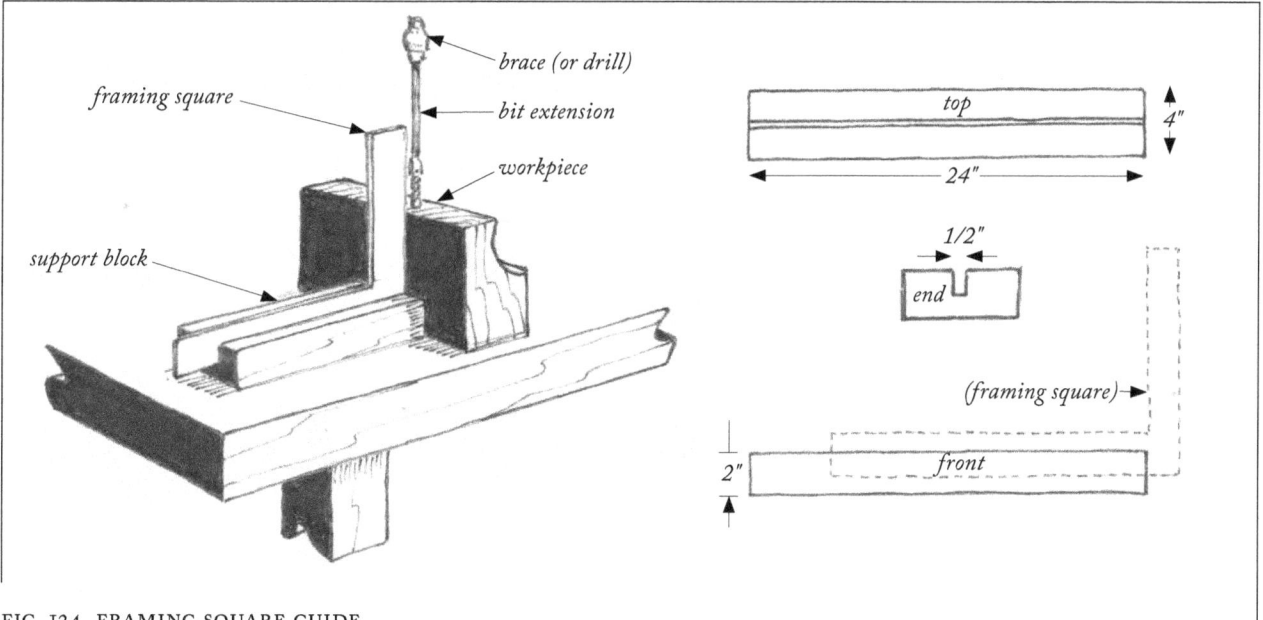

FIG. 124 FRAMING SQUARE GUIDE

FRAMING SQUARE GUIDE

FOR ESPECIALLY DEEP HOLES THAT MAY REQUIRE being bored with a bit extension a carpenter's framing square, if one is available, mounted in a grooved support block provides even greater visual reference than a simple trysquare.

To make the support block that will hold the framing square upright on edge, a length of two-by-four, long enough to support either the short arm (typically 18 in. long) or the long arm (typically 2 ft. long) of a standard framing square, is all that is necessary. Make a groove in the center of its 4 in. width deep enough to hold the square upright, but note that care should be taken to ensure that the groove is absolutely perpendicular to the bottom of the two-by-four, and at the same time also narrow enough to hold the square with no sideways wobble so that the free arm stands up straight.

VERTICAL BORING GUIDE

IN THE ABSENCE OF A FRAMING SQUARE A suitable length of 1/2 in.-diameter dowel can be quickly bored (perhaps using the block boring guide illustrated on the next page to ensure a vertical hole) into a piece of scrap substantial enough to hold it upright.

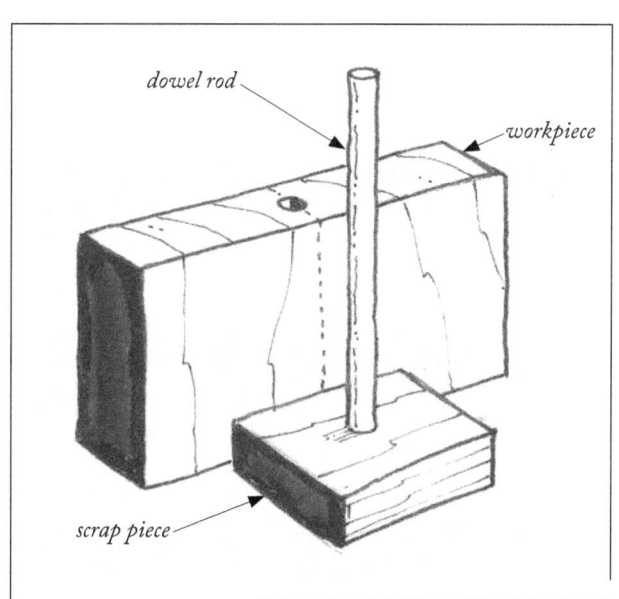

FIG. 125 VERTICAL BORING GUIDE

THIN-STOCK BORING GUIDE

FOR VERY THIN OR NARROW STOCK WORKPIECES perhaps no more than 2 in. or 3 in. square — there is an even better solution than using a single framing square — which only provides a visual reference in one direction.

This consists of two guide strips of thin, flat stock that are clamped to the workpiece 90° apart so that the bit (especially if mounted in a bit extension) can be fed directly into the workpiece

BORING

TRADITIONAL JIGS & FIXTURES

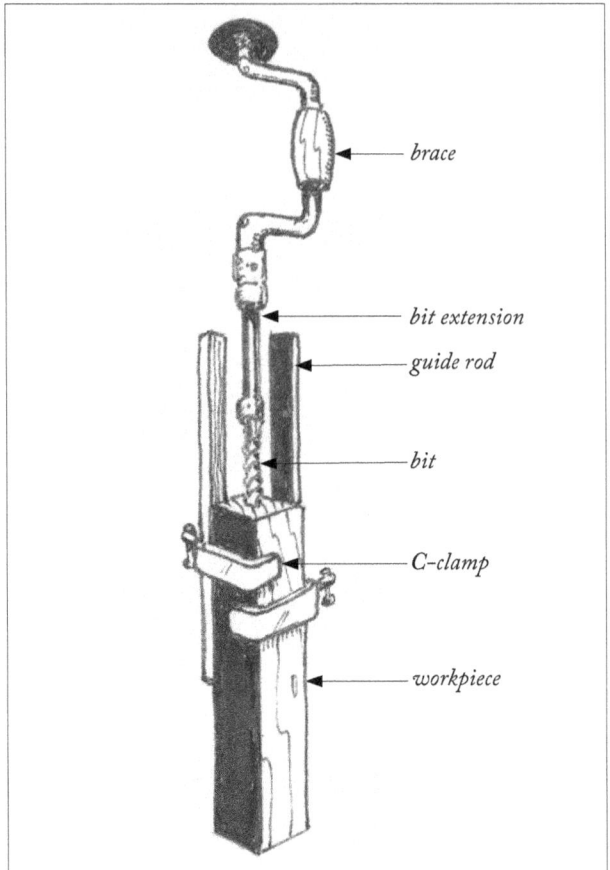

FIG. 126 THIN STOCK BORING GUIDE

Since this jig is theoretically the very jig that should be used to make itself, extreme care should be used in making it before such a jig exists. Start by preparing the block of the hardest and densest wood available (the better to withstand wear) to be perfectly rectilinear (perhaps by shooting all four faces with the aid of a shooting board, q.v.). Next, square around the block at the places where the guide holes are to be made and use a marking gauge (always registered against the same face of the block) to mark the entrance and exit points. Using a bit smaller than the size hole ultimately required, bore in from both sides until both holes meet in the middle. If they meet perfectly aligned you can now use the right sized bit to enlarge the hole to the required diameter. If the meeting points are offset use either a round file or another bit one size smaller to align them, taking care not to alter the entrance and exit points, after which you can now use the right size bit to enlarge the hole to the required diameter as before.

as both sideways and back-and-forth positioning is checked. Take care to ensure that the strips are not only straight, but are also clamped to the workpiece so that they are indeed parallel and perfectly vertical.

BLOCK BORING GUIDE

MANUFACTURED DOWELLING AIDS ARE OFTEN furnished with short tubes or sleeves of variously sized diameters to guide drill bits or auger bits into the workpiece; a block of wood, bored with the right size hole and sufficiently large to be clamped to the workpiece will do the same thing. While the taller the block the better the guide will be, it should not be so tall that any bit used with it has insufficient length actually to penetrate the workpiece. It is therefore generally most useful for guiding auger bits mounted in a brace, although extra long twist bits are obtainable that can be used with hand drills (or electric drills).

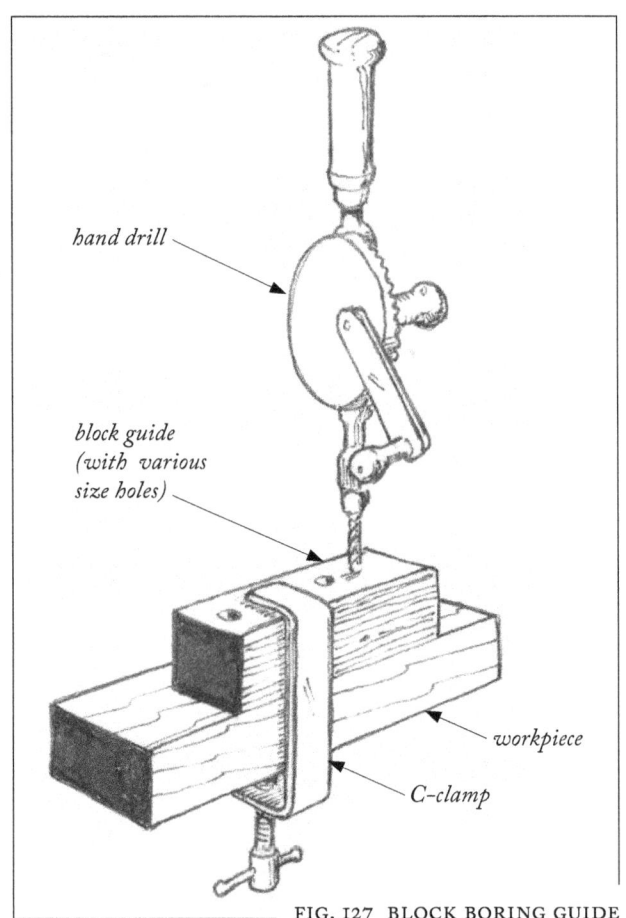

FIG. 127 BLOCK BORING GUIDE

TRADITIONAL JIGS & FIXTURES

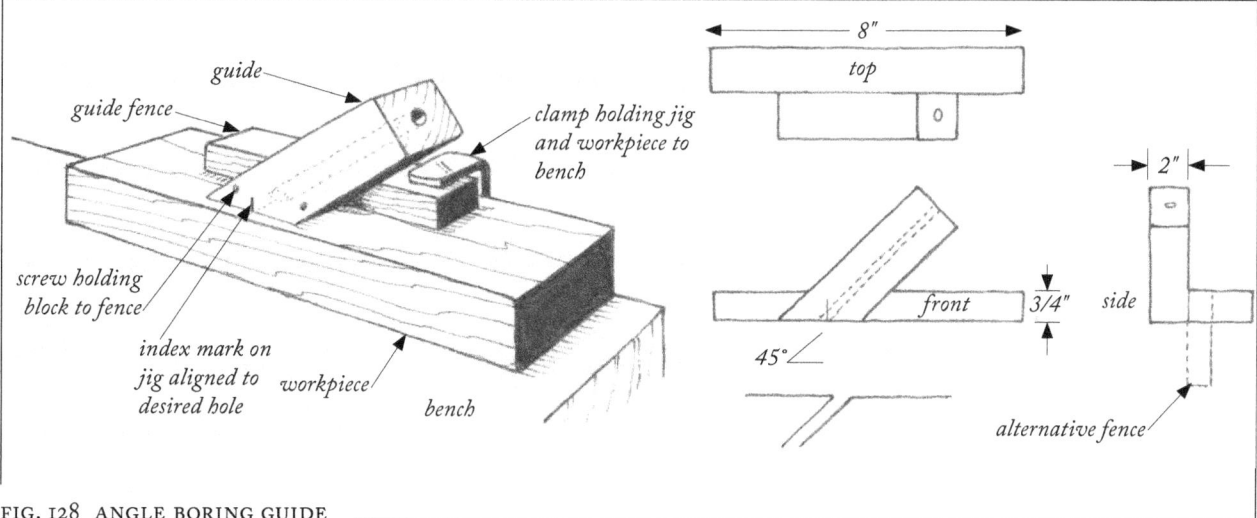

FIG. 128 ANGLE BORING GUIDE

ANGLED & SPACED GUIDES:

ANGLE BORING GUIDE

IT IS FAR MORE DIFFICULT TO JUDGE AN ANGLED operation than one that is perfectly vertical or horizontal — for which reason it is good practice whenever possible to secure the workpiece so that the desired operation (whether sawing, planing, or boring) can be effected either vertically or horizontally. Should this, however, not be possible, prepare a guide block to lead the bit at the required angle by boring a vertical hole in a rectangular block (using one of the jigs mentioned above), and then sawing the bottom of this block at the required angle. To use this guide, attach a fence that may be clamped either to the top of the workpiece as shown, or alternatively to the side of the workpiece. Square a line from the center of the bored hole in the jig to the side of the jig and use this to align the hole with the required position in the workpiece as shown. Such a jig will also ensure that the hole will be started correctly — something that is often difficult to do with various bits when beginning to bore at an angle.

SPACED-HOLE BORING GUIDE

SLIGHTLY MORE COMPLICATED THAN BORING A hole at the correct angle is the problem of boring a line of holes at a predetermined distance from one another, such as the holes that might be needed for shelf supports in a cabinet or bookcase. The problem is further compounded by the fact that four such lines of holes may be needed, all of which must match, even if the holes are not evenly spaced, in order that any shelving resting on supports inserted in these holes does not rock. The solution

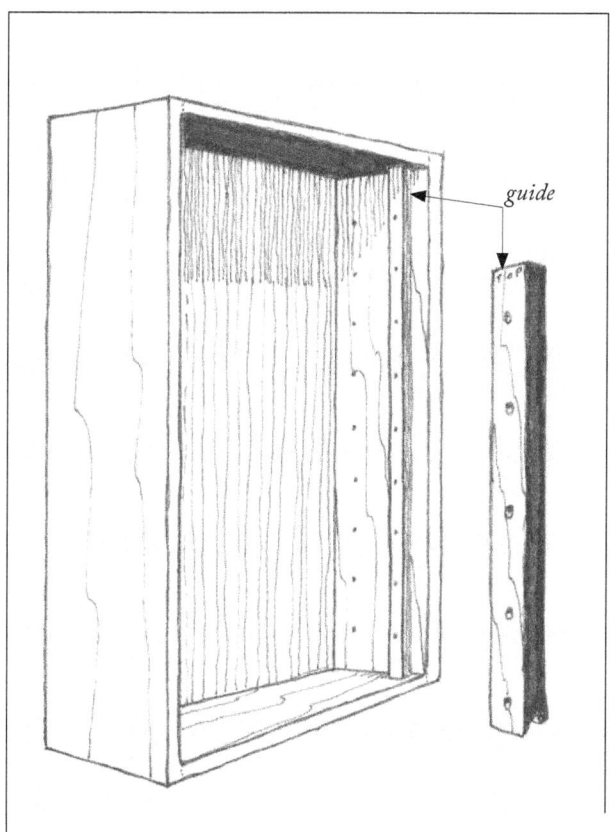

FIG. 129 SPACED HOLE GUIDE

BORING

TRADITIONAL JIGS & FIXTURES

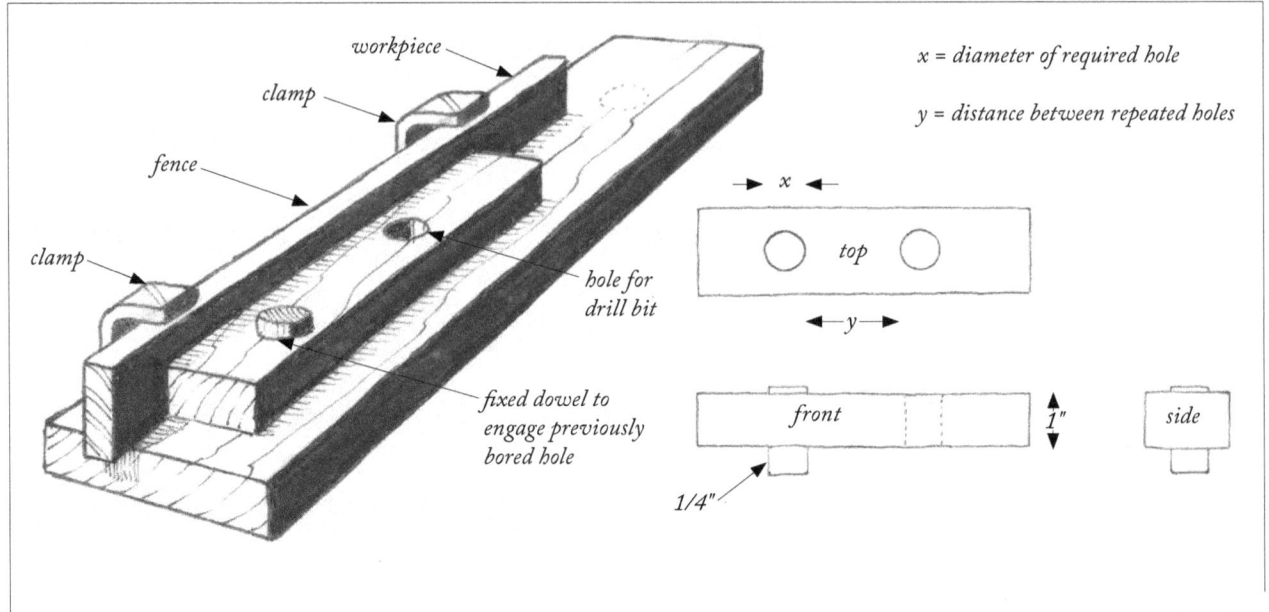

FIG. 130 EVENLY-SPACED HOLE GUIDE

is to bore a line of holes in a strip of hardwood, spaced one from the other as required, having laid this out as carefully as possible; and in the event that the holes are not evenly spaced being sure to mark one end of this strip so that it may always be oriented in the same direction.

In order to extend the life of this guide as long as possible when using an electric drill be sure not to start the drill until the bit is in the guide. This is not a problem, of course, with a hand drill or brace since the bits are typically inserted before being turned.

EVENLY- SPACED HOLE GUIDE

TO ENSURE THAT REPEATED HOLES SUCH AS those used in the previous jig are the same distance from one another, bore two holes the required distance apart in a block of hardwood, and insert a dowel into the first hole that protrudes a little to act as an indexing pin to be inserted into each previously bored hole in turn. To keep the holes aligned in a straight line it is further recommended to use this guide pressed against a separate fence that has been clamped to the workpiece. In order not to damage previously bored holes, gently round the bottom edge of the indexing dowel — a good habit to get into when inserting any dowel.

CORNER BORING GUIDE

TO ENSURE THAT CORNER HOLES SUCH AS MIGHT be needed for dowelling or attaching a lid or cabinet base with screws to a rectilinear carcase are all bored the same distance from each corner, a corner boring guide is needed. The lid or base to be bored is placed into the corner of the fixture, and a prebored platen is superimposed, also firmly positioned into the corner of the fixture. The platen, if perfectly square, may have a series of guide holes of varying diameters as needed bored along diagonal lines extending from each corner.

Fix two guide strips or fences high enough to contain both the workpiece and the prebored platen, arranged so as to form a right-angle on a base, and then prepare a square platen at least 3/4 in. thick to fit into the corner thus formed. On a 45° diagonal drawn from one corner to the opposite corner of the platen bore a hole of the required diameter and at the required distance from the corner.

The entire fixture need not be much larger than is sufficient to contain the platen, regardless of the size of the workpiece, provided that the workpiece can be held securely in the fixture, with the addition of a spacer block the same thickness as the base of the fixture if necessary, and the whole assembly then securely clamped to the worksurface.

TRADITIONAL JIGS & FIXTURES

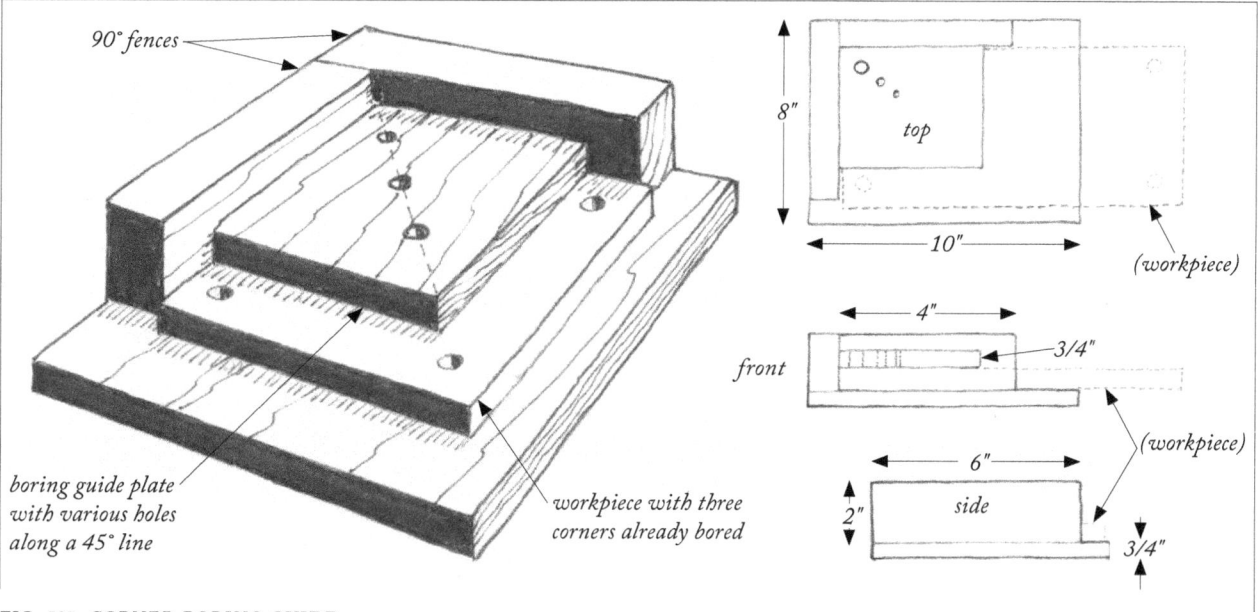

FIG. 131 CORNER BORING GUIDE

Once this principle is grasped it will be easily understood that it is equally possible to prepare similar corner-boring guides for shapes other than rectilinear — such as triangles, pentagons or other polygons — simply by altering the angle of the corner fences and preparing appropriately angled platens to fit in them.

DEPTH STOPS:

NOT ALL THE HOLES YOU BORE NEED TO BE completely through-bored. For such holes some form of depth stop is usually needed, especially if the hole is to bored to a precise depth. This is one case where most usermade items are superior to manufactured metal items, since there is always the danger of damaging the surface of the workpiece with metal depth stops designed to be tightened on the bit, especially when boring at an angle.

TAPE DEPTH GUIDE

THE SIMPLEST METHOD, ESPECIALLY USEFUL when using small twist bits in hand drills, is simply to wrap a short length of bit of masking tape or something similar, around the bit, leaving the required depth exposed.

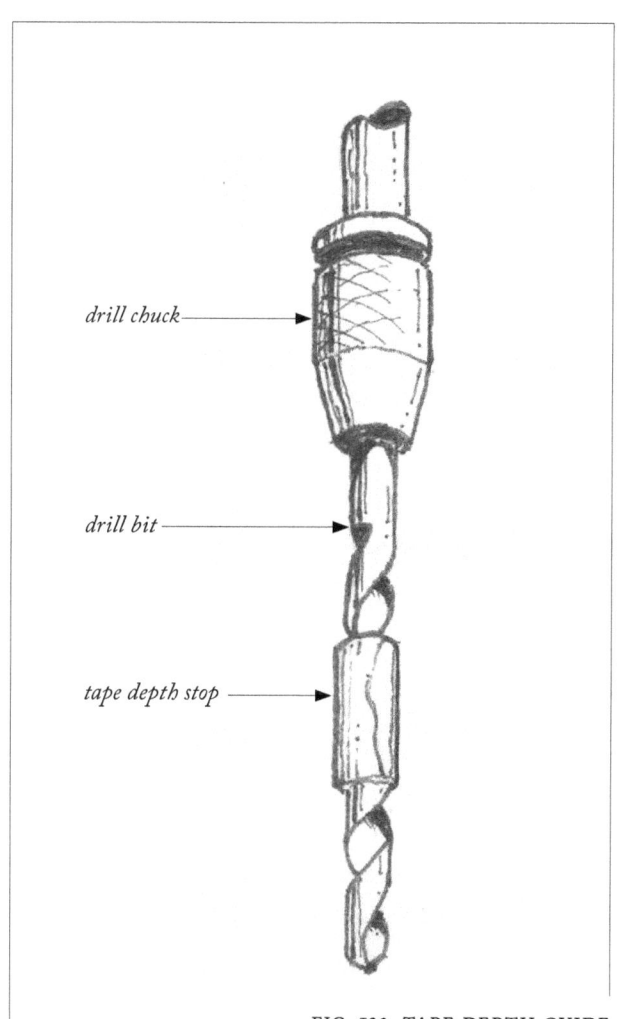

FIG. 132 TAPE DEPTH GUIDE

BORING

BLOCK DEPTH GUIDE (BLOCK STOP)

WHEN BORING WITH LARGER BITS, SUCH AS auger bits held in a brace, a block of wood bored to fit the bit and cut to a length that will stop the bit entering more deeply is all that is needed. To minimize any damage to the workpiece gently round the outside edges of the bottom of the guide. To avoid having the block stop revolve on the workpiece as the brace is turned until the auger bit has entered the workpiece to the required depth — at which point the block stop should be riding against the bottom of the brace's chuck — secure the block stop in its final position by inserting a blunted screw through its side in order to bear against the auger bit's shank.

ADJUSTABLE DEPTH STOP

A LITTLE LESS CLUMSY, AND MUCH MORE USEFUL for different boring depths than preparing a different size block stop every time, is to use an adjustable depth stop that may be secured at any point along the bit's twist section.

Bore a hole the same size as the diameter of the auger bit into a narrow piece of scrap and then saw this piece in half through the center of the bored hole. The saw kerf will have removed enough wood so that the two halves, when placed over the bit and screwed together, will tighten securely enough not to move. Be sure to round the bottom of the stop as well as to bevel the outside ends so that even if boring at an angle the stop does not damage the workpiece.

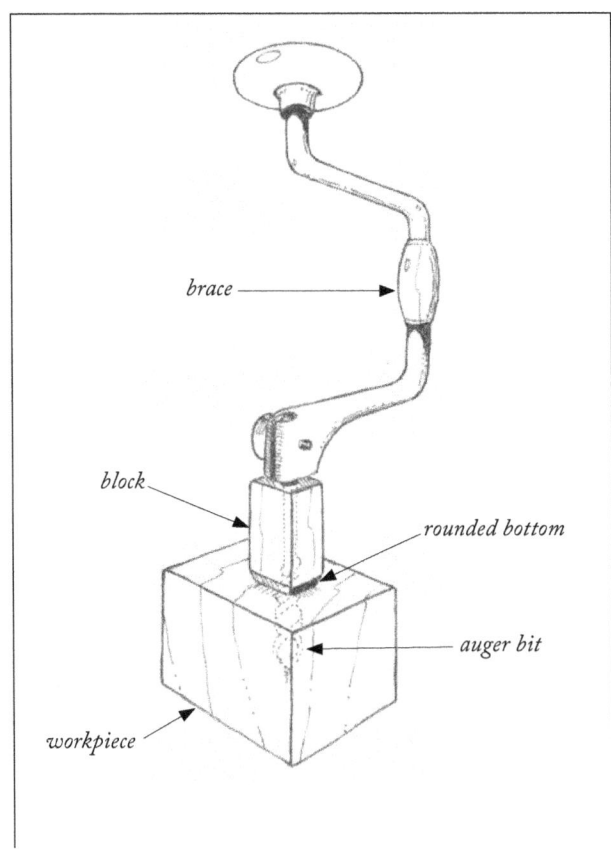

FIG. 133 BLOCK DEPTH GUIDE

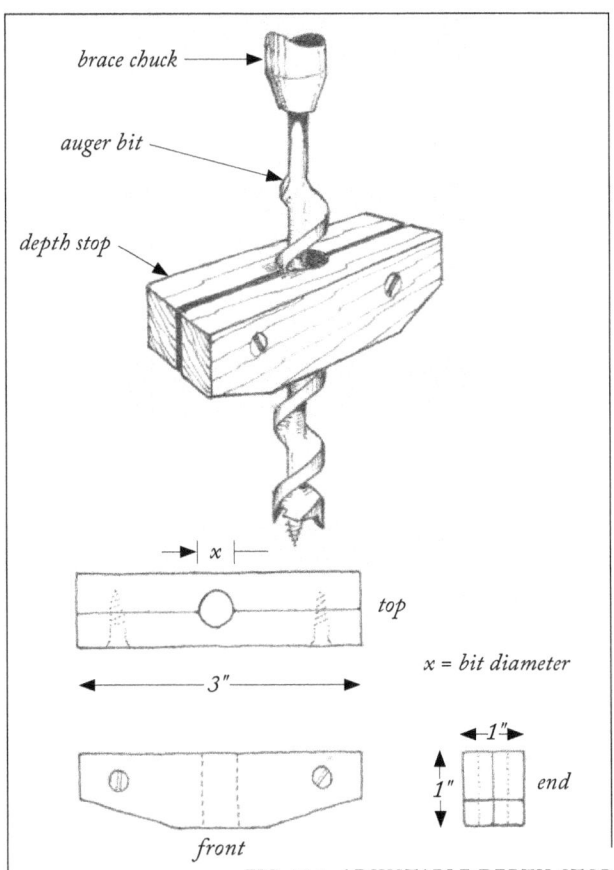

FIG. 134 ADJUSTABLE DEPTH STOP

7

JIGS & FIXTURES FOR ASSEMBLY & FINISHING

FROM A 2OZ. TACK HAMMER TO A 10LB. COMMANDER THERE ARE NUMEROUS TOOLS DESIGNED TO ASSEMBLE THE VARIOUS PARTS OF MOST WOODWORKING PROJECTS. AS THE FINAL, OR PERHAPS PENULTIMATE STAGE OF A PROJECT IF FINISHING IS INCLUDED, OF WHAT MAY HAVE BEEN a long and careful expenditure of time, it makes little sense to jeopardize the project's successful completion by risking dents and dings and other finishing mistakes.

This chapter is therefore divided into two parts: the first dealing with assembly and the second with various finishing procedures.

I. ASSEMBLY

DENT PROTECTION:

ONE DEFINITION OF A WELL-CUT JOINT IS THAT although easily assembled it should be tight enough so that it does not fall apart of its own accord. This can mean that sometimes a certain amount of assistance in the form of carefully applied force, using mallets or hammers, is necessary. In these cases, assuming the parts of the joint do indeed match and fit, the chief concern should be to avoid damaging the various parts.

HAMMER SHIELD

ALTHOUGH A PROPERLY DESIGNED HAMMER will have a slightly crowned face, which will make it possible to 'bounce' the nail being driven below the surface of the surrounding wood without the face of the hammer actually touching the wood until the nail head reaches the point at which this can be effected, it is worth while to employ some form of guard to protect the surrounding wood from any

TRADITIONAL JIGS & FIXTURES

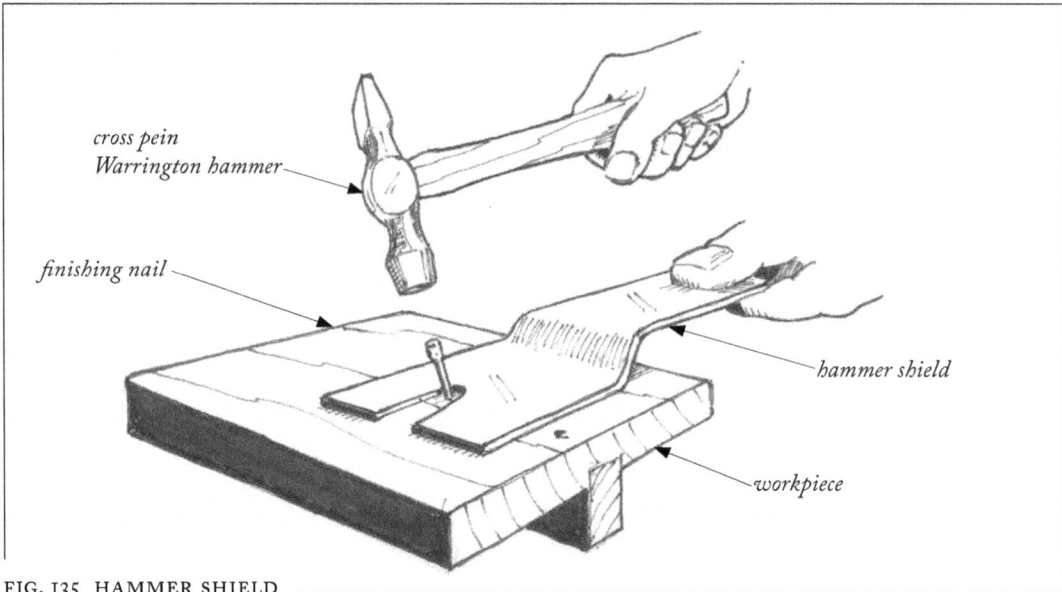

FIG. 135 HAMMER SHIELD

so-called moons caused by misplaced or missed hammer blows. A slotted piece of thin metal, such as aluminum flashing or thin tin, that can be placed around the fastener, if sufficiently broad and provided with softened edges will provide just such protection.

To make its use easier it is well to dog-leg bend the edge opposite the slot upwards a little so that it may be held while in use.

PLIERS SHIELD

ROUND-FACED PLIERS MAY BE VERY EFFICIENT when removing small nails, tacks, brads, and even

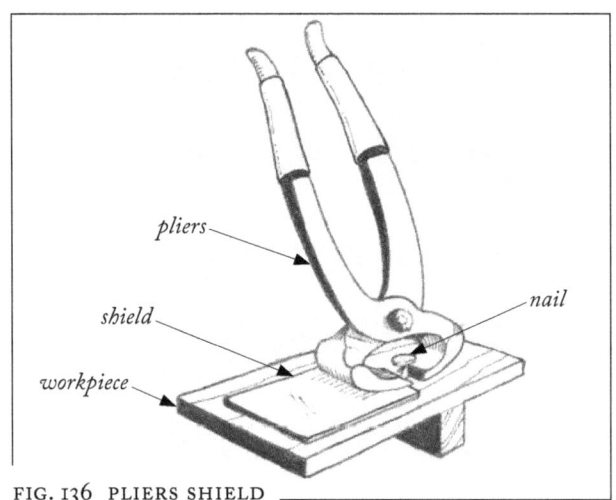

FIG. 136 PLIERS SHIELD

staples that have not been completely inserted below the surface of the wood, but if used without any protection these tools will invariably damage the surrounding wood — as will claw hammers (not normally part of any fine woodworker's toolkit) when levered against the workpiece. A thin piece of scrap wood, sufficiently broad to spread the effect should therefore always be used if dents are to be avoided.

FULCRUM RAISER

DESPITE WHAT IS WRITTEN ABOVE REGARDING the inappropriateness of claw hammers in the fine woodworker's toolkit, such tools are sometimes necessary. On such occasions, both to prevent damage as well as to increase the tool's efficiency when used to withdraw nails, it is essential to raise the level of the tool's fulcrum as the fastener is extracted, especially if the nail continues to maintain its grip to the point where greater force than normal is needed.

A small block of scrap softwood such as pine is ideal, provided once again that it is large enough to spread the pressure evenly so that the edges (which in any case should be rounded) do not dig into the surface of the workpiece. Softwood is preferable to hardwood since although it may be dented by the levering action of the hammer's claw it is less likely

TRADITIONAL JIGS & FIXTURES

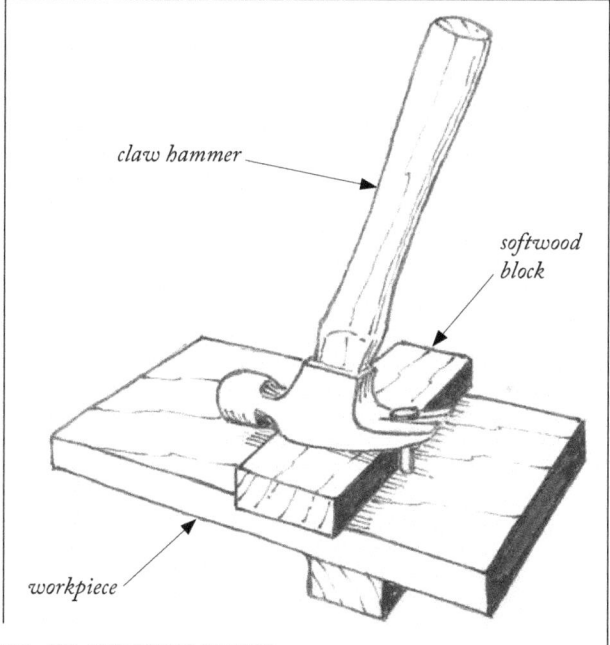

FIG. 137 FULCRUM RAISER

FIG. 138 STRIKING BLOCK

than a piece of hardwood to transmit this damage to the underlying workpiece.

STRIKING BLOCK

THERE ARE VARIOUS TOOLS SPECIFICALLY DESIGNED to knock components together without damage, such as rubber mallets, brass hammers, and shot-filled plastic hammers, but often a heavier tool is required. For these tools use of an intermediate striking block is recommended. If such a block is furnished that itself is accurately planed, it will also serve the function of aligning adjacent parts, such as shelving in casework, to a perfect flushness.

CLAMPING:

FLOOR FRAME-CONTAINER

A DIFFICULTY SOMETIMES ENCOUNTERED WHEN assembling framework is to ensure and maintain the required rectilinearity. Simply applying clamps

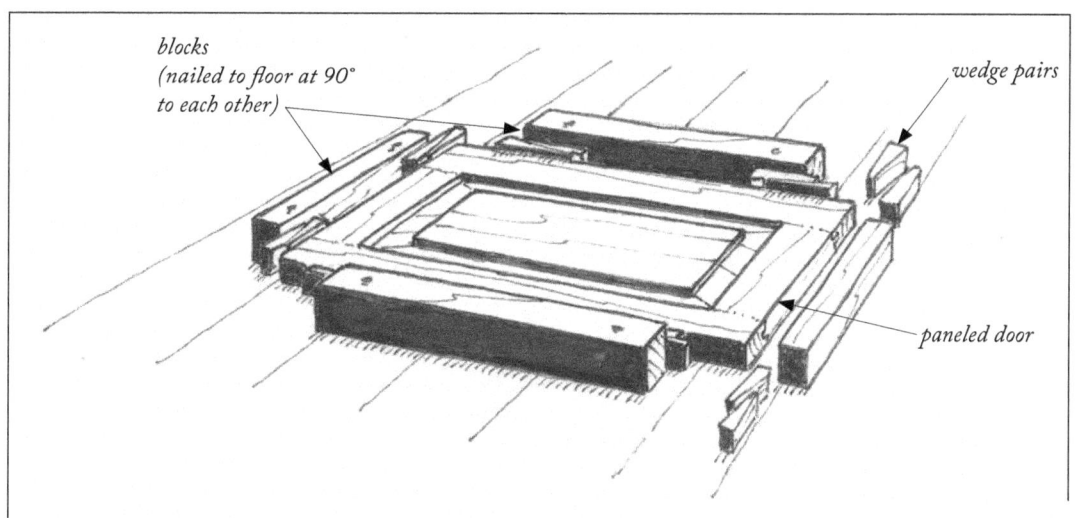

FIG. 139 FLOOR FRAME-CONTAINER

ASSEMBLY & FINISHING

across an assembly may pull joints together but does little to avoid pulling the piece out of square. A better method is to use a slightly larger fixed frame — such as, in the case of large assemblies, blocks laid out at exactly 90° to each other and securely nailed to the shop floor — into which the workpiece can be placed, and then by means of wedges driven in to close up the parts continue to maintain a perfect rectilinearity. Note that it is important to use wedges in pairs in order that the piece being clamped is not dented — because the face of the wedge next to the workpiece is always parallel to its workpiece — nor become wedged out of rectilinearity as might happen if a single wedge were used.

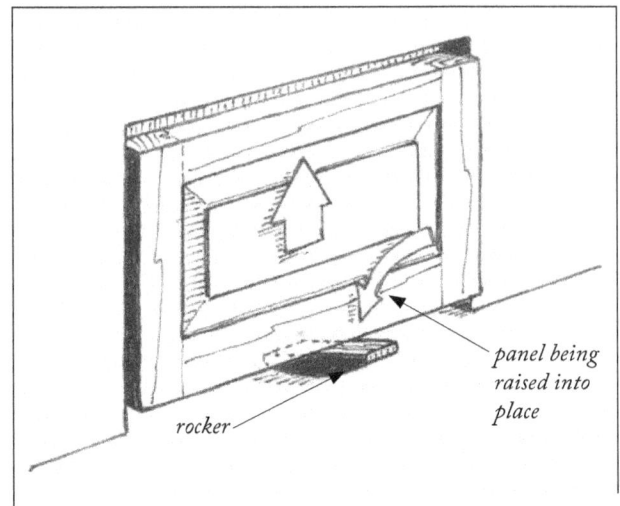

FIG. 141 DOOR ROCKER

FRAME CLAMP

IF BLOCKS NAILED TO THE FLOOR ARE NOT AN option, consider something similar on a large base such as a sheet of plywood or even a large assembly table. For workpieces measuring no more than two or three feet in any one direction this fixture may be simplified by making one corner closed and using wedges only on the opposite sides.

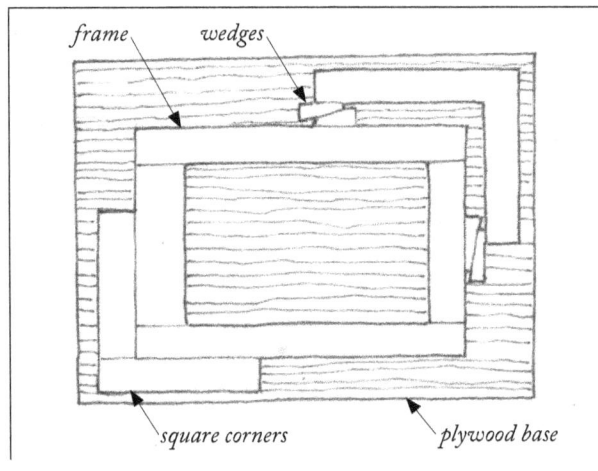

FIG. 140 FRAME CLAMP

DOOR ROCKER

THIS SIMPLE JIG CAN BE INVALUABLE IN THE assembly of large pieces when an extra pair of hands is unavailable. Depending on the size of the piece being assembled it consists of a larger or smaller crowned length of scrap that can be inserted crown-down under or between adjacent parts, and then stood upon in order to raise the workpiece to its correct position. Besides being extremely useful when positioning paneling, framing parts, or sections of large casework such as tallboys and highboys, its most obvious use (and the use for which it is named) is to raise heavy doors to the required position within their frames so that they may be marked for hinging and subsequently hung.

GLUING AIDS:

EDGE CLAMP

ALTHOUGH PROPERLY SURFACED EDGES SHOULD need little clamping when glued (glue is not any more effective under pressure, the strength of the joint being primarily a function of how well the glued surfaces mate — something which is easier to achieve with a hand-planed surface than one from a jointer whose rotating knives, no matter how sharp or finely adjusted necessarily leave a surface consisting of repeated cups rather than a continuously smooth surface), it is sometimes necessary to hold the two parts in position while the glue cures. This becomes critical when very thin pieces are glued since they may have insufficient mass to maintain their position on their own. The solution is an edge clamp.

The edge clamp is a three-part jig consisting of two outside strips against which the outside edges of the

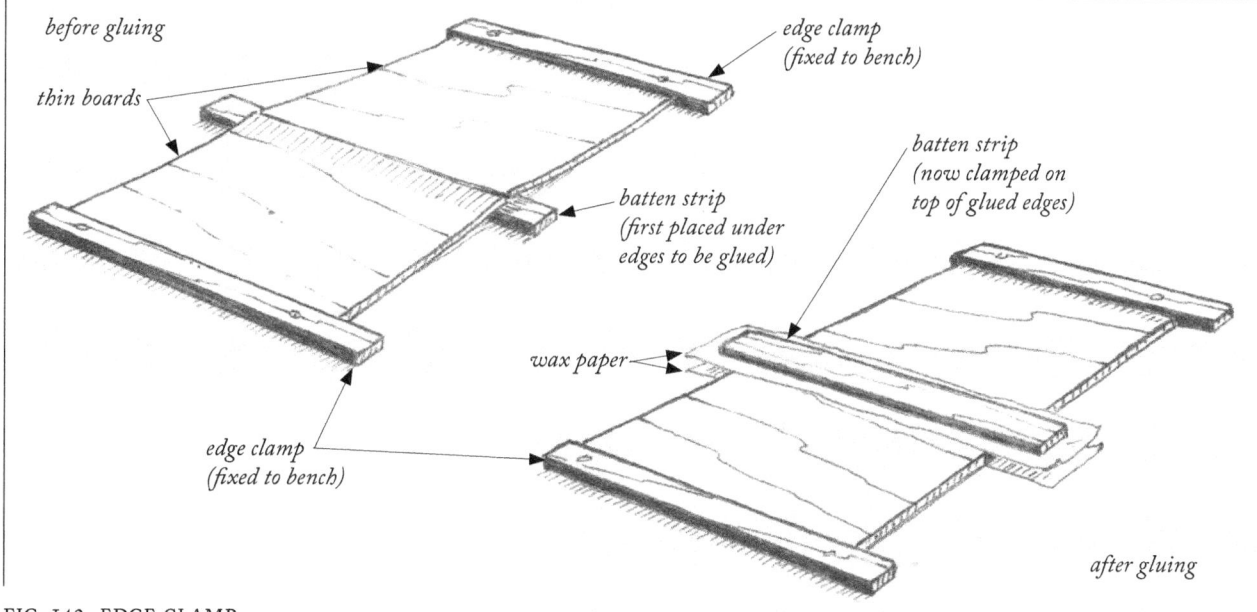

FIG. 142 EDGE CLAMP

pieces to be glued bear, and a broad but relatively thin (1/2 in.) piece — the batten — placed on top of the joint after glue has been applied. When you are ready to glue, start by positioning the outside strips against the pieces to be glued with a thin broad batten placed under the joint. If the two pieces are arranged so that with this batten underneath they touch lightly, when the batten is removed they will be forced together in what is now slightly less space.

After applying glue remove the batten from beneath the workpieces and use it to press the edges down flat and together, keeping it in this position by weights or even by clamping it to the worksurface. Be sure to use wax paper immediately above and below the glued joint so that the batten does not become part of the assembly. After the glue has cured first remove one of the outside strips before removing the batten — or the workpiece may spring up and damage the just completed joint.

PEG FORM

WHEN GLUING UP LAMINATE STRIPS OR HOLDING steamed wood in position while it dries a bending form is essential. The simplest device is a backing board as large as the workpiece, and which is bored with a variety of holes into which pegs that can

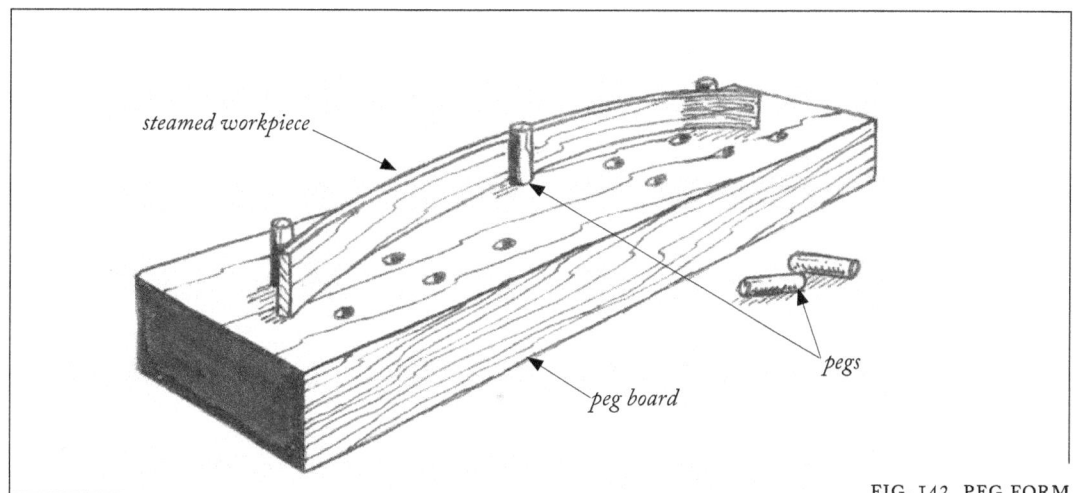

FIG. 143 PEG FORM

ASSEMBLY & FINISHING

be moved incrementally until the desired shape is attained may be inserted in order to keep the workpiece in the desired position.

As well as being large enough to contain the entire workpiece, the backing board should also be thick enough to hold the pegs. Medium density fiberboard (MDF) can be a good choice since flatness is essential, although solid wood, provided with cleats to keep it flat if it is not massive enough to remain stable, may be a better choice to avoid wear on peg holes becoming so great that the pegs can no longer be held in position.

WALL FORM

NOTE ALSO THAT THE PEG FORM CAN BE USED vertically as well as horizontally, transforming it into a so-called wall form, thus taking up less space in the shop.

SOLID BENDING FORM

WHILE AN ALL-PURPOSE PEG FORM MIGHT BE generally useful for a variety of projects, should

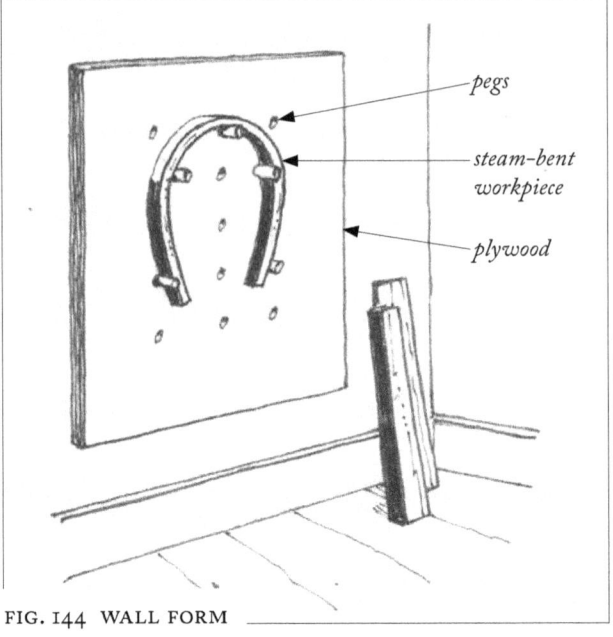

FIG. 144 WALL FORM

the same shape be needed repeatedly — as when repeatedly forming bent backs for a set of chairs or other production articles — a purpose-built form should be constructed. Such a form will provide a solid shape against which the workpiece can

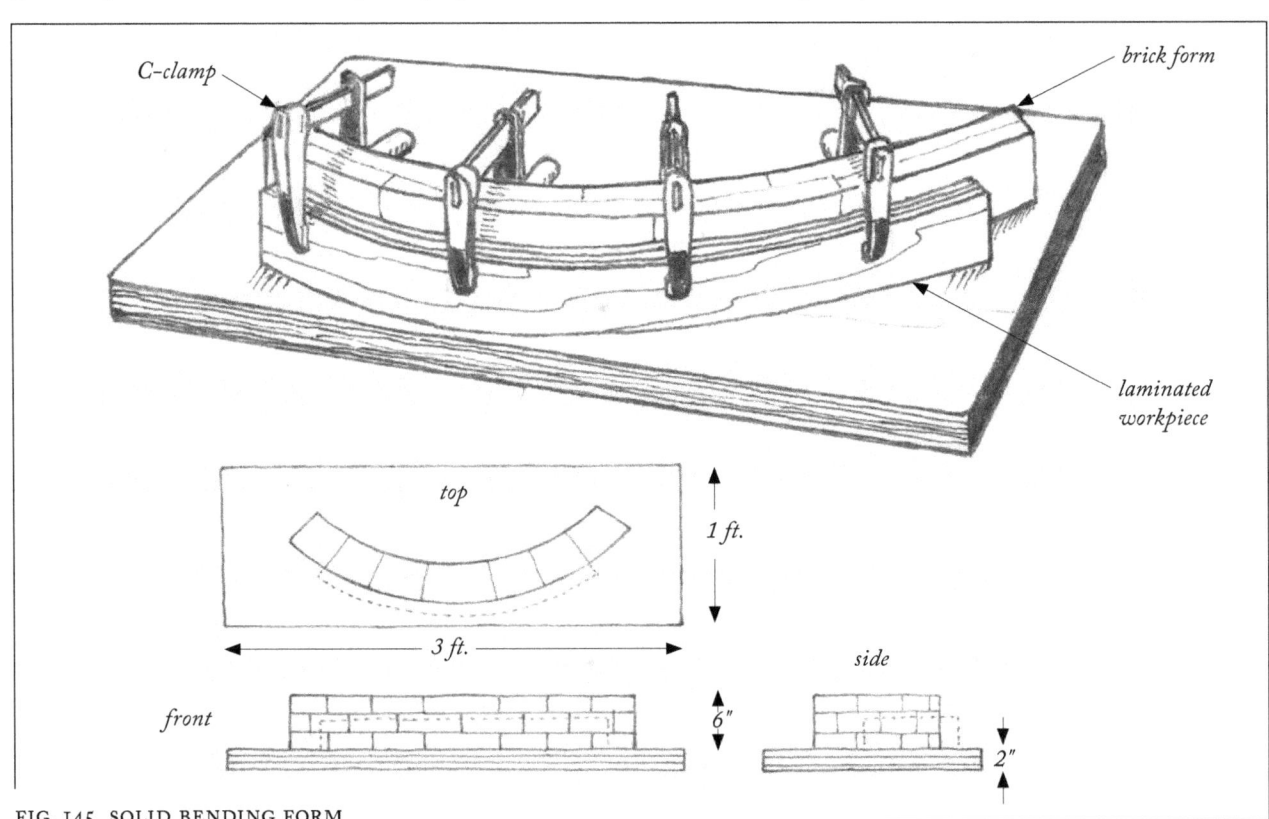

FIG. 145 SOLID BENDING FORM

be clamped, and eliminate the need to measure repeatedly or provide more holes.

A solid form can be made either by being sawed out from a solid piece or by being built up from brick-like sections glued into a rough approximation of the required form which is then sawed and sanded into the finish profile.

The entire form should be mounted on its own backing board which, of course, should be perfectly flat. Make the actual form part strong and wide enough to clamp any steamed workpiece or glued-up laminates to it without risk of deformation.

GLUING & ADHESIVE TAPE:

WATERPROOF ADHESIVE TAPE HAS MANY USES connected with the glue-up part of assembly, and as such adhesive tape may be thought of as multi-purpose disposable shop jig.

GLUE-BLOCK PROTECTOR

THE PRIMARY USE OF A GLUE-BLOCK protector is to prevent glue from inadvertently attaching parts not required to be attached — such as blocks and cauls used in glue-up — where the use of wax paper is not possible.

SQUEEZE-OUT PROTECTOR

EQUALLY OBJECTIONABLE TO DISCOVERING THAT your glue-up blocks or clamp spacers have become glued to the workpiece is, after everything has dried and you are ready to start the finishing stage of the project, to find glue squeeze-out in especially hard-to-clean corners such as the interior areas of dovetailed casework, the insides of small drawers, and partition joints.

A little tape judiciously applied in these places before assembly can be more easily removed than cleaning up any squeeze-out.

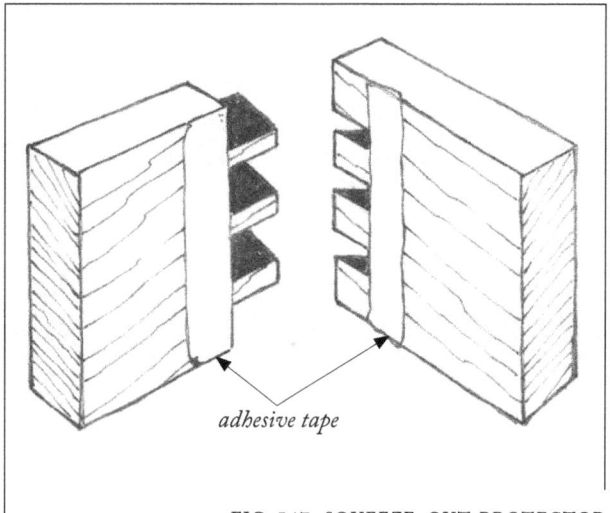

FIG. 147 SQUEEZE-OUT PROTECTOR

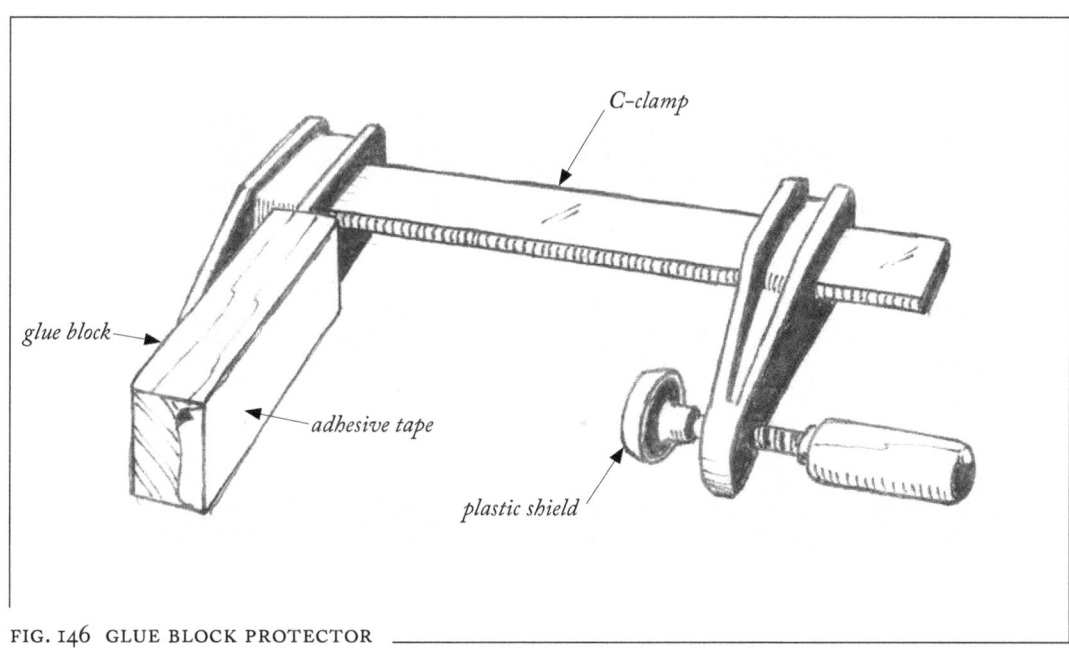

FIG. 146 GLUE BLOCK PROTECTOR

GLUE-SURFACE PROTECTOR

IT IS OFTEN EASIER TO APPLY FINISH TO constituent parts of a project before assembly, but finish in the wrong place can, depending on the kind of glue used, impair glue adhesion. Thus tape applied in areas to be glued can protect them from excessive finish. The tape should be removed, of course, before glue-up, perhaps to be replaced by tape instead now protecting the finished areas from glue.

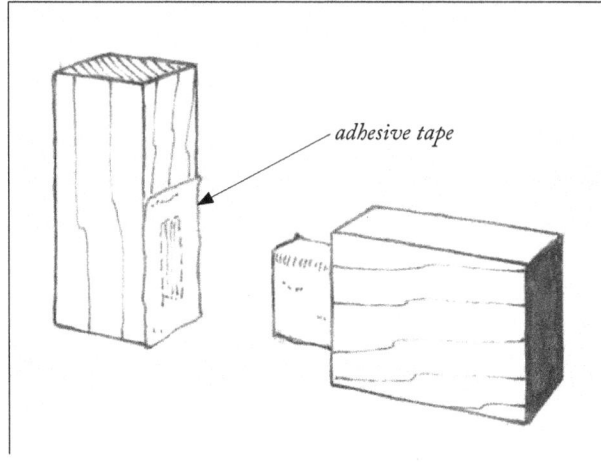

FIG. 148 GLUE-SURFACE PROTECTOR

TAPE REPAIR

TAPE CAN ALSO BE USED TO KEEP PARTS TOGETHER that are too small to be clamped. It can be especially useful for gluing small repairs such as splinters that may have been inadvertently chipped off during assembly.

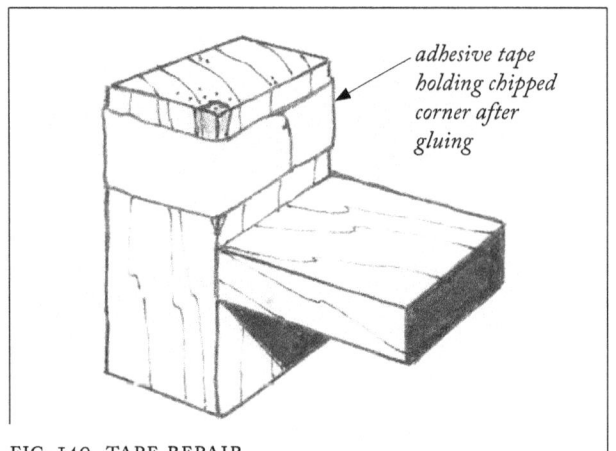

FIG. 149 TAPE REPAIR

II: FINISHING:

SANDING:

THE TRADITIONAL WOODWORKER MAY ESCHEW electric sanders in favor of the superior finish obtainable by proper planing but still find reasons occasionally to use abrasive paper. Although sandpaper is generally available in sheets of standard sizes, one of the first jobs is often to reduce a sheet to a more usable size.

SANDPAPER DIVIDER

YOU WILL OFTEN FIND IT CONVENIENT TO USE abrasive paper of various kinds in smaller pieces than whole sheets, transverse thirds being among the most common size needed. Speed and consistent uniformity in making such strips can be greatly improved with the use of this simple jig, rather than risking torn and uneven pieces separated by hand.

For the most efficient use of this jig, illustrated on the opposite page, it helps to place the sheet of abrasive paper against the fence and then fold it before placing it face down on the base and tearing it against the edge.

Not all abrasive-paper manufacturers produce sheets to the same size, so measure those you use carefully before making this jig. One of the more common sizes will use a jig that measures 12 in. long by 4-1/2in wide from the edge of the fence to the edge of the base. Whatever size you need, provide a flat base that is as long as the paper, and wide enough so that with the central fence attached (which fence need be no more that 1/2in. to 1in. wide), a width equal to exactly one third of the paper's width (or one half if this is preferred) is left on both sides. Plywood may be a particularly good choice for the base since, if cut cleanly to size, the edge against which the paper is torn will remain sharp longer than a piece of softwood, such as pine.

SANDPAPER HOLDERS:

ALMOST ALL SURFACES THAT MAY NEED TO BE sanded will benefit from the use of holders or

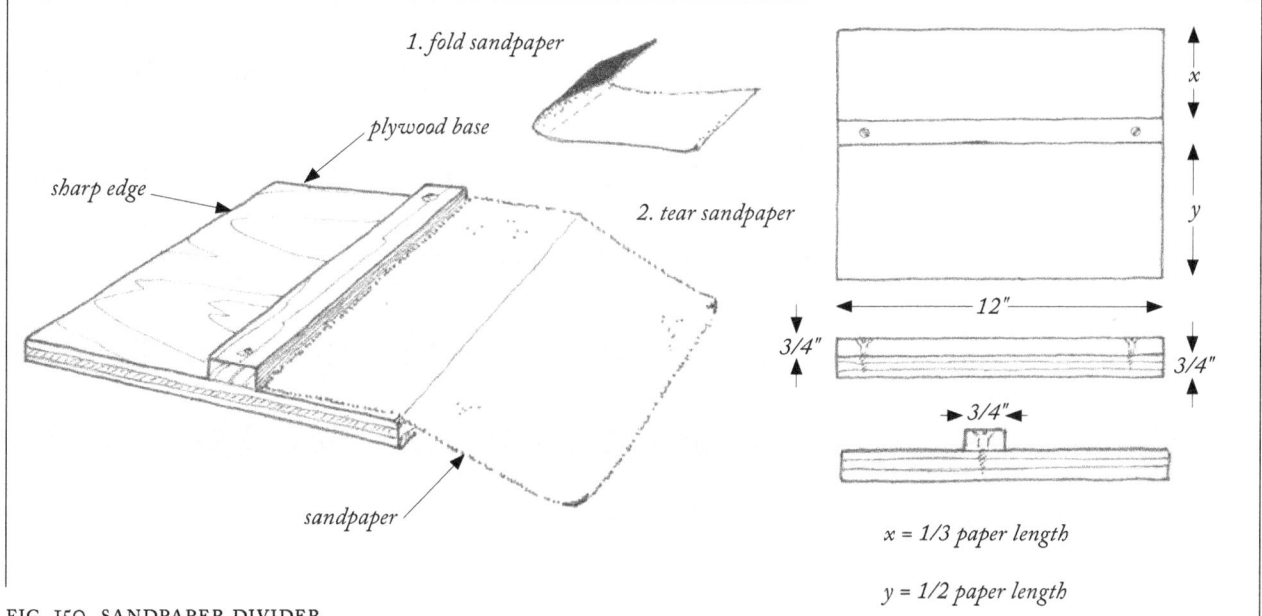

FIG. 150 SANDPAPER DIVIDER

rubbers which distribute the pressure evenly rather than being sanded freehand.

Flat surfaces especially are best sanded with abrasive paper wrapped around a flat block in order to maintain the flatness of the surface being sanded. Large areas are most easily sanded if a sanding plane as described below is used.

SANDING PLANE

MAKE THE BASE FROM SOLID WOOD AT LEAST 1 in. thick and approximately 7 in. wide by 11 in. long, so that a standard 9 in. by 11 in. sheet of abrasive paper may be torn in half with enough paper left at the edges to be pushed into narrow grooves.

Cut these grooves using a narrow grooving plane or even a simple scratch stock or even a hand router into the sides of the block.

Paper pushed into these grooves can be easily held in place with a long thin wedge. For a more easily used fixture recycle old plane totes and front knobs. If these are attached by screws through the underside of the plate be sure to countersink them well so they do not damage whatever abrasive paper you use.

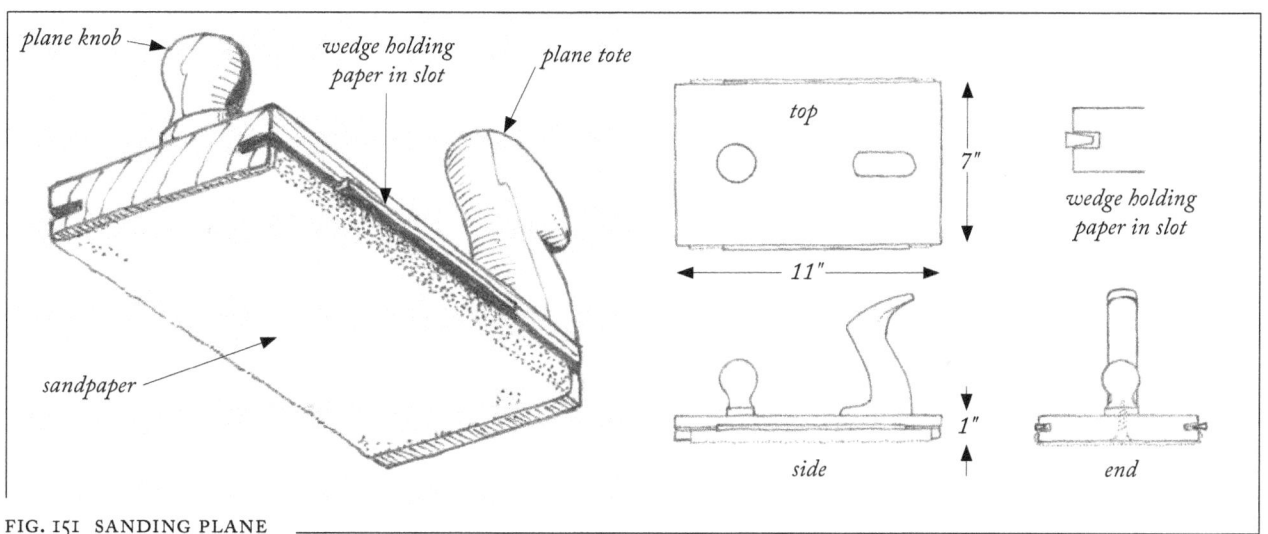

FIG. 151 SANDING PLANE

TRADITIONAL JIGS & FIXTURES

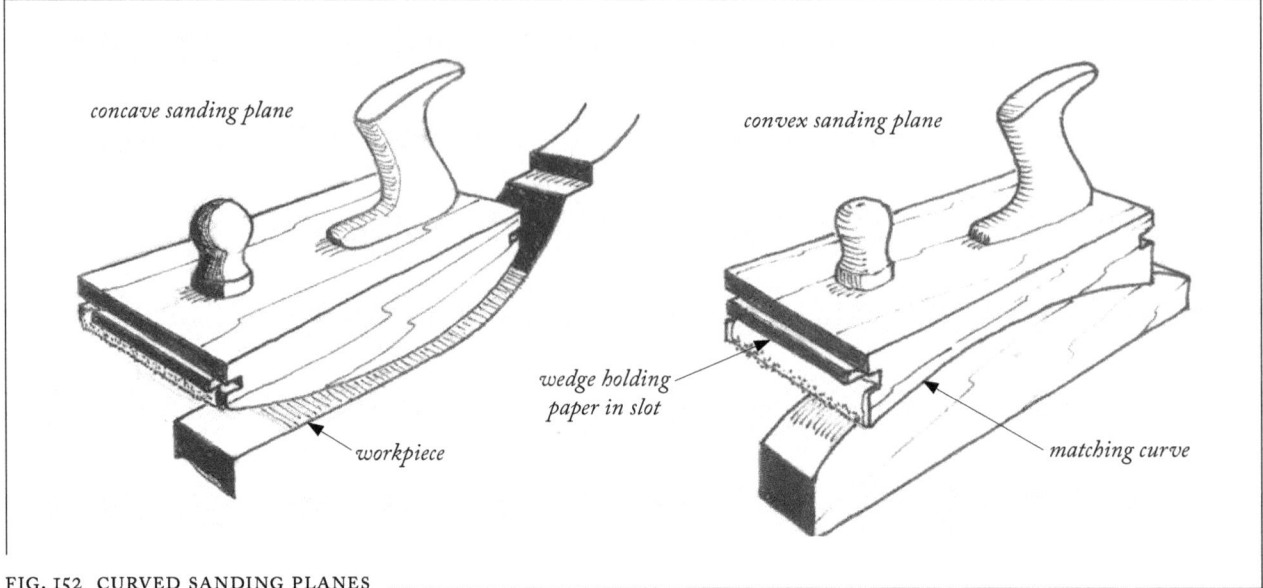

FIG. 152 CURVED SANDING PLANES

CURVED SANDING PLANES

CURVED OR OTHERWISE SHAPED SURFACES ARE similarly best sanded with the abrasive paper wrapped around a sanding plane made with a base matching the shape to be sanded.

SANDING RUBBERS

THE CHIEF RISK IN SANDING MOULDED PROFILES lies in dubbing over crisp edges. Just as complicated mouldings can be built up by using several simpler shapes, so can rubbers — small pieces of hardwood carefully finished to mirror a particular profile — of simple shapes such as coves, rounds, and quirks be used successively in combination to finish complicated profiles.

SANDING SHOOTING BOARD

THE TRADITIONAL APPROACH TO A MODERN powered sanding wheel with an attached and

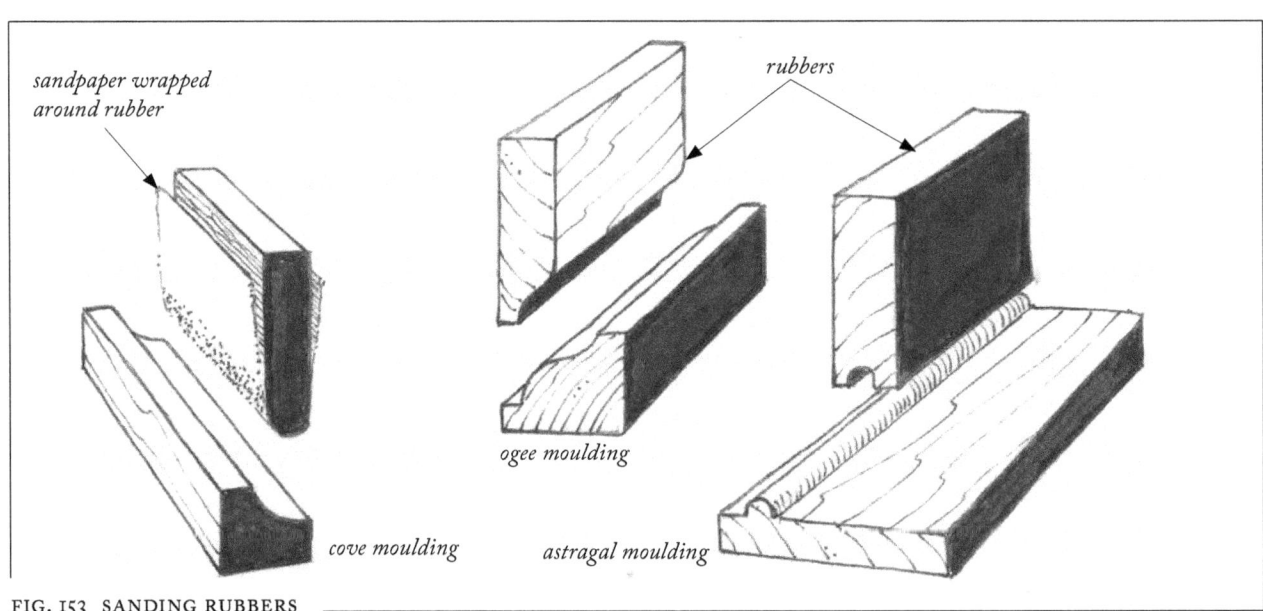

FIG. 153 SANDING RUBBERS

TRADITIONAL JIGS & FIXTURES

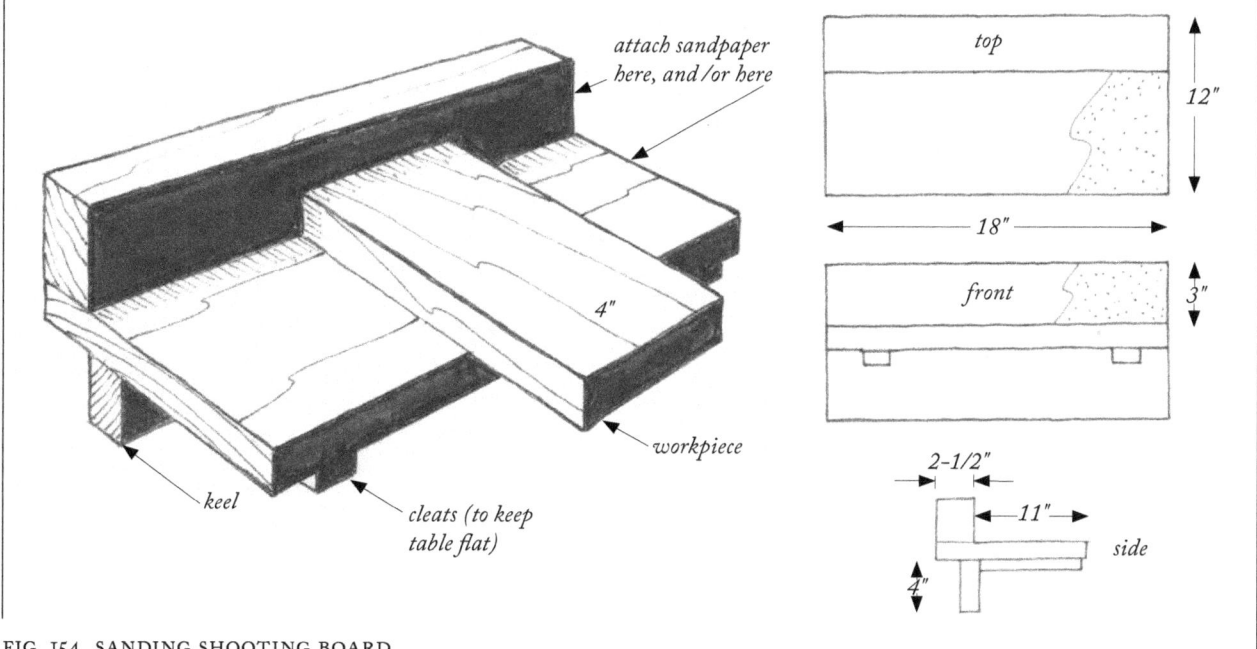

FIG. 154 SANDING SHOOTING BOARD

adjustable table that allows adjacent surfaces to be sanded at precise angles to each other is a far simpler fixture known as the sanding shooting-board. Similar to a bench hook in construction, the sanding shooting-board has sandpaper fixed either to the surface of the board or to the inside of the hooks allowing the workpiece to be shot smooth while maintaining perfect flatness or — when abrasive paper is attached (with rubber cement) to the hooks — a perfectly square edge. Similarly to shooting boards used for planing, a sanding board may also be made with either its hook or its bed at an angle other than 90°, or alternatively, when edges at angles other than at 90° need to be sanded, be used with an angled or wedged bed.

LIPPING SANDER

SANDING ANY KIND OF VENEER, INLAY, OR marquetry work is always fraught with the danger of sanding through the thin applied layer. This is

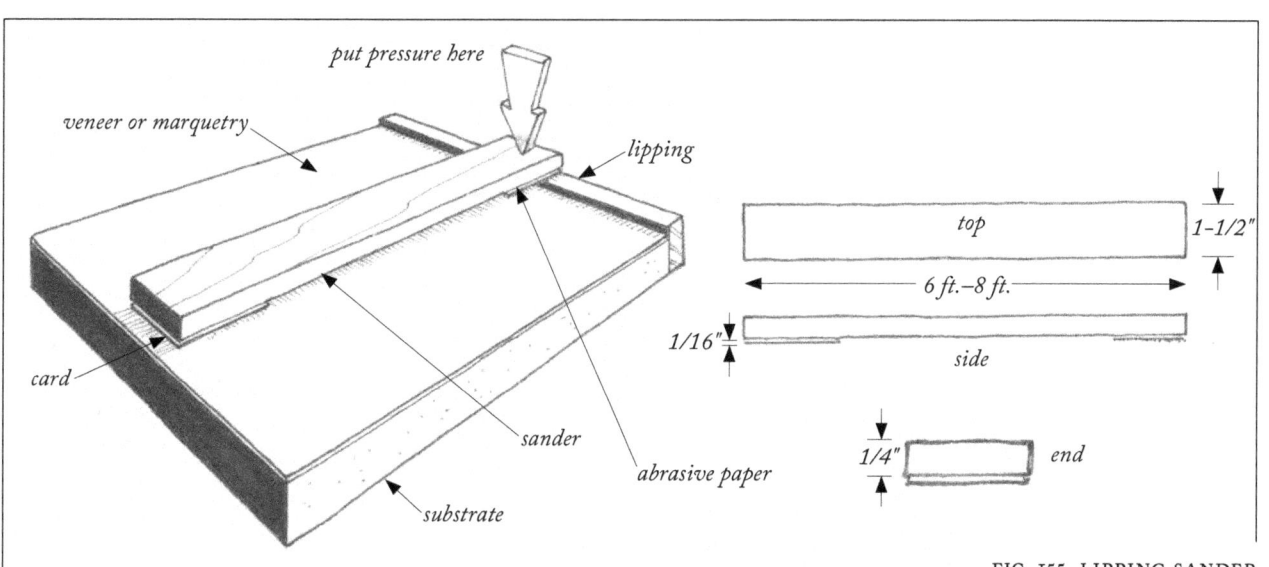

FIG. 155 LIPPING SANDER

ASSEMBLY & FINISHING

especially true when attempting to level surrounding solid wood material such as lippings, edgings, or mouldings with the veneered surface. The danger can be largely overcome with the use of the lipping sander, which permits flush leveling without damaging the veneer. Pressure on the abrasive end when applied to the area to be sanded is relieved at the other end by the protective masking tape which is thereby prevented from damaging the workpiece.

A strip of relatively narrow material, perhaps 1-1/2in. wide, thin enough to be slightly deformed under moderate pressure, and about 8in. long, is faced at one end with adhesive abrasive paper of the desired grit, or stuck on with double-sided tape. At the other end of this strip, and on the same face, a couple of layers of masking tape or a piece of thin card are applied sufficient to prevent the strip from rubbing the surface but still keep the area being sanded essentially level with the overall surface of the workpiece.

STRADDLE SANDER

SIMILAR IN CONCEPT TO THE PREVIOUS JIG is the straddle sander, which, as its name implies, allows for levelled sanding of a given interior area of inlay without impacting the surrounding area. The differences between the two jigs are that the straddle sander has abrasive paper attached to a similarly narrow and relatively inflexible strip in the center of the strip rather than at one end, and that both ends are furnished with layers of masking tape or perhaps a piece of thin card.

FINISH PROTECTION:

FINISHING SUPPORT BOARD

IN ORDER TO AVOID DRY-LINES AND UNEVEN coverage it is often advisable to apply finish to the entire piece at the same time. This is sometimes difficult to do, however, since part of the piece may necessarily always be in contact with some other surface, such as the floor or a wall. A board provided with appropriately spaced pins or small pyramids of wood can be an invaluable fixture in the finishing shop. Touch-up of the tiny areas that may have rested on the pins or pyramids is usually far easier than refinishing an entire surface.

FINISH PROTECTORS

IT IS OFTEN NECESSARY TO CONTINUE WORK ON a piece after finish has been applied. One or two scrap blocks covered with carpet, clean excess toweling, or some other soft fabric on which the workpiece can be supported without danger of being scratched or dented can save a lot of retouch time.

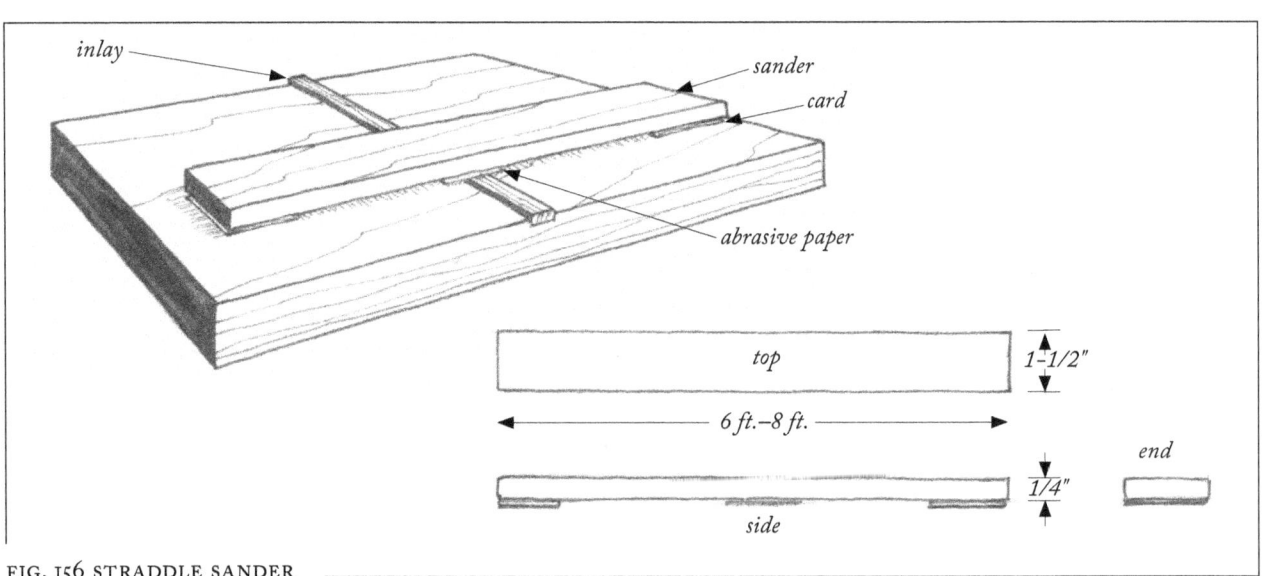

FIG. 156 STRADDLE SANDER

TRADITIONAL JIGS & FIXTURES

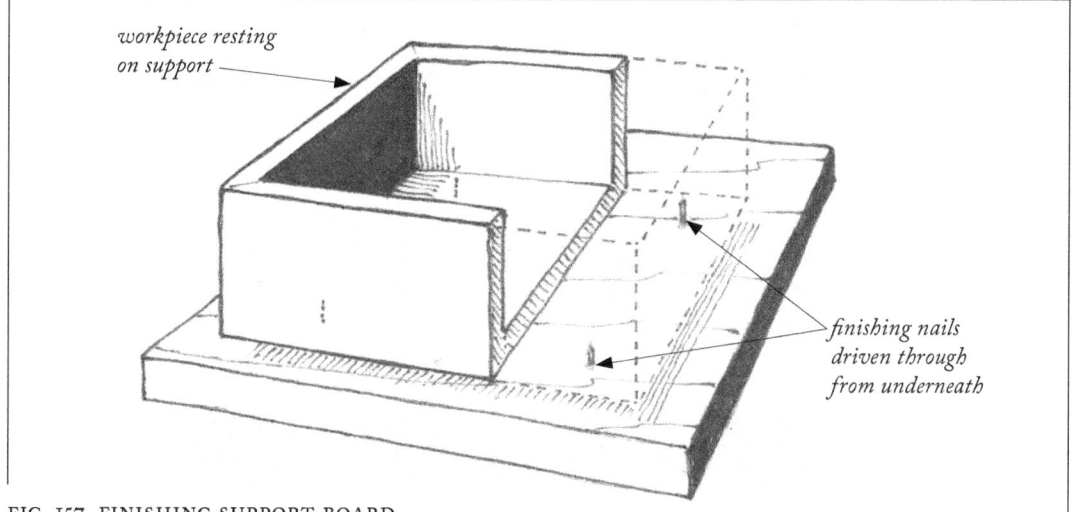

FIG. 157 FINISHING SUPPORT BOARD

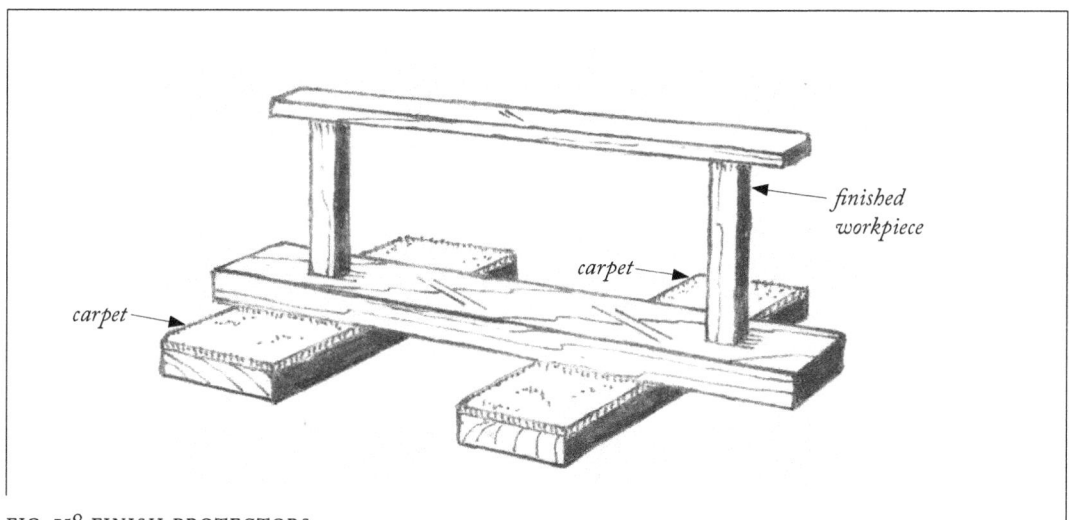

FIG. 158 FINISH PROTECTORS

ASSEMBLY & FINISHING

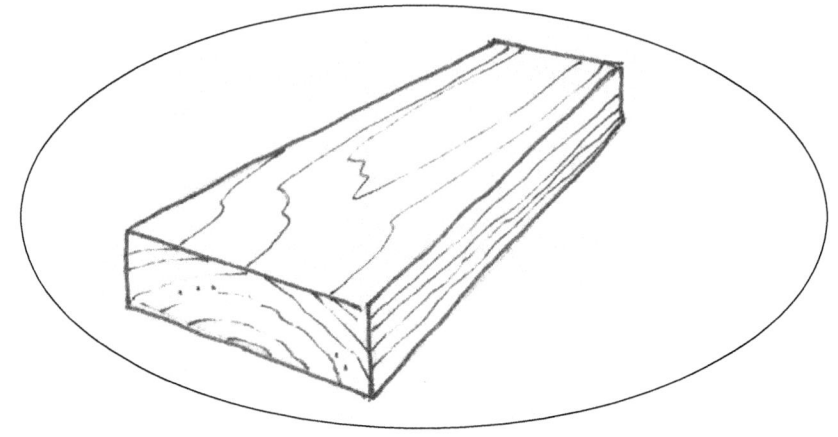

APPENDICES

1

SHARPENING

Sharpening lies at the very heart of traditional woodworking. While powertools may be able in some instances to work by force, being so much more powerful than the human hand or arm, most handtools — apart from various striking and holding tools — invariably require sharpening. And, as every traditional woodworker sooner or later discovers, the better they are sharpened the easier they are to use and the better they work.

There are, of course, many ways to sharpen, many theories, and much equipment, but some things remain the same — metal and edges. One only has to look at masterpieces from the past to realize that, strange as it may seem, fine work was somehow accomplished without the most recent, high-tech toys we enjoy today. Fundamental to the process are sharpening stones and the edges they produce. Without wishing to impugn other techniques, far less to deny the validity and usefulness of more modern methods, what follows are a few traditional approaches that are guaranteed to work.

Sharpening is essentially the process of reducing the cutting edge of a metal blade from whatever thickness it may be down to the thinnest possible dimension before it no longer exists. The thinner the edge the sharper the blade may be said to be. But there is a trade-off to be borne in mind: the thinner the edge the sharper it is but the quicker it will wear down — and become blunt again.

Three things affect the rate at which this ultimate sharpest edge breaks down: the quality of the metal comprising the blade, the length of the bevel that forms the edge, and, of course, the material the edge is being asked to cut. This last being also a function of various factors such as the hardness of the wood, its particular grain structure, and the amount of mineral content that may be present in any particular species.

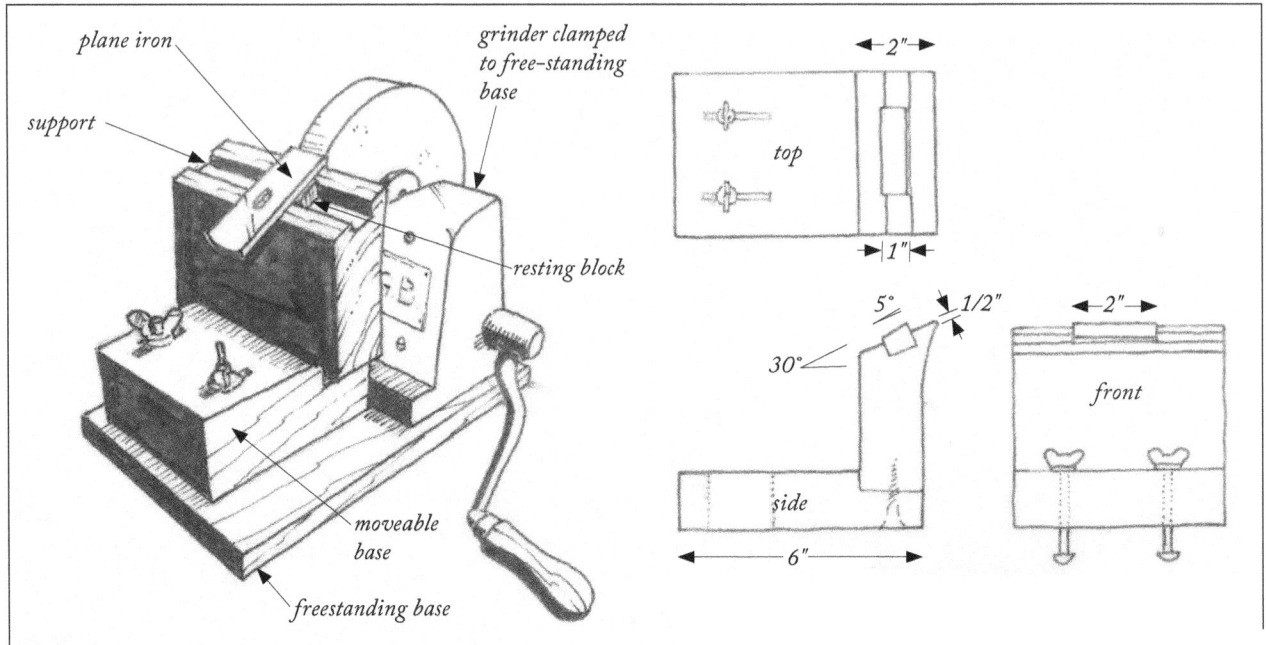

FIG. AI HAND-GRINDER BLADE SUPPORT

HAND-GRINDER BLADE SUPPORT

As a consequence of so many variables certain compromises have been established over time that reflect more useful approaches to a situation that may change as you go from project to project. The first of these has to do with the actual bevel, since the longer the bevel the sharper the edge, but as we have already noted, the sharper the edge the quicker it breaks down. Averaging most situations out — the quality of the metal and the material being cut (and incidentally, strictly speaking we are never *cutting* the material so much as separating the cellular structure that comprises the wood) — bevels formed between 25° and 35° tend to last, and remain efficient, the longest. Here is where we may meet our first sharpening jig: the hand-grinder rest.

The lowly hand-grinder as used by the traditional woodworker possesses one significant advantage over motorized grinders: it is very difficult to draw the temper of a blade being ground on a hand-grinder because it simply does not turn fast enough to generate any temper-destroying heat. It is, however, difficult to use since one hand is always employed in turning the grinder and the other hand is all that is left to hold the blade being sharpened at the critical angle. Some hand-grinders may be furnished with a small metal bracket on which to rest the tool being ground, but results are never as satisfactory as they are with the following jig.

THERE ARE TWO IMPORTANT PARTS TO THIS JIG. The first is the moveable base, which allows the support to be adjusted right up to the wheel, and the second is the actual resting block (often one of several, designed to produce differently angled bevels), which slides from side to side in a groove cut in the top of the support. The blade to be sharpened can be held with one hand on the sliding resting block and moved across its entire width against the wheel without fear of being skewed as it is moved. In this way the bevel, and the transverse angle at which it is formed on the end of the blade, remain constant.

An almost universal feature of many of today's contemporary hand-grinders is the clamp that secures them to a horizontal board, bracket, or shelf. They can with this clamp be secured now to a separate, free-standing 6 in.–8 in.-wide base to which is also secured a sliding L-shaped part, the base of which is slotted and secured with adjustable screws (or bolts and wingnuts) to the free-standing base — which in turn can be mounted somewhere convenient in the shop, possibly to its own purpose-built grinding stand.

The upright part of the L-shaped part is bevelled at approximately 30°, and abuts the grinding wheel when positioned as closely to it as possible some little way below the center of the wheel. This upright part should be thick enough — 2 in. or so — to allow a 1 in. wide groove no more than 1/2 in. deep to be cut in it from side to side. A separate block, about 2 in. wide, sufficient to support comfortably both chisels as well as most plane irons, is made to fit snugly but moveably in the slot. The top of this sliding block may be further bevelled to produced any required angle on the cutting edge. It is usually most convenient to have two or three such blocks, so that cutting-iron bevels of 25°, 30°, and maybe even steeper, can be ground.

If the sides and bottom of the block and groove are waxed, it will be easy with one hand to hold the blade being sharpened securely against the block, and at the same time be introduced against the wheel without the angle of the required bevel being compromised in any way by rocking or tilting.

SHARPENING STONES:

USING A HAND-GRINDER TYPICALLY CONSTITUTES the first stage in sharpening, whereby the basic straightness and bevel is established by rapid but coarse removal of metal. Once the tool's cutting edge has been thus correctly formed, all that remains is the elimination, so far as possible, of the scratches left by the coarse composition of the grinding wheel. This is achieved by the use of a series of graduated sharpening stones, each possessing progressively finer grit than the previous one. In order to do this without altering the bevel formed on the grinder and in addition both to form and maintain a perfectly flat back on the opposite side of the cutting tool from its bevel, two things are necessary: one, a perfectly flat surface of the stone — since you cannot sharpen anything flatter than the flatness of the stone on which it is being sharpened — and two, some way of consistently holding the tool at the required angle without rocking, so that the bevel remains flat as formed on the grinding wheel.

OILSTONES

THE DEDICATED TRADITIONAL WOODWORKER WILL eschew powered sharpening machines, and will primarily use sharpening stones of one sort or another. Many people make the mistake of believing (probably because they have observed previous generations of woodworkers using them) that using an oilstone is a more traditional method than using the recently introduced waterstones.

The truth of the matter is that for a long time before the introduction of oilstones all stones used water both as a lubricant and a medium for washing away broken-down stone particles and removed metal. It was primarily with the advent of large scale whaling operations in the nineteenth century that whale oil began to be used as a lubricant thanks to the enterprising advertising of those involved in its marketing. It is true that being considerably finer than much commercially produced mineral oil whale oil worked well, but it has been a long time since

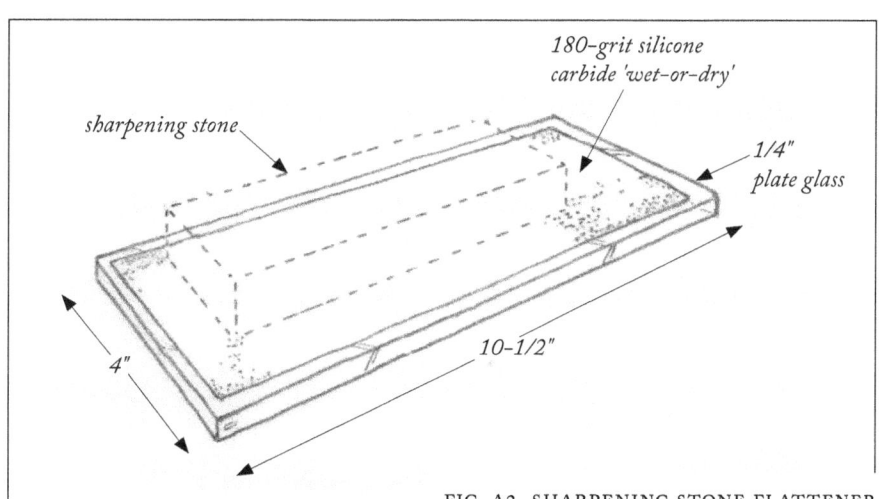

FIG. A2 SHARPENING STONE FLATTENER

whale oil has been generally available, and probably longer since anyone used it for lubricating those stones used for sharpening woodworking tools. As a result, the typical oilstone when unearthed from your grandfather's workshop is invariably a messy affair, its surface clogged with frequent applications of heavy proprietary oils such as 3-in-One™, and its flatness long since a thing of the past. And yet very often these are still useful stones. What needs to be done is first to bake out the old oil by leaving them in the oven at 350° for a couple of hours (preferably in a metal tray to catch the extruded oil) and then to flatten them with the sharpening stone flattener as described below.

SHARPENING STONE FLATTENER

REGARDLESS OF THE KIND OF STONE BEING USED it should be kept as flat as possible, bearing in mind that absolute flatness is always lost the moment any cutting tool is passed across it the first time. It therefore helps enormously if the stone is dressed frequently during use by being rubbed on a known flat surface. Depending on the hardness as well as the grit composition of any given stone it is not unreasonable to spend as much time flattening the stone as it is using it.

All that is needed for a sharpening-stone flattener is a piece of quarter-inch-thick plate glass a little larger than the stone itself, and a piece of 180-grit wet-or-dry silicone carbide sandpaper as shown in FIG. A2 on the previous page.

Cut the sandpaper to match the glass and attach it with a smear of silicone adhesive (because this is waterproof). Both items are commonly available and more than adequate for the job, although more expensive stone-dressing blocks and diamond encrusted flattening plates can also be bought.

You now possess an abrasive surface flat enough to keep your stones flat — which you can recognize by observing the surface of the rubbed stone: when it is evenly clean across its entire surface it will be flat.

WEDGED STONE-HOLDER

NOTE THAT ONCE CLEAN AND FLAT, OILSTONES, JUST like waterstones, may be used with water as a lubricant, just as did Thomas Chippendale's workers in that most famous of British cabinetmakers' shops over two hundred and fifty years ago. But something that will make the process easier, both for oilstones as well as waterstones is a wedged stone-holder set in a shallow waterproof tray.

USING A SHARPENING STONE

BEFORE STARTING TO REMOVE THE SCRATCHES left by the grinding wheel on any newly formed

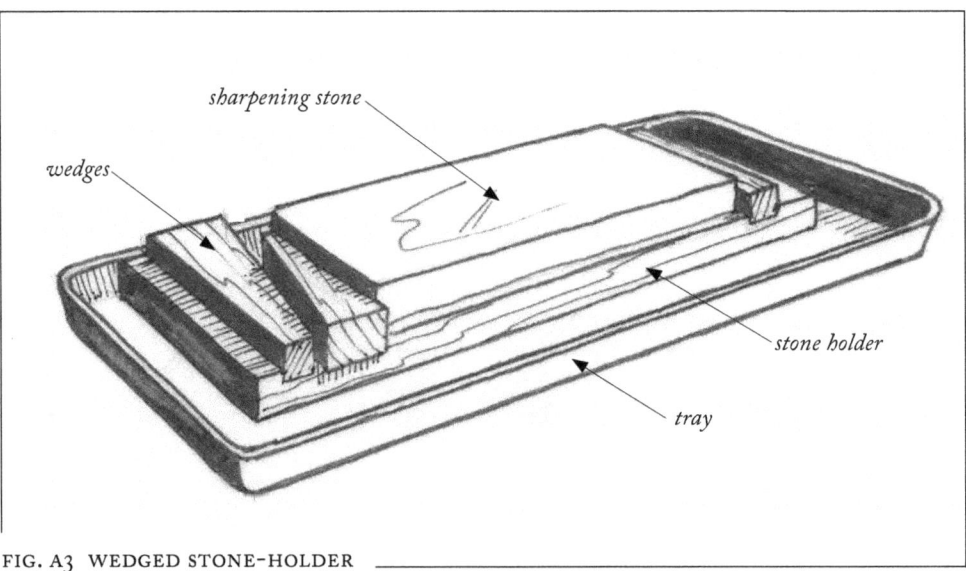

FIG. A3 WEDGED STONE-HOLDER

bevel you should make sure that the back of the cutting tool (chisel, plane iron, etc.) is perfectly flat.

Holding the back of the tool back-side down on the sharpening stone flattener will quickly show how flat the back is. If it is perfectly flat, then scratches left by the wet-or-dry will show up across the entire surface of the back where it is rubbed. Note that you do not need to flatten the entire back, but only from the tip to an inch or so up the back. If, however, scratches show only in the middle of this area then you have a little more work to do before addressing the bevel, because a curved back meeting a flat bevel will produce a thickening edge rather than a uniformly thin edge.

Once you are sure that bevel and back are both flat and meet at an arris that is nicely perpendicular along its length to the sides of the tool being sharpened you are ready to start the process of making these two surfaces as smooth as possible on an actual sharpening stone. But one other thing to bear in mind is that not all tools with a cutting edge have parallel sides, so measuring the perpendicularity just mentioned may not be possible with a trysquare. Rather, you should aim to have this edge perpendicular to a longitudinal center line imagined down the length of the blade.

Begin by working on the bevel. There are three ways to ensure that this remains flat while being rubbed on the stone. The first and ultimately the best way, for reasons to be explained a little further on, is simply to use finger pressure alone. If the bevel and the stone are indeed flat, then it should be possible to place a finger (or two, depending on the size of the blade being sharpened) on the back of the blade behind the bevel and press so that the two surfaces make perfect contact. When you are sure you can feel this then you can start to move the bevel against the stone, but remain vigilant about being able to feel that the contact is complete between the two surfaces. With a little practice this becomes second nature, but if you move too fast in the beginning you will surely lose the awareness of how perfect the contact is, and the bevel will inevitably become rounded over.

The second way is to buy a so-called honing guide. While this may ensure that the bevel remains constant it has three disadvantages. First is that the majority of manufactured honing guides require the blade to be moved backwards and forwards, with the result that scratches left by the stone being used, no matter how fine a grit and how fine the resultant scratches, run right off the end of the cutting edge.

Look at such an edge under a magnifying glass and you will see that this translates into a serrated edge, the tips of which serrations are easily broken off resulting in bluntness. To avoid this the edge might be moved not backwards and forwards but from side to side — something impossible when using a honing guide. Of course, a sideways motion producing scratches parallel to the cutting edge is also not ideal since while no scratch will run off the edge, a single such parallel scratch is especially vulnerable to being broken off completely, leaving a wide blunt edge. The compromise is to sharpen at a 45° angle to the length of the stone — something more easily done by hand than using the guide.

The second disadvantage of a honing guide is that there is always a risk of the edge digging into the stone with consequent damage both to the tools's edge and the flatness of the stone.

The third disadvantage, which can intensify the second disadvantage, is that there is a tendency to put too much downwards pressure on the cutting edge. Such pressure in no way increases the cutting action of the stone and may in fact simply render the stone less efficient. The pressure needed to keep the bevel flat against the stone exerted by one or two fingers alone is perfect.

BEVEL SUPPORT

THE THIRD AND BEST WAY IS TO USE A PURPOSE-made bevel support, made from a block of ideally close-grained hardwood such as boxwood, although coarser-grained species will also serve. The cutting tool can then be held against this block and the two items moved as one over the entire surface of the sharpening stone while at the same time being held at 45° to the longitudinal axis of the stone.

Two things to consider when making this jig are that the support should be wide enough and big enough comfortably to support the item being sharpened, and that the angle should be appropriate.

For most purposes 25° will be found to be ideal. If, after having been sharpened completely at this

TRADITIONAL JIGS & FIXTURES

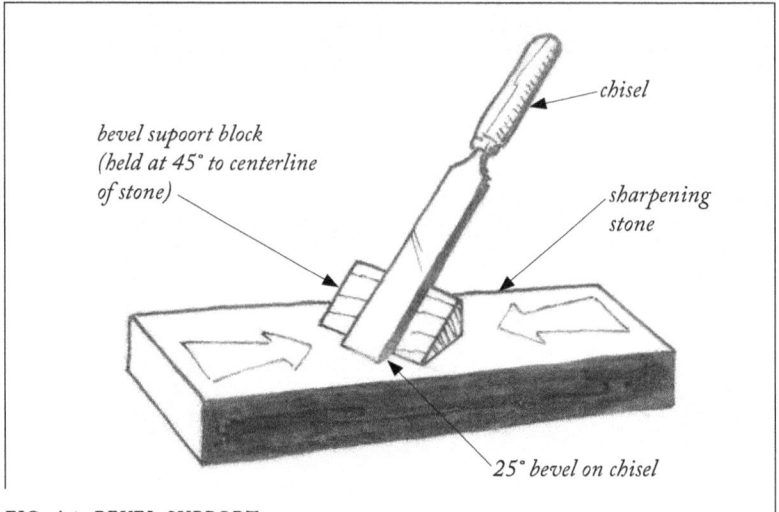

FIG. A4 BEVEL SUPPORT

angle and then used for a time it is discovered that the edge breaks down too quickly (depending of course on the species of wood it is being asked to cut) then make another block with a steeper angle — perhaps 30°. On the other hand if the cutting edge seems to last a long time, then this may be an indication of a better-quality metal which might now be profitably sharpened at a lower angle — since the longer the bevel the more easily the edge will separate the cellular structure of the wood.

When all the scratches left by the grinding wheel have been replaced by scratches resulting from the first stone you use — ideally fairly coarse, perhaps 1000-grit, since a finer grit stone will simply take longer to remove coarser scratches — resist the temptation to feel for a wire edge on the back of the blade, since this may result in breaking off the wire edge, leaving you with a blunt edge. Instead, place the back of the tool on the stone carefully, and wear, rather than break, the wire edge off. You will know this has been done when the back, just like the front, no longer shows any of the original coarse scratches.

The remainder of the sharpening process is simply a matter of progressing through a series of increasingly finer grit stones. Stones may be found with extremely fine grits, but there is little point in sharpening with a stone whose grit is finer than the cellular structure of the particular species you are planing to cut. In general this means that edges sharpened with 8,000-grit to 10,000-grit stones are more than sufficient.

One last aspect of the sharpening process bears mentioning, and involves perhaps the simplest jig or fixture of all — the heel of your hand. Stropping the finished tool against the heel of your hand by alternately dragging both sides of the tool off your hand will wear off the most minuscule remaining wire edge. This is a technique that is also useful for a stop-gap resharpening if you find yourself in the middle of a planing or cutting operation and do not want to stop work to go through the entire sharpening process. Note however, that using an old-fashioned barber's strop of the kind once used for sharpening traditional so-called 'straight razors' is not a good idea because such action will round over the cutting edge; this may be fine for carving tools, but it is less than ideal for paring chisels and plane irons.

SCRAPER PLANE BLADE SUPPORT

AN IMPORTANT EXCEPTION TO THE TYPICAL angles of bevels formed on single-edge cutting tools is the angle found on the blades used in scraper planes. In actuality, the scraper plane blade is not a plane iron, but rather a scraper held in a plane-like body. As such it does not work exactly like a plane, either single-iron or double-iron, but instead uses a short, 45° bevel, the edge of which is sometimes turned, with the plane being used to scrape rather than cut. Such a blade can nonetheless have its bevel formed similarly to that of other cutting edges, but

TRADITIONAL JIGS & FIXTURES

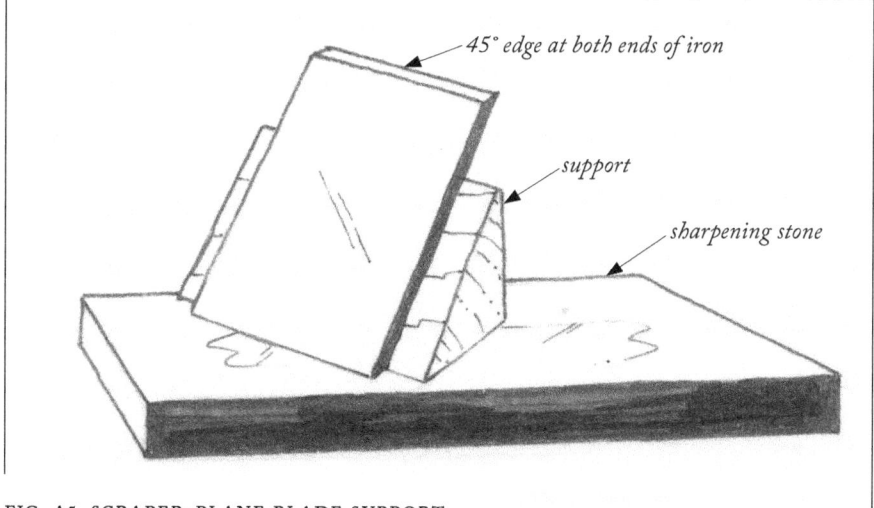

FIG. A5 SCRAPER-PLANE BLADE SUPPORT

it must be sharpened at such a steep angle (45°) that a blade support is almost an absolute necessity.

The scraper-plane blade support is similar in all respects to the bevel support described opposite except for size and dimensions.

SPOKESHAVE SHARPENING HOLDER

SPOKESHAVE BLADES ALSO NEED TO SHARPENED with a bevel, but being so small it is more convenient to place them into a holder rather than to attempt to hold them against an angle block. If such a block is made large enough in additional to being held easily by hand, it can also be held against a bevel support as described above.

As well as being slotted so as to hold securely the spokeshave blade, the holder may also be fitted with a screw to tighten both sides of the slot down against the blade. In order to be used with the bevel support, the holder block should also be carefully made with a back that is perfectly parallel to the back of the blade itself.

DRAWKNIFE REST

WHEN IT COMES TO SHARPENING TRADITIONAL woodworking cutting edges, the drawknife presents the greatest challenge. These tools are virtually all different, as a look at any traditional woodworking tool catalogue will show; every variety has a different

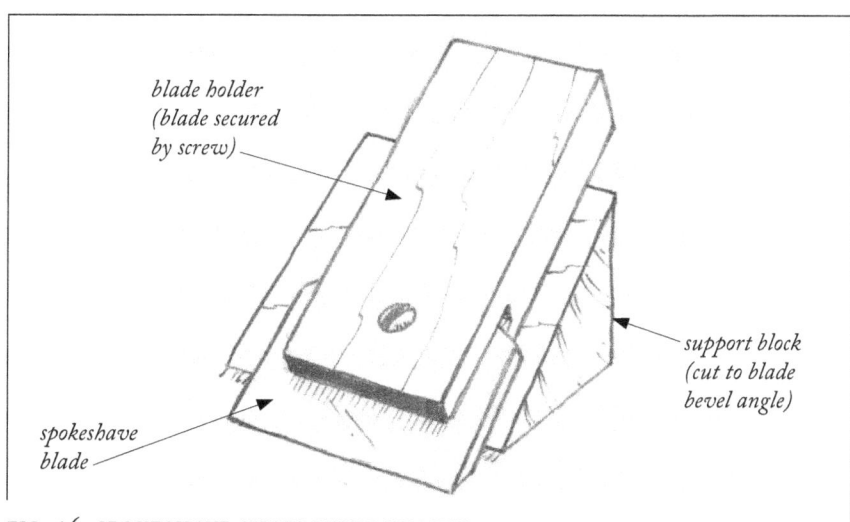

FIG. A6 SPOKESHAVE SHARPENING HOLDER

SHARPENING

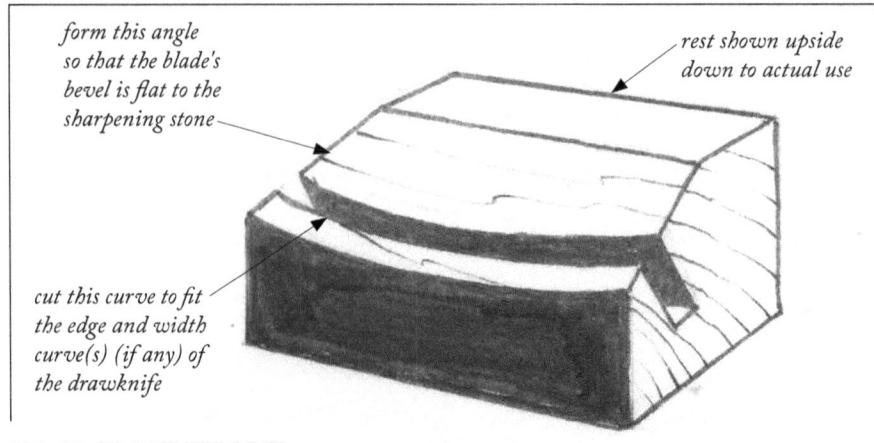

FIG. A7 DRAWKNIFE REST

profile and a different curve. It was common therefore to sharpen these tools freehand in much the same way that an axe or hatchet is sharpened: by bringing the sharpening stone to the tool rather than the other way round. Nevertheless, if you have a particular favourite it will be found useful to make a custom fitted rest that will allow the tool to be presented to a stone at the optimum angle for the desired bevel. By also mirroring the lateral curve of the drawknife at the base of the holder it becomes possible to maintain the bevel angle across the entire width of the tool.

2

SELECT BIBLIOGRAPHY

TRADITIONAL JIGS & FIXTURES FOR THE HANDTOOL WOODWORKER IS THE FIFTH VOLUME IN THE ILLUSTRATED WORKSHOP SERIES, EACH PREVIOUS VOLUME OF WHICH I HAVE INTENDED TO BE READ AS A STAND-ALONE WORK, BUT ALL OF WHICH TAKEN TOGETHER CONSTITUTE a useful and logically sequential understanding of the traditional handcraft of woodworking.

What follows is a brief description of the previous four volumes together with some of my favorite books that I have enjoyed over the years and which may augment and possibly clarify the contents of this particular work.

It should be noted that while not all the following titles may still be in print, and some, subsequent to their original publication, may well have been reissued by other publishers, even in other formats, such as e-books and the like, a search of the Internet will most likely turn up other editions both new and second-hand.

THE ILLUSTRATED WORKSHOP:

VOLUME I
THE ILLUSTRATED ENCYCLOPEDIA OF WOODWORKING HANDTOOLS, INSTRUMENTS & DEVICES
Bearsville, New York: Blackburn Books, 2000

Originally published in 1974 as an illustrated book of thosechandtools that might be found in the average carpenter's toolbox this book has evolved through various editions into a much more comprehensive alphabetical pictorial index to the tools of various woodworking trades common in the United States and Great Britain from the eighteenth century to the present.

VOLUME II

TRADITIONAL WOODWORKING HANDTOOLS: A MANUAL FOR THE WOODWORKER, A GUIDE FOR THE ENTHUSIAST

Bearsville, New York: Blackburn Books, 1998

Organized by major tool classes, this is the basic user manual for the tools described in the previous volume, explaining how to tell good from bad, how to tune and recondition them, together with basic techniques for their successful use.

In an age of increasing technology, ever less accessible to most people except the experts of particular fields, this book satisfies many people's basic urge to practice a craft over which they can be in complete control themselves — and thereby understand the production of many of the masterpieces of woodworking produced during the golden age of woodworking — as represented by designers such as Chippendale, Sheraton, and Hepplewhite, to mention but three masters whose efforts resulted in objects of enduring value without having had to plug anything in, far less rely on complicated technologies such as CNC machines.

VOLUME III

TRADITIONAL WOODWORKING TECHNIQUES: FUNDAMENTALS OF FURNITUREMAKING

Bearsville, New York: Blackburn Books, 2004

After learning what the various tools are and what they are designed to do, this book focuses on how to use them successfully. It is thus a practical introduction to the methods and techniques of furnituremaking, including chapters on design, function, and specific applications, such as mitering, moulding, running carving, frame-and-paneling, and drawer making.

VOLUME IV

FURNITURE DESIGN & CONSTRUCTION: CLASSIC PROJECTS & LESSONS OF THE CRAFT

Bearsville, New York: Blackburn Books, 2019

A thorough introduction to both the craft and the art of furnituremaking by hand, describing the underlying design principles and offering an opportunity to practice many of the more interesting aspects of the craft by means of a series of graduated projects ranging from a simple box to a linenfold-decorated throne, each progressively illustrating the previously described techniques.

No woodworking bibliography of woodworking by hand would be complete without reference to three of the most important books ever published, even though now several centuries old.

MECHANICK EXERCISES: OR THE DOCTRINE OF HANDY-WORKS

by Joseph Moxon, London 1703

A useful reprint has been published by the Astragal Press, Morristown, New Jersey, 1975

Generally regarded as the first record of British (and the subsequent American adoption) of woodworking tools and techniques.

L´ART DE MENUSIER EBENISTE

by J. A. Roubo, Paris , 1774

For French woodworking what Moxon did for Britain but focusing on more sophisticated branches of the trade.

MECHANICAL EXERCISES; OR THE ELEMENTS AND PRACTICES OD CARPENTRY, JOINERY, BRICKLAYING, MASONRY, SLATING, PLASTERING, SMITHING, AND TURNING

by Peter Nicholson, J. Taylor, London, 1812

Moxon's nineteenth century successsor; my personal favorite and greatest inspiration.

The following works should be part of every woodworker's library as a matter of course. They deal with jigs and fixtures as well as techniques in general:

PRACTICAL WOODWORK

by Charles Hayward, London, Evans Brothers, 1968

Just one of numerous titles by the man described as 'the most important workshop writer and editor of the twentieth century', and long-time editor of the seminal British woodworking magazine 'The Woodworker'.

THE WORKBENCH BOOK

by Scott Landis, Newtown Connecticut: The Taunton Press, 1987

Argualby the fist book you should read when setting up a shop.

WOODEN PLANES IN 19TH CENTURY AMERICA, VOL. I AND II *and* SOME 19TH CENTURY ENGLISH WOODWORKING TOOLS
by Kenneth D. Roberts, Ken Roberts Publishing Co., Fitzwilliam, New Hampshire, 1982
The best books for understanding what handtool use is all about.

WOOD-WORKING TOOLS; HOW TO USE THEM: A MANUAL
by The Industrial School Association, Ginn, Heath & Co., Boston, 1884
Little has changed in the century and a half since this book first appeared, but much has been forgotten.

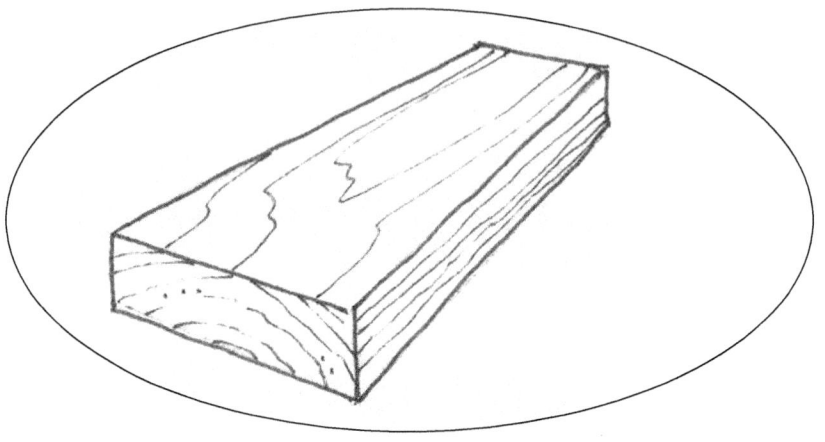

3

FIGURES

An alphabetical list of all figures, both in the main text as well as in the Sharpening Appendix.

ADJUSTABLE DEPTH STOP FIG. 134 PAGE 84
ANGLE BORING GUIDE FIG. 128 PAGE 81
ANGLE GUIDE FIG. 75 PAGE 49
ANGLED CIRCLE-CUTTING GUIDE FIG. 120 PAGE 75
ASYMMETRICAL STRAIGHTEDGE FIG. 36 PAGE 26
AVOIDING SPLIT-OUT FIG. 121 PAGE 78
BASIC HOLDFAST FIG. 11 PAGE 8
BASIC SHOOTING BOARD FIG. 90 PAGE 60
BEAM COMPASS FIG. 41 PAGE 28
BEAM COMPASS WITH TRAMMEL POINTS FIG. 42 PAGE 29
BENCH DOGS FIG. 8 PAGE 6
BENCH HOOKS FIG. 10 PAGE 7
BENCH STOPS FIG. 1 PAGE 2
BEVEL SUPPORT FIG. A4 PAGE 107
BEVELED WIDTH STOP FIG.102 PAGE 66
BLOCK BORING GUIDE FIG. 127 PAGE 80
BLOCK DEPTH GUIDE FIG. 133 PAGE 84
BORED TRYSQUARE FIG. 49 PAGE 32
BOSSED CURVE GAUGE FIG. 44 PAGE 30
BOX JAWS FIG. 27 PAGE 17
BRICK BATTEN STOP FIG. 37 PAGE 26
BRIDGE CLAMP FIG. 14 PAGE 9
CABINET DOOR-HANDLE GUIDE FIG. 52 PAGE 35
CAM-FIXED BENCH STOP FIG. 3 PAGE 3

CAM-FIXED STOP DETAILS FIG. 4 PAGE 4
CAMMED PLANING BOARD FIG. 86 PAGE 57
CLAMPING WITH TALL JAWS FIG. 26 PAGE 17
COMPOUND ANGLE SHOOTING BOARD FIG. 93 PAGE 61
COMPOUND MITERBOX FIG. 78 PAGE 51
CORNER BORING GUIDE FIG. 131 PAGE 83
CORNER SCRIBE FIG. 56 PAGE 37
CRADLE INTERNAL ANGLES FIG. 89 PAGE 59
CURVED SANDING PLANES FIG. 152 PAGE 94
CYLINDER GAUGING CRADLE FIG. 55 PAGE 37
DEPTH & WIDTH STOPS FIG. 101 PAGE 65
DEPTH STOP FIG. 72 PAGE 48
DIAGONAL STRIPS FIG. 33 PAGE 34
DONKEY'S EAR SHOOTING BOARD FIG. 95 PAGE 62
DOOR ROCKER FIG. 141 PAGE 88
DOVETAIL MARKING GUIDE FIG. 58 PAGE 39
DOVETAIL PARING GUIDE FIG. 113 PAGE 71
DOWEL GROOVER FIG. 108 PAGE 69
DOWEL LENGTH STOP FIG. 73 PAGE 48
DOWEL MARKER FIG. 110 PAGE 70
DRAWER-PULL CENTERING POSITIONER FIG. 51 PAGE 34
DRAWER-PULL GUIDE FIG. 50 PAGE 33
DRAWKNIFE REST FIG. A7 PAGE 106
DUTCH ZAAG-BOK FIG. 66 PAGE 45

TRADITIONAL JIGS & FIXTURES

EDGE CLAMP FIG. 142 PAGE 89
EDGE-PLANING CLAMP FIG. 84 PAGE 56
END BRACKET FIG. 18 PAGE 12
EVENLY-SPACED HOLE GUIDE FIG. 130 PAGE 82
FACE-PLANING STOP FIG. 81 PAGE 54
FIELDING GUIDES FIG. 99 PAGE 64
FINISH PROTECTORS FIG. 158 PAGE 97
FINISHING JAWS FIG. 20 PAGE 13
FINISHING SUPPORT BOARD FIG. 157 PAGE 97
FIXED DEADMAN FIG. 15 PAGE 10
FLEXIBLE STRAIGHTEDGE FIG. 35 PAGE 25
FLOOR CLAMP FIG. 29 PAGE 19
FLOOR FRAME-CONTAINER FIG. 139 PAGE 87
FRAME CLAMP FIG. 140 PAGE 88
FRAMING-SQUARE GUIDE FIG. 124 PAGE 79
FREE-STANDING DEADMAN FIG. 16 PAGE 11
FRETSAWING BLOCK FIG. 71 PAGE 47
FRETSAWING BRACKET FIG. 70 PAGE 47
FULCRUM RAISER FIG. 137 PAGE 87
GLUE BLOCK PROTECTOR FIG. 146 PAGE 91
GLUE-SURFACE PROTECTOR FIG. 148 PAGE 92
GRASSHOPPER GAUGE FIG. 54 PAGE 36
HAMMER SHIELD FIG. 135 PAGE 86
HAND-GRINDER BLADE SUPPORT FIG. A1 PAGE 109
HAND-ROUTER SHOE FIG. 119 PAGE 75
HANDSCREW JAW EXTENDER FIG. 30 PAGE 19
HORIZONTAL CRADLE JAWS FIG. 24 PAGE 16
KERFED BENCH HOOK FIG. 69 PAGE 46
LIPPING SANDER FIG. 155 PAGE 95
MATCHING TAPER JAWS FIG. 22 PAGE 14
METAL BENCH STOP FIG. 6 PAGE 5
MITER BLOCK FIG. 76 PAGE 50
MITER BOX FIG. 77 PAGE 50
MITER SHOOTING BOARD FIG. 94 PAGE 64
MITERED DOVETAIL PARING BLOCK FIG. 114 PAGE 72
MITERED MOULDING GUIDE FIG. 112 PAGE 71
MITERED SAWING SADDLE FIG. 80 PAGE 52
MITERED STUCK MOULDING FIG. 111 PAGE 70
MITERED-DOVETAIL BLOCK FIG. 79 PAGE 51
MITERED-DOVETAIL GUIDE FIG. 100 PAGE 65
MORTISING BLOCK FIG. 115 PAGE 73
MORTISING HANDSCREW FIG. 116 PAGE 73
MULLET FIG. 39 PAGE 27
NOTCHED PRESET GAUGE FIG. 88 PAGE 32
NOTCHED PRESET GAUGES FIG. 47 PAGE 31
PANEL & DOWELLED CURVE-GAUGE FIG. 45 PAGE 30
PARALLEL MARKING GAUGE FIG. 46 PAGE 31
PATTERNS & TEMPLATES FIG. 40

PEG FORM FIG. 143 PAGE 89
PENCIL GAUGE FIG. 43 PAGE 29
PINCH RODS FIG. 32 PAGE 23
PIVOTING SAW STOP FIG. 68 PAGE 45
PLANING BOARD FIG. 85 PAGE 56
PLANING CRADLE FIG. 88 PAGE 59
PLANING PUSH BLOCK FIG. 104 PAGE 66
PLIERS SHIELD FIG. 136 PAGE 86
RABBETING GUIDE FIG. 98 PAGE 64
REPLACEMENT VISE FACINGS FIG. 19 PAGE 13
RIGHT-ANGLE BRACKET FIG. 28 PAGE 18
RIPPING HORSE FIG. 64 PAGE 44
ROMAN PEGS FIG. 81 PAGE 55
ROUNDED-EDGE SCRATCH STOCK FIG. 107 PAGE 68
SANDING PLANE FIG. 151 PAGE 93
SANDING RUBBERS FIG. 153 PAGE 94
SANDING SHOOTING BOARD FIG. 154 PAGE 95
SANDPAPER DIVIDER FIG. 150
SAW BENCH FIG. 60 PAGE 42
SAW BENCH DAMAGE FIG. 67 PAGE 45
SAW BENCH DIMENSIONS FIG. 61 PAGE 42
SAW HORSE FIG. 62 PAGE 43
SAW HORSE DIMENSIONS FIG. 63 PAGE 43
SAW HORSE DOWEL GROOVER FIG. 109 PAGE 69
SAWBUCK FIG. 65 PAGE 44
SCRAPER-PLANE BLADE SUPPORT A5 PAGE 108
SCRATCH STOCK BLADE FIG. 106 PAGE 68
SCREW HOLDFAST FIG. 13 PAGE 9
SCREW-FIXED BENCH STOP FIG. 5 PAGE 4
SHARPENING STONE FLATTENER FIG. A2 PAGE 102
SHOOTING BLOCK FIG. 96 PAGE 63
SHOOTING END GRAIN FIG. 91 PAGE 61
SHOULDER GUIDE FIG. 74 PAGE 49
SIDE DOVETAIL GUIDE FIG. 59 PAGE 39
SIMPLE SCRATCH STOCK FIG. 105 PAGE 68
SLIDING BEVEL SPACER FIG. 57 PAGE 38
SLIDING DEADMAN FIG. 17 PAGE 11
SOLID BENDING FORM FIG. 145 PAGE 90
SPACED HOLE GUIDE FIG. 129 PAGE 81
SPLINTERING GUARD FIG. 122 PAGE 78
SPOKESHAVE SHARPENING HOLDER A6 PAGE 105
SQUARE-EDGE GUIDE FIG. 103 PAGE 66
SQUEEZE-OUT PROTECTOR FIG. 147 PAGE 91
STICKING BLOCK FIG. 138 PAGE 87
STICKING BOARD FIG. 87 PAGE 58
STORY STICK FIG. 38 PAGE 27
STRADDLE SANDER FIG. 156 PAGE 96
STRAIGHTEDGE FIG. 31 PAGE 22

FIGURES

TRADITIONAL JIGS & FIXTURES

STRIP CLAMP FIG 83 PAGE 55
TALL JAWS FIG. 15 PAGE 16
TAPE DEPTH GUIDE FIG. 132 PAGE 83
TAPE REPAIR FIG. 149 PAGE 92
THIN STOCK BORING GUIDE FIG. 126 PAGE 80
TOP VIEW OF CABINETMAKER'S BENCH FIG. 12 PAGE 8
TRYSQUARE GUIDE FIG. 123 PAGE 78
TURNING BOX FIG. 117 PAGE 74
TURNING BOX DIMENSIONS FIG. 118 PAGE 74
USERMADE SHOOTING BLOCK FIG. 97 PAGE 63

V-BLOCK BENCH STOP FIG. 7 PAGE 5
VARIOUS BENCH STOP DIMENSIONS FIG. 2 PAGE 3
VERTICAL BORING GUIDE FIG. 125 PAGE 79
VERTICAL CRADLE JAWS FIG. 23 PAGE 15
VERTICALLY TAPERED JAWS FIG. 21 PAGE 14
WALL FORM FIG. 144 PAGE 90
WEDGED SHOOTING BOARD FIG. 92 PAGE 61
WEDGED STONE-HOLDER FIG. A3 PAGE 102
WINDING STICKS FIG. 14 PAGE 25
WOODEN & METAL BENCH DOGS FIG. 9 PAGE 6

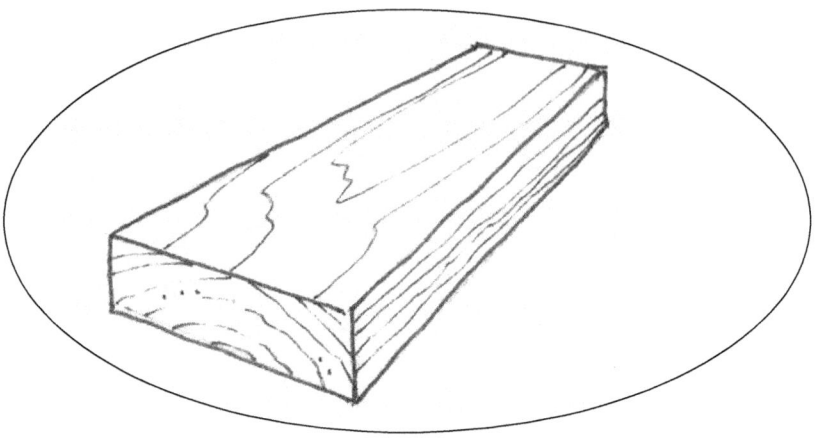

4

INDEX

Index of tools, techniques, jigs, and fixtures
*Numbers in boldface (e.g., **32**) indicate pages with illustrations.
References to ranges greater than two pages (e.g., **98–100**) may
also include illustrations.*

A

Angled circle-cutting guide, **75**
Assembly, 85–92
Auxiliary vise jaws:
  box jaws, **17**–18
  cradles:
    horizontal, **16**
    vertical, **15**
  finishing, **13**
  matching taper, **14**–15
  replacement facings, 12–**13**
  tall, 16–**17**
  vertically tapered, **14**

B

Beam compass, **28**–29
Bench clamp *(see V-block)*
Bench dogs, **6**
Bench hook:
  regular, **7**
  kerfed, **46**
Bench stops:
  cam-fixed, **3**–4
  capped & pinned, **3**
  for sawing, **45**
  manufactured, **5**
  pivoting, **45**
  round, **2**
  screw-fixed, **4**
  square, **2**
Bending forms, 89–91
Boring:
  avoiding split-out, 78
  guides:
    adjustable depth stop, **80**, **84**
    angle, **82**
    block, **84**
    corner, **82**–**83**
    evenly-spaced hole, **82**
    framing square, **79**
    spaced hole, **81**–82
    straight, **78**–80
    tape depth stop, **83**
    thin-stock, **70**–80
    trysquare, **78**
    vertical, **79**
  splintering guard, **78**
Brick batten stop, **26**
Bridge clamp, **9**

C

Chute boards *(see under Shooting boards)*
Clamping, 87–88
Corner scribe, **36**–37

Cylinder gauging cradle, 36–37

D

Deadmen:
   fixed, **10**
   free-standing, 10–**11**
   sliding, **11**
Dent protection, 85–87
Door rocker, **88**
Diagonal strips, 23–**24**
Dovetail guides:
   mitered-dovetail block, **51**
   mitered-dovetail guide, **65**
   paring guide, **71**
   sawing guide, **49**
   dovetail marking, 38–**39**
   side, **39**
Dowelling:
   dowel box, **58**
   dowel length stop, **48**–49
   groover, **69**
   marker, **70**
   mitered-dovetail paring block, **72**
   saw horse groover, **69**
Drawknife rest, 105–**106**

E

Edge clamp, 88–**89**
End bracket, **12**

F

Fielding guides, **64**
Finish protectors, 96–**97**
Finishing support board, 96–**97**
Folding rule, 21–**22**
Floor clamp, **19**
Floor frame-container, 87–**88**
Fluting box *(see under Turning box)*
Frame-and-paneling:
   checking groove, **27**
Frame clamp, **88**
Fretsaw, **47**
Fretsawing guides:
   fretsawing block, **47**–48
   fretsawing bracket, **47**
Fulcrum raiser, 86–**87**

G

Gauges:
   bossed curve, 29–**30**
   dowelled curve, **30**
   grasshopper, **36**
   handrail *(see grasshopper)*
   panel, **30**
   parallel marking, **31**
   pencil, **29**
   preset:
     bored trysquare, **32**
     cabinet door-handle guide, 34–**35**
     drawer-pull centering positioner, 33–**34**
     drawer-pull guide, 32–**33**
     notched, **31**
     rabbeted, **32**
     shelf-support layout guide, **53**
Gluing aids, 88–92
   glue block protector, **91**
   surface protector, **92**
   squeeze-out protector, **91**

H

Hammer shield, 85–**86**
Hand-grinder blade support, 100–**101**
Hand-router shoe, **75**
Handscrew jaw extender, **19**–20
Holdfasts:
   basic, **8**
   screw, **9**

I

Internal measurements, **23**

K

Keeled fielding guide, **64**
Kerfed bench hook, **46**

M

Marking knife, 21
Mitering:
   compound miter box, **51**
   miter block, **50**
   miter box, **50**–51
   mitered-dovetail block, **51**
   mitered-dovetail paring block, **72**
   miter-sawing saddle, 51–**52**
   moulding guide, 70–**71**
   template *(see under moulding guide)*
Mitre *(see under Mitering)*
Mortising:
   handscrew, **73**
   mortising block, **72**–73
Moulding block *(see under Turning box)*
Mullet, **27**

P

Patterns & Templates, **28**
Peg form, **89**
Pinch rods, 22–**23**
Planing:
   cammed planing board, **57**–58
   depth & width stops, **65**–66
   dowel box, **58**
   edge planing clamp, **56**
   face-planing stop, 53–**54**
   fielding guides, **64**
   mitered-dovetail guide, **65**
   planing board, **56**–57
   planing cradle, **59**
   push block, **66**
   rabbeting guide, **64**
   Roman pegs, 54–**55**
   rounding cradle *(see under Dowel box)*
   sanding planes, **94**
   scraper plane, 104–**105**
   square-edge guide, **66**
   shooting boards:
     basic, 59–**62**
     compound angle, **61**
     donkey's ear, 62–**63**
     miter, **62**
     wedged, **61**
   strip clamp, **59**
Pliers shield, **86**

R

Rabbet plane, **65**

Rabbeting guide, **64**
Rectilinearity, **23–24**
Right-angled bracket, **18**
Ripping horse, **44**
Roman pegs, **54–55**
Rounding cradle *(see under dowel box)*

S

Sanding:
   curved sanding planes, **94**
   holders, **92–94**
   lipping sander, **95–96**
   planes, **93**
   rubbers, **94**
   sanding shooting board, **94–95**
   sandpaper divider, **92-93**
   straddle sander, **96**
Saw bench, **41–42**
Saw buck, **44–45**
Saw-goat *(see under sawbuck)*
Saw horse, **42–43**
Sawing guides:
   angle guide, **49–50**
   depth stop, **48**
   dowel length stop, **48–49**
   pivoting saw-stop, **45–46**
   ripping horse, **44**
   shoulder guide, **49**
Scratch stock:
   rounded-edge, **68–69**
   simple, **67–68**
Sharpening:
   blade bevel-support, **103–104**
   drawknife rest, **105–106**
   grinder blade support, **101**
   spokeshave holder, **105**
Sharpening stones:
   flattener, **101–102**
   oilstones, **101**
   using, **102–104**
   wedged stone-holder, **102**
Shooting boards:
   basic, **59–62**
   compound angle, **61**
   donkey's ear, **62–63**
   miter, **62**
   sanding, **94–95**
   scraper plane blade support, **104–105**
   wedged, **61**
Shooting block, **63**
Side hook *(see under Bench hook)*
Side rest *(see under Bench hook)*
Sliding bevel spacer, **38**
Sliding dovetail, **71**
Solid bending form, **90–91**
Spokeshave sharpening holder, **105**
Sticking board, **58**
Story stick, **27**
Striking block, **87**

Straightedge:
   asymmetrical, **26**
   basic, **22**
   flexible, **25–26**

T

Tape measure, **21**
Tape repair, **92**
Top clamp *(see under V-block)*
Turning box, **74**

V

V-block, **5**
V-board *(see under V-block)*
Vise fixtures, **10–18**

W

Wall form, **90**
Wedged stone-holder, **102**
Winding sticks, **24–25**
Workbench, **1–2**
Workbench aids, **1–9**

Z

Zaag-boc, **45**

ABOUT THE AUTHOR

Graham Blackburn was born and educated in London, England before moving to New York City to continue his studies at the Juilliard School. While pursuing a career as a professional musician, he built his first house in Woodstock, NY. Since then, he has published more than twenty books, including both novels and books on all aspects of house building, interior carpentry, traditional woodworking, cabinetmaking, furniture making, handtools, and design.

While running his own custom furniture-making shop, he also became a regular contributor to leading woodworking publications, including *Fine Woodworking, Popular Woodworking,* and *Woodwork*—of which he was also the Editor-in-Chief for a number of years.

In addition to being a writer and illustrator, he has been the subject of several books on crafts and design. He was featured in Maxine Rosenberg's *Artists of Handcrafted Furniture at Work* (Lothrop, Lee & Shepard) and Jane Smiley's *Catskill Crafts: Artisans of the Catskill Mountains* (Crown Publishers) and has made numerous television appearances, including serving as the national spokesperson for Boyle-Midway's media campaign: *Secrets of the Master Craftsmen.* He was a featured speaker at the nationwide Woodworking Shows for over a decade and a frequent lecturer at woodworking schools, guilds, and colleges across the country.

Visit Graham at BlackburnBooks.com or, better yet, take a class with him at the Graham Blackburn School of Traditional Woodworking in Woodstock, NY.

MORE GREAT BOOKS *from* CEDAR LANE PRESS

Discover the entire *Illustrated Workshop* series

Over 1,300 pages of essential handtool information and original hand-drawn illustrations from the workshop of the master woodworker, Graham Blackburn.

Illustrated Encyclopedia of Woodworking Handtools
$24.95 | 206 Pages

Traditional Woodworking Handtools
$29.95 | 384 Pages

Furniture Design & Construction
$24.95 | 256 Pages

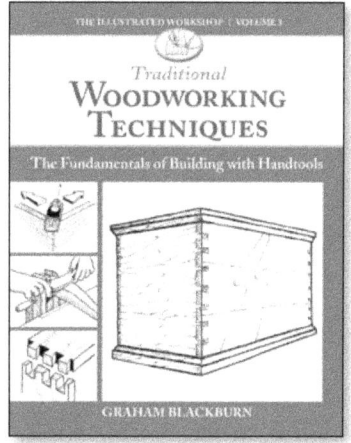

Traditional Woodworking Techniques
$24.95 | 352 Pages

CEDAR LANE PRESS

Look for these titles wherever books are sold or visit www.CedarLanePress.com.

finis

www.ingramcontent.com/pod-product-compliance
Lightning Source LLC
Chambersburg PA
CBHW051551220426
43671CB00025B/2996